FAT YEARS
AND LEAN

Other books by Bernard D. Nossiter

THE MYTHMAKERS: AN ESSAY ON POWER AND WEALTH

SOFT STATE: A NEWSPAPERMAN'S CHRONICLE OF INDIA

BRITAIN: A FUTURE THAT WORKS

THE GLOBAL STRUGGLE FOR MORE: THIRD WORLD CONFLICTS
WITH RICH NATIONS

FAT YEARS AND LEAN

The American Economy Since Roosevelt

Bernard D. Nossiter

1817
HARPER & ROW, PUBLISHERS, NEW YORK
Grand Rapids, Philadelphia, St. Louis, San Francisco
London, Singapore, Sydney, Tokyo, Toronto

FIRST EDITION

Designed by Erich Hobbing

Library of Congress Cataloging-in-Publication Data

Nossiter, Bernard D.
    Fat years and lean : the American economy since Roosevelt /
Bernard D. Nossiter.—1st ed.
        p.   cm.
    ISBN 0-06-435853-4
    1. United States—Economic conditions—1918–1945.   2. United
States—Economic conditions—1945–   3.   United States—Economic
policy.   I. Title.
HC106.3.N596   1990
330.973'092—dc20   89-46110

---

90 91 92 93 94 AC/HC 10 9 8 7 6 5 4 3 2 1

For Ellie

Contents

Preface

"Why are they sitting on the sidewalk?" I asked. It was 1931 or 1932 and I was staring at some pale-faced families huddled around sticks of furniture on Columbus Avenue in New York.

"They've lost their homes," I think my father said. "They couldn't pay the rent."

"Why not?"

"Well, they lost their jobs. There's a depression."

It wasn't much of an answer but it was about all anybody could have told me, even Mr. Hoover in the White House. I have a clear memory of being unsatisfied. Perhaps I decided then that someday I'd find out for myself.

So, after the war, I studied economics at college and in graduate school. By then, almost everybody knew how to cure a depression although there is still no agreement about its causes. War spending was an overwhelming, unmistakable lesson that would not be forgotten, at least for twenty-five years. Counter-cyclical fiscal and monetary policies worked so well I gave up my idea of going to Washington to help avert another depression. I wasn't needed. Instead, I went to Washington to report on the use and abuse of the new economic wisdom.

The business cycle had not been repealed but all administrations, Republican and Democrat, acted on the new knowledge to keep recessions brief and employment high. Eisenhower sensed there was something wrong when prices rose despite idle men and plants. Kennedy was the first to deal directly with union and corporate power—incomes policy it was called later—to restrain prices at high employment levels.

But in the seventies, things clearly went sour. Doing the research for my last book I was impressed with how many key indicators turned down in the single year of 1973 and stayed down thereafter. There was a sharp break with the past. The hard-earned wisdom to manage economic affairs was devalued. Public policy was a bust.

Now a new synthesis has emerged. We are told that all is well when growth is far below potential, that unemployment and price increases are tolerable though well above the levels of the postwar quarter century. The new-model commentators fret about budget and trade deficits, although they have trouble explaining why, and not about idle resources. Public policy appears to rest largely on the use of the money supply to control inflation and expansion of the economy.

On Columbus Avenue, the dispossessed families have given way to boutiques and smart restaurants. But in other streets, the pavements have been taken over by battalions of sidewalk dwellers. I still think it is important to understand how and why, and particularly why the lessons of the post-Depression years have been scrapped so casually.

In a very real sense, this book is an attempt to understand what has happened in economic affairs in my life. As it happens, my life coincides with a cycle in public policy. It begins with the Hoover-Roosevelt efforts to cope with catastrophe and their unwitting prolongation of disaster. It rises through the more or less successful war and postwar management of the economy. The cycle returns to its starting point with the unacknowledged repeal of the 1946 Employment Act by the Reagan administration.

I am deeply grateful to a pair of splendid editors at the *Washington Post*, Alfred Friendly and Ben Bradlee, who frequently indulged my whims and let me pursue paths less adventurous editors would have blocked. Several others have strongly influenced my work. At the Fieldston School, Elbert Lenrow taught me to read a text critically and listen to the sound of a written sentence. Michael Choukas at Dartmouth cultivated skepticism for public discourse. Gardiner Means and John Blair gave me a vocabulary and abundant evidence to describe the behavior of firms with market power. Above all, I owe a deep debt to my dear friend Charles Keith, a founder of the CIO seaman's union, fighter in Spain for the Republic, real-estate tycoon, the most astonishing autodidact. He daily demonstrated that events are related, cohere. He was a genuinely good man.

Adam Nossiter, a fellow reporter, read my manuscript and made very useful suggestions. At Harper & Row, Cass Canfield, Jr., has been a wise and sympathetic editor. Fiona Maclachlan has checked the manuscript for accuracy and compiled the end notes.

I am also grateful to the Lionel Robbins library at the London School of Economics, where the staff was as helpful as the excellent collection. I finished the book in the Allen Room of the New York Public Library, a blessing for any writer.

London and New York, 1989

FAT YEARS
AND LEAN

I

The Hoover – Roosevelt Depression

On the eve of the 1936 campaign, Franklin Roosevelt turned to Samuel Rosenman and asked his close adviser to draft a "good and convincing explanation" of Roosevelt's speech in Pittsburgh four years earlier. There he had promised to halt the profligacy of Herbert Hoover, cut Federal spending by 25 percent, and balance the budget. But after four more years of depression, spending had risen nearly 70 percent and the budget was further than ever from balance.

"Deny categorically that you ever made it," Rosenman quipped. FDR roared in delight.[1]

The story reveals more than Roosevelt's glee over political duplicity. It shows that after wrestling with the worst slump in the nation's history for a full term, the President still did not know what he was doing, did not yet understand the economic dimensions of a New Deal. Some elements like the Works Progress Administration (WPA) and the Public Works Administration (PWA) were already in place. A dramatic amount of social reform had become or would soon become law. But FDR lacked a theory, an understanding of cause and effect, to explain what had gone wrong with the economy and why it was still

1

depressed. Almost in exasperation, he described early in 1936 all that he had done to "stop the downward spiral." He had, he said,[2] taken simultaneous action on a dozen fronts, to protect bank deposits, save homes and farms from foreclosure, increase farm prices, give credit to railroads, provide useful work to the jobless, raise prices generally but cut interest rates, start large-scale public works. Taken together, they had not worked. There had been a mild recovery from the depths of the Depression, but unemployment still stood at a terrifying 16.9 percent;[3] output of all goods and services at $99.5 billion was well below the 1929 peak of $104.4 billion.[4]

The President still did not understand the role of aggregate demand, of expanding incomes to raise a slumping economy. He had only the dimmest perception of how a government adds to or subtracts from that demand. Indeed, much of his first term was spent chasing after irrelevancies. He experimented with corporatism, cartels sought by businessmen to curb output and lift prices. Hoover had rejected this notion but it was at the heart of Roosevelt's National Recovery Act. Characteristically, FDR had added an unexpected balancing feature at the demand of unions. This was the charter the NRA gave workers to organize unions with representatives of their own choosing, protected from harassment by the National Labor Relations Board. But, like many other Roosevelt innovations, old-age pensions or outlawing child labor, this was social reform. It tended to make life more bearable, more just, but contributed little if anything to expanding demand, enlarging incomes, the force needed to pull the economy from slump.

Roosevelt's understanding was fogged by the economic cant of his day. The Pittsburgh speech was not sheer demagoguery. FDR, like most in his class and those who taught them at Harvard, Columbia, and Chicago, believed that a nation must run like a household, along Micawber's lines. He had said, "Annual income twenty pounds, annual expenditure nineteen nineteen six, result happiness. Annual income twenty pounds, annual expenditure twenty pounds ought and six, result misery." Virtually all businessmen, bankers, and economists agreed that this was so and therefore it must be so. As shrewd a politician as Roosevelt probably sensed that a good deal of self-interest was wrapped up in the business view that deficits were always evil. A government running ever-increasing deficits would expand its power, its control over private firms. A spending government can make or break firms by granting or withholding contracts and can impose many onerous conditions on the contracted job.

Moreover, bankers especially are seldom in any hurry to cure a slump. Some may possess the economic wit to appreciate that a deficit will put idle resources to work. But depression and deflation better suit those financiers who do not go under. A loan made in good times is made with relatively cheap dollars; a loan repaid in bad times, when prices have fallen, is repaid with dear dollars that buy more. To lend cheap dollars and receive dear ones in return is a banker's dream.

Roosevelt was willing to confront bankers over inflation; he believed higher prices would somehow restore prosperity. Apart from the NRA, which tried to lift nonfarm prices, his farm program was built almost exclusively around efforts to raise farm prices. But he was not willing to challenge orthodoxy over the budget. An unbalanced budget, a deficit, an excess of spending over receipts would frighten businessmen and discourage their spending for new plants and machines. A balanced budget was Roosevelt's goal. Until 1938, he held to it as passionately as Herbert Hoover.[5]

There is a remarkable identity in the budget behavior of these two conservative Presidents. During the 1930s, government budgets at all levels provided a strong antidepression stimulant only twice and then despite the White House. The 1931 budget spurred income, employment, and output only because Congress approved a speedup in the payment of bonuses to World War I veterans. The legislators overrode Hoover's veto and put cash in the hands of those who would spend it quickly. Much the same thing happened in 1936. Congress rejected FDR's veto and gave veterans cash. But apart from the stimulus supplied by the veterans' bonus, Federal, state, and local governments gave little help to demand throughout the thirties.[6] Budgets acted as a brake on recovery and the balanced budget fallacy dominated what was essentially a single period, the Hoover-Roosevelt era of 1929–37.

Indeed, had Roosevelt lost to Landon in 1936, had the New Deal ended after one term, economic historians might well have judged that Hoover's assault on the Depression was bolder and more imaginative than his successor's. It was Hoover, not Roosevelt, who was the first American president to assume responsibility for the state of the economy, who did not rely on blind market forces, the natural appetites of businessmen, or Divine Providence to bring about recovery. Hoover tried to make the Federal government an actor, insisting that it had a role in restoring output, income, jobs. Hoover was chastised for his "socialistic legislation" by at least one prominent Democrat, Bernard Baruch,[7] a stock market millionaire. It was Hoover who prescribed, no matter how timidly, many of the remedies that FDR was later to adopt with gusto. Rexford Guy Tugwell, an early Roosevelt brain truster, said: "We didn't admit it at the time but practically the whole New Deal was extrapolated from programs that Hoover started."[8] But Hoover lacked the courage of his intellect. When his cautious measures failed to achieve recovery, he succumbed to the orthodox views of the financiers around him, especially Andrew Mellon, the multimillionaire Treasury Secretary who had welcomed the Depression. "It will purge the rottenness out of the system," Mellon told Hoover. "High costs of living and high living will come down. People will work harder, live a moral life. Values will be adjusted, and enterprising people will pick up the wrecks from less competent people."[9]

Hoover recoiled from Mellon's view that a depression improves morals. But he subscribed implicitly to Mellon's prescription as the slump deepened. At last Hoover became as rabid a budget balancer as the Roosevelt of 1936–37 and with equally catastrophic results. The great difference, perhaps, is that Roosevelt learned in time from disaster and listened to other voices. Catastrophe drove Hoover into a shell where he could hear only those at hand.

Earlier, as Secretary of Commerce in the 1920s, Hoover made plans to combat a slump. He reasoned, with no underlying economic theory in support, that spending on public works could provide useful employment and income. The business recession of 1921 and the slowdown in 1923 strengthened his view. To be sure, Hoover's approach was modest. He did not favor Federal financing of national public works. Instead, the states should have on their shelves plans for useful projects to be started when recession struck. This was no call for deficit spending, no call for an extra increment of Federal demand. But in its cautious way it contained two central ideas. One was that slumps are not preordained phenomena to be endured by sinful men but unnecessary breaks with prosperity that could be ended by state action.

Hoover's second idea was a crude foreshadowing of the multiplier that R. F. Kahn developed at Cambridge in 1931 and

Keynes was to incorporate into his *General Theory of Employment, Interest and Money* in 1936. The multiplier is shorthand for the strong likelihood that a given input of new income will yield some multiple of itself. A new $1 million outlay for a bridge will produce in the end perhaps $2 million in added incomes. Bridge workers, foremen, materials suppliers, engineers, designers will all share in the first million-dollar round of spending. These people will save a portion of their extra income and spend the rest on groceries, clothes, medicines, cars, radios, movies, homes. These expenditures become income for grocers, garment makers, farmers, druggists, auto dealers, bankers. The process then repeats itself in continuing rounds. In the end, more income is created than the initial $1 million spent on the bridge. This is the multiplier.

At a conference of businessmen in 1921, Secretary Hoover displayed a diagram that showed how this worked and called it the "Multiplying Effect of Successive Use of Funds in Circulations."[10] All that was ten years before Kahn and fifteen before Keynes. In the business slowdown of 1923, Hoover repeated his proposal for a public-works speedup. The president of the American Construction Council, a New York lawyer, Franklin Roosevelt, applauded.[11]

Again, in those earlier recessions and in the Great Depression, Hoover pleaded with businessmen not to cut wages. He understood that purchasing power must be maintained to avoid a slump; he did not see that businessmen unaided could not and would not heed his plea for long. Hoover, a voluntarist, was too cautious to employ direct Federal action to sustain demand, but he knew that it should be maintained.

In the depths of the Depression, Hoover left as a legacy some notable institutional innovations that the New Deal later embraced. Hoover's Federal Farm Board paid farmers to take crops off the market and raise prices. This peculiar notion was borrowed by FDR's Agricultural Adjustment Act, which went further and paid farmers not to produce. (Like NRA, it rested on a money illusion, that if only producers could get higher prices for their products, prosperity would somehow return. Of course, this approach did tend to increase prosperity for the richest and best-off, the largest producers, but that was not the advertised goal.)

In the Depression's worst hours, Hoover abandoned voluntarism and yielded to congressional pleas. He created a great loan agency, the Reconstruction Finance Corporation. This was his single most important action to undo the slump. At first, RFC was allowed to lend only to banks and to railroads, whose shaky bonds imperiled the banks. Eventually, reluctantly, Hoover responded to public pressure. RFC was allowed to lend to all troubled corporations. This was a major step forward, open government intervention in the marketplace on a wide scale. To be sure, it was aid for the best-off, the great corporations. It aimed at achieving trickle-down prosperity, rescuing businessmen in hopes that they would create more jobs for the destitute. Sometimes RFC's favoritism reached scandalous proportions. It approved a $90 million loan for the Chicago bank of Charles Dawes, a former Republican vice president and first head of the RFC, at the very moment that the agency turned down the city of Chicago, which had sought $70 million to pay teachers and other workers.[12] Hoover tried to keep the loans secret but congressional Democrats frustrated him. Even so, RFC was a considerable advance.

Hoover, however, strenuously resisted putting Federal dollars directly into the hands of the jobless, against placing the unemployed on a Federal payroll. That, he feared, would breed corruption and waste.[13]

7

Hoover was less insensitive than he sounded. He simply had a limited vision. "No one went hungry or cold" in the slump, he said, "if our committees knew of it."[14] But that was the trouble. Neither Hoover nor his agents saw the miserable thousands, plainly visible to city dwellers like me, living in tarpaper shacks in public parks. These were called, not inappropriately, Hoovervilles.

Even so, if the state could finance ailing business, the state's power to intervene in the economy was limitless. The Federal government lost its chaste free-market character under Herbert Hoover. Walter Lippmann, the distinguished conservative commentator of the day, recognized as much. He chided Hoover for interfering with natural economic law, for urging businessmen in the slump to avoid wage cuts.[15] Indeed, economic thought generally disapproved of the Hoover remedies as affronts to received theory. Sumner Slichter, who became Harvard's oracle on labor affairs, protested that Hoover's public works would interfere with the very wage reductions the economy needed.[16] Until Keynes, the prevailing wisdom in the academies held that unemployment represented an unstable equilibrium, an unnatural state that could be cured if sticky wages came unglued, if workers would recognize that demand for their labor had fallen and so accept wage reductions. This remedy, suitable in an inflation, when resources are fully employed, is self-defeating in a slump. It further cuts demand, thereby reducing the need for workers. Hoover understood this; most departments of economics did not.

Hoover's break with conventional wisdom must not be exaggerated. If he anticipated some New Deal notions, he often lacked the will to act on his own ideas. He not only presided over the disaster of 1929–32, he helped deepen it. He welcomed and signed the Smoot-Hawley tariff bill of 1931, a measure that raised barriers against foreign goods by about 50 percent.[17] It was the most formidable engine of protection imposed by any administration until Ronald Reagan took power. Protection, whether it is a tax or tariff, import quota or artificial "health" or other standard, forces consumers to subsidize corporations. It is also enormously popular with workers and managers faced with shrinking jobs and markets they can blame on foreign competition. It almost always leads to retaliation. Foreign nations respond by strengthening their restraints on trade and so reduce sales, output, and jobs of the protectionists. Protectionism is a form of Federal interference with markets that had long been sanctioned by conservative politicians who thought outlawing child labor was pernicious socialism. Hoover said he didn't like cheap foreign competition[18] and so helped wreck world trade.

Again, he did not lift a finger when the Federal Reserve tightened money, drove up interest rates, and made borrowing for demoralized business harder at the depths of the slump in 1931. Hoover's man Eugene Meyer, another multimillionaire stock speculator who bought the bankrupt *Washington Post* as an eleemosynary gesture, was governor of the central bank. Meyer objected to tight money, but he was overridden.[19] George Harrison, president of the powerful New York Federal Reserve, said: "Some temporary recession, even admitting that it might be severe for the time being, might in the long run prove to be the cheaper price to pay."[20] Take the Depression's deflationary medicine, Harrison was saying. He and many fellow bankers were safely employed at well-paid tasks.

Harrison and the others who overruled Meyer's plea for easier money had a peculiar logic. Britain had gone off gold, refused to tie its supply of money to the amount of yellow metal it possessed. Other nations still had gold deposited in New York vaults, and they worried lest the U.S. follow Britain, abandon gold, and pay them dollars for their holdings. They threatened to take metal from New York. But that would force the U.S. to drop its gold link, to devalue the dollar. So, to encourage foreigners to leave their gold in New York, to preserve the dollar's tie to gold, the Federal Reserve drove up interest rates. The central bank ignored the consequences of tighter money for ten million unemployed, for levels of output that now must shrivel even further, for misery on a massive scale. If the Fed had worried about jobless men, it would have driven interest rates down sharply. Then there would have been enough credit at an affordable price to tempt some businessmen to borrow. Their borrowing would have financed new orders and new jobs, reversing the cycle of misery. But that was not the central bank's concern. It feared a lowering in the exchange rate of the dollar.

There are times when monetary and fiscal policy can march in opposite directions, when credit should be tightened while spending is relaxed. This was not one of them; curing slump was the overwhelming need. It was not an occasion when one foot should press the accelerator and the other the brake.

If Hoover did nothing to stop the Federal Reserve from hastening the caravan over the cliff, he helped prolong disaster in his final year in office. Late in 1931 he called for a large tax increase.

Budget deficits, despite Hoover, had become inevitable. The sharp fall in employment and output meant deep cuts in income. As the incomes of citizens dropped, they paid less taxes, or, in the case of the jobless, no taxes. Unless government expenditures were drastically cut—and that policy ran against the strategy of former Commerce Secretary Hoover—receipts must drop below spending. These deficits gave the economy some limited relief, acting like a flow of needed added income.

But Hoover and those around him did not see things that way. Businessmen do not like deficits. The deficit, therefore, must stop to revive business confidence and investment.

Hoover, a sophisticated politician, somehow failed to see through the special pleas of businessmen who claimed that their willingness to invest rested on reduced government spending. Business investment to enlarge capacity, spending for new plants and machines, does not vary inversely with Federal deficits. It depends on a businessman's assessment of future demand. The nation's most confident businessman will not enlarge his plant by one toolshed unless he thinks he will have customers for its future production. Hoover and the Republicans had the wrong end of the stick. Demand should have been expanded to encourage investment, not the other way around. By raising taxes, Hoover delivered a swift crushing blow to demand. He guaranteed the stifling of investment. He killed off the customers' purchasing power. His $900 million tax increase was particularly savage. In percent, it was the biggest peacetime increase in American history, and it consisted largely of excises or sales taxes.[21] It was, therefore, regressive, placing most of the burden on those of middle and lower incomes whose spending is swiftest and greatest.

When reporters asked Babe Ruth if he thought it right that he made more money than the President, the slugger replied, "I had a better year."[22]

Hoover, no doubt, had blundered badly, although FDR would leave the tax increase untouched. At the start of 1933, the Federal Reserve deepened the disaster. It sold government paper or i.o.u.'s to the commercial banks. This is how central banks tighten money. The commercial banks pay for the paper with the deposits they keep as reserves at the Fed. As reserves fall, so does the banking system's capacity to make loans. With less money available, its price, the rate of interest, climbs.

Milton Friedman, a major historian of monetary economics, says flatly that the Depression was created by the central bank's ruthless squeeze on money, that a policy of expansion instead of contraction could have averted the catastrophe.[23] The central bank had slashed $700 million from the money supply in the first six months of 1930.[24] Overall, the quantity of money fell more than one-third from August 1929 to March 1933,[25] from two months before shares fell until Roosevelt's inauguration. Thanks to this tightening vise, income per person fell to the level of 1908; two decades of gain were thrown away.[26] Monetary policy reinforced fiscal policy and both ran in exactly the wrong direction.

Hoover was thoroughly demoralized by 1933. On the eve of the inaugural, with banks collapsing everywhere, he tried to pledge FDR not to resort to easy money and unbalanced budgets. Roosevelt ducked.[27] Once in office, the new President began undoing some of the worst excesses of monetary policy. He began scrapping the platform on which the Fed had rested its perverse policies. FDR even tinkered with the sacred price of gold.

"We must be free to establish our own price level, regardless of the foreign exchange rate," Roosevelt wrote Cordell Hull, his Secretary of State.[28] The new President had it mostly right. Freed of the obligation to buy gold at a fixed price, much like the obligation to maintain a fixed exchange rate, the new administration could now pursue the money and spending policies it wanted to restore the economy. Dean Acheson, the Treasury undersecretary, thought that altering gold was immoral and resigned.

Roosevelt's gold game—he arbitrarily set the price each

morning over coffee in his bedroom—finally freed the Fed and its new governor, Marriner Eccles. The central bank had lost its excuse to deepen the Great Depression. Now it could expand credit.

Nevertheless, Roosevelt's approach to the gold price, no matter how playful, typified a basic misconception. FDR believed that if only a proper relationship between prices could be found—more important, if only the level of prices could be raised by main force—happy days would come again. In the Depression, it was easy to fall for the money illusion. Wholesale prices in commerce tumbled 23.4 percent from 1929 through 1932; farm prices fell a staggering 56 percent.[29] Since falling prices went hand in hand with misery, there must be a cause and effect. Much business and academic thought ran along similar lines, although a few of the more rigorous professors insisted that deflation had not gone far enough. Jacob Viner and Frank Knight of Chicago, distinguished economists, thought prosperity lay in further wage cuts.

So Roosevelt listened to Gerald Swope of General Electric and the omnipresent Baruch and tried to create great cartels in all branches of industry. This was the National Industrial Recovery Act, which urged business to carve up markets and raise prices. It was, of course, an American version of Mussolini's corporate state, and Norman Thomas called it "capitalist syndicalism . . . in essence, fascist."[30]

Today, the most important sectors of the modern economy—finance, computers, electrical machinery, autos, chemicals, drugs, entertainment, aluminum, copper, oil, and more—resemble cartels. A handful of competitors follow a leader in setting prices and output. But this goes on without the sanction of law. NRA gave cartel arrangements government blessing. It did nothing to stimulate recovery. Indeed, studies of the act agree that it raised costs and decreased output, precisely the opposite of what is wanted in a slump.

Hoover at least had resisted such proposals for industry although he adopted them for farmers. FDR followed Hoover's farm lead with similar results, higher costs and reduced output. The simplest way to relieve farm distress is to give farmers money directly. Britain did that until it joined the European Community's cartels. But unlike price supports, direct payments do not necessarily reward the biggest producers and they are a visible political target. So Roosevelt adopted Hoover's approach, attempting to support prices, paying for smaller crops.

To be sure, Roosevelt scrapped great portions of the Hoover heritage. Direct relief now went to millions of jobless, through jobs created by the WPA. FDR, no economist, could not understand how the economy or morale could be harmed by employing on simple tasks men who wanted but could not find work. These grants injected on a modest scale some additional purchasing power, some extra aggregate demand.

FDR also threw overboard Hoover's insistence that antidepression public works were a proper task only for states. The PWA built schools, post offices, dams, libraries, and more, enlarging incomes, expanding employment, increasing the nation's capital.

The administration also won far-reaching social reforms to raise living standards for the weakest. Limits were placed on the maximum number of hours a worker could work before receiving overtime; a minimum wage was established; farms were electrified; workers were protected in their attempts to join unions; employers and workers were required to contribute to a pension scheme for the aged. These and other measures launched a welfare state but they did little if anything to relieve the Depression. Unemployment at the depth in 1933 was 12.9

million, 25 percent; four years later, it was still 9 million, 17 percent.[31] Total output had risen from $74.8 billion to $99.5 billion* but was still below the level of 1929.[32] In Roosevelt's first four years, the economy ran far below its potential. The nation lost $154 billion in goods and services, about one and a half times the entire gross national product of 1929.[33]

There had been some recovery from the Depression's trough. Output rose slowly after 1933. But this modest revival had more to do with resilience in the private economy than with the assortment of limited Roosevelt measures. In FDR's first term, the New Deal was a poor argument for compensatory fiscal policy.

"Our policy is succeeding," FDR told the Congress in 1936. But the policy he spoke of was the policy of balancing the budget, of making receipts match spending. "The deficit of today . . . is making possible the surplus of tomorrow," Roosevelt said.[34] He promised to balance the fiscal 1937 budget, to make good the Pittsburgh pledge, provided relief outlays were not counted.

In his public addresses and his policy decisions, Roosevelt seemed to have learned little from his first term. He was still far more concerned with balancing the Federal budget than with the national economy.†

Even so, he had been listening to some heretics. He had picked up the multiplier concept and, in a Detroit campaign speech, explained it to a cheering audience in terms of a pop-

---

* The amounts are calculated in dollars of 1929 buying power.

† Harvard Sitkoff has reached the same conclusion.[35] In FDR's hectic early months in office, he launched seventeen major measures. Eight had little to do with the fight on slump—the NRA and the Securities Exchange Commission, for example. Seven were of some limited help, like the Agricultural Adjustment Act and the Rural Electrification Administration. Only two were of major help—the Works Progress Administration and the Civil Works Administration, which became the WPA.

ular song of the day. Federal spending for drought relief or cattle is spent in turn by its recipients, who buy goods that lead retailers to place orders with wholesalers, whose suppliers hire more workers. "The music went round and round," FDR said, "and a lot of it came out right here in Detroit."[36] But the President was not ready to overturn the prevailing wisdom, to act on his own insights.

Heartened by the modest recovery from the 1933 trough, Roosevelt proudly celebrated his reelection by presenting Congress with a balanced budget. This time, there were no qualifications for relief. For the twelve months beginning June 30, 1937, he planned to reduce Federal spending and increase taxes slightly to produce a surplus of $1.5 billion. The President even proposed to retire $400 million of the national debt.[37] This sounded grand, but it ignored the horrendous 7.7 million still unemployed,[38] a level of factory output still 4.4 percent under 1929, a failure to overcome the Depression.[39] Or rather Roosevelt's economics were still so primitive that he did not understand how his budget would kill the fragile recovery. Like Hoover, he continued to believe that a balanced budget would soothe businessmen and inspire outlays for new plant. He had not yet discovered that business confidence, business investment, depended on cash customers, and their incomes depended in part on whether government was expanding or contracting employment. In any event, Roosevelt was convinced that a balanced budget was good politics, appealing to those moneychangers he had once scourged. His audacious plan to stack the Supreme Court had met with wide condemnation. He needed to restore his orthodox credentials, and a balanced budget was the vehicle.

There is, of course, nothing inherently bad or good in a balanced budget, just as a deficit is neither inherently virtuous nor evil. The utility or disutility of a surplus or a deficit depends entirely on the state of the economy. An economy with fully employed resources, in which all those seeking jobs can find them, with plants producing at their most efficient levels close to capacity, is in danger of overheating, of inflation. The Federal government must not inject added funds into such an economy, either by increased spending, lower taxes or easier credit. The extra funds can't be employed to put idle resources to work; there are none. The extra money will only cause prices to rise. If one million men are working at $20,000 a year each and none are idle, injecting an extra $2 billion will only raise wages and prices by 10 percent at first, more later. A budget surplus, withdrawing funds from the economy, would be the best policy, cooling off demand.

But if 100,000 of those men are idle and 20 percent of the nation's plant is not working, then a very different state of affairs obtains. Now the injection of extra funds—expanded outlays for schools and roads, a tax cut, easier credit—will be spent to hire some of the jobless men and put them to work in the unused plants. Incomes, employment, and output will increase. Here, when resources are lying idle, proper policy is a budget deficit. The government should pour resources into the economy.

At the start of 1937, Roosevelt had it exactly wrong. Resources were still idle on a huge scale but he proposed to depress demand with a surplus. As it happened, one of his chief reforms also worked against him, reinforcing the depressing effect of a surplus. Pensions for the aged, a landmark in social welfare, were about to bring the U.S. nearer to the Germany of Bismarck. But taxes to finance old-age insurance were collected from employers and workers several years before any payments went to the aged. During this period, the system was a great economic depressant, sucking out income, putting nothing in its place.

17

A few weeks after his budget message, Roosevelt delivered his second inaugural address, one of his most eloquent. "Democratic government has innate capacity to protect its people against disasters once considered inevitable," FDR said. "I see one-third of a nation ill-housed, ill-clad and ill-nourished."[40] It was moving, but the President had taken a stance, his insistence on a balanced budget, that must increase misery, add to the army of ill-housed, ill-clad, and ill-nourished.

Roosevelt's deflation froze the gentle recovery and produced a new slump. The economy began turning down in the spring of 1937; by the fall, the evidence of a slump on top of depression was plain. The stock market crashed again, falling 40 percent from its March peak to the trough of late October.[41] The stock market's ability to predict the past is uncanny. Between May and October, industrial production fell 14 percent. More than half a million jobs were lost in October alone.[42] The cancer had developed a tumor.

There now began a decisive battle for Roosevelt's soul, a clash of advisers and policy proposals on a grand scale. The outcome would determine whether history would record Roosevelt as a second Hoover, an interesting man with some decent instincts who failed in the crisis, or a leader with the insight to see a way out. More important, the outcome might determine whether democracy and private property would survive in the United States.

Orthodoxy was led by Henry Morgenthau Jr., Roosevelt's Treasury Secretary, a friend of long standing, a Duchess County neighbor and confidant. "My husband no doubt often treated Henry as a younger brother," Eleanor Roosevelt wrote.[43] "They differed and were annoyed with each other and probably said things neither of them meant on occasion." Both, as John Morton Blum observed,[44] loved the land, had a patrician instinct for public service, and were conservative in ideology. Neither could ever be accused of being an intellectual. Morgenthau had grown up in New York City, the son of a wealthy German Jewish real-estate operator. He was not much interested in school and left Cornell after three semesters. He was unhappy in the business jobs his father picked for him. Morgenthau bought a tract in Duchess County and developed a taste for scientific farming.

Perhaps because he had abandoned them, he never lost his awe of what he called "the big boys," the New York financial community. He believed in their wisdom, including their simple, self-interested solution for an ailing economy, a balanced budget. Roosevelt, his friend and neighbor, drew Morgenthau into Democratic politics, into state government, and finally placed him in the Treasury. There he regularly met with bankers and stock-market moguls, the "big boys," and remained persuaded of their philosophy. He was one in a long line of rich Treasury secretaries, from Andrew Mellon through Ogden Mills to George Humphrey and Robert Anderson, who lacked much understanding of the larger workings of an economy. They thought it should be run like their banks, steel mills, or brokerage houses, or, in Morgenthau's case, his farm: receipts must match, or better, exceed expenses. Deficits hurt the government's credit, compel the use of a printing press to create money, must breed inflation. Deficits strengthen a power-hungry government at the expense of private enterprise. Deficits encourage moral slackness.

Nobody has ever explained why it is sinful for the government to employ a printing press to create money but virtuous for business cartels to raise prices. Government-created inflation is doubtless a bad thing; somehow, it is thought better when inflation results from oligopolistic power.

Morgenthau may not have understood why a reduction of government spending in a slump, a drop in demand, could revive business confidence shattered by a cataclysmic fall in purchasing power. No matter, this is what the "big boys" thought and they must be right.

Against the background of slump on slump, the 1937 descent, Morgenthau was scheduled to deliver a critical speech to leading businessmen at the Academy of Political Science on November 10. The President carefully edited every line of the text. With this speech, Morgenthau hoped to slay the dragon of deficits. He would, he believed, commit his friend and neighbor to balance forever. Morgenthau showed drafts to his key advisers, Jacob Viner, the distinguished international trade specialist, and Harry Dexter White who was to create with Keynes the International Monetary Fund, a monument to conservative deflationist thought. Viner thought Morgenthau's draft was too soft on budget balancing, had unnecessarily conceded there were circumstances when a deficit was warranted.[45] White, however, suggested that Morgenthau's balanced budget in a slump would intensify deflation.[46]

Morgenthau, an honorable man, showed a draft to Marriner Eccles, FDR's governor of the Federal Reserve and Morgenthau's principal administration opponent over the balanced budget.

Eccles was an odd New Dealer.[47] A wealthy Mormon from Utah with inherited interests in profitable banking and sugar enterprises, he was a maverick in the business world. He was the son of a tough Scots immigrant who had made his millions in the West before he learned to read. Young Marriner served his apprenticeship in an inheritance fight when he was twenty-two. He successfully fought off his older half brothers, sons of his polygamous Mormon father's first wife, and preserved his inheritance. When the Depression struck, Eccles saved his banks from the common collapse, but that was not good enough. He had, he wrote, been active in finance and production since 1917, but "I knew less than nothing about its economic and social effects."[48] He had the wit to recognize there is a vast difference between a well-run firm and a properly run national economy. He also knew that the Eastern financiers, the "big boys," had little to tell him.

Eccles turned to the writings of William T. Foster who, with Wadill Catchings, had written *The Road to Plenty* in 1928. Here was a work for a maverick. The book contended that Say's Law, a staple of conventional economists, was wrong. The law held that production created its own demand, implying that there could be no genuine unemployment. Instead, Foster and Catchings argued that demand could fall short because income was absorbed by too much savings that never found its way into investment, into plants and machinery. A lack of consumption, of demand, of aggregate purchasing power, led to leaks from Say's tidy little circle where production and consumption chased each other in equal and identical streams. The leaks led to unemployment, the two radicals wrote. Government spending must close the circle, compensate for inadequate demand.*

This was heady stuff. Roosevelt scrawled in his copy of the book, "Too good to be true. You can't get something for nothing."[49] But Eccles, who thought for himself in these matters, thought otherwise. The message made sense to him and he needed no other authority.

As early as 1931, Eccles was saying some peculiar things. The slump, he insisted, was not made by God's writ and there was nothing holy in the rules of the marketplace. The Depression, as Foster asserted, was due to riotous saving, the saving created by the Federal attempt to make falling taxes exceed outlays, the

* J. M. Keynes, another maverick, but respectable, acknowledged his debt to Foster and Catchings.[50]

savings of fearful businessmen unwilling to invest when there were no customers, and the savings of frightened consumers unwilling to buy postponable goods because their jobs had or would soon disappear. The Depression was not due to wild spending. The crucial element in an economy is aggregate demand. Balance the economy and a balanced Federal budget will follow. Raise aggregate demand. Put idle men and plants to work with government outlays. "An unbalanced budget could help counteract a depression on a downswing," Eccles said.[51]

This was shocking, a proposal for compensatory fiscal policy five years before Keynes's text, *The General Theory of Employment, Interest and Money*. Indeed, Eccles was using the term "compensatory instruments" a year before Keynes published.[52] To be sure, Eccles's insight must not be exaggerated. He had not worked out—as Keynes did—an elaborate, coherent theory that linked savings and investment, the tendency to consume at different income levels, interest and liquidity preference into a might engine explaining employment and unemployment. Moreover, Keynes mapped out his new territory inside the atlas of classical economics, assuring the ultimate support of most of the profession.* But Eccles, with uncommon shrewdness and a refusal to accept conventional foolishness gladly, had seen through to the heart of the matter: a government deficit lifts demand and puts jobless resources to work.

Eccles's views made him attractive to New Dealers, who

---

* Herbert Stein concludes that "no substantial influence from Keynes on the New Deal has been found."[53] The shapers of FDR's 1938 turn to a New Deal—Eccles, Currie, Lubin, Henderson, Ruml—had reached some of the key Keynesian conclusions about appropriate policy in a slump, but they mostly got there without Keynes's map. This is not surprising. Thoughtful men, unbound by dogma, often arrive at similar conclusions, even novel ones, about great affairs. Keynes showed economists why these men were doing the right thing, and the economists then left the universities for Washington to convert the converted.

invited him to Washington. He was introduced to Morgenthau, a large enough man to recognize Eccles's talent. The Treasury Secretary made Eccles his special assistant for monetary and credit problems. When Eugene Black resigned as head of the Federal Reserve, Morgenthau put in a word for Eccles; FDR gave him the job. Now it was unlikely that the central bank would again tighten money at the expense of jobs and output. Indeed, Eccles told a press conference that he favored easy money as long as unemployment was high.

As matters neared a climax in the fall of 1937, Eccles directed a stream of advice at Roosevelt. He had objected vainly to Roosevelt's budget balancing earlier in the year; now that the economy was slumping so badly, FDR was more receptive. Early in November, Eccles gave FDR a powerful memo[54] written by three of the New Deal's star economists, Isador Lubin, Leon Henderson, and Lauchlin Currie.* The memo demonstrated that the cuts in Federal spending had depressed demand and created the new slump. Eccles told the President he must increase consumer demand and business investment by increasing government outlays. Why not housing?

Eccles and his team thought they had won over the President. So they were shattered by Morgenthau's speech at the Academy of Political Science. To a disbelieving audience of business leaders, Morgenthau twice promised that the New Deal would seek balanced budgets. Roosevelt had inserted a sentence in the draft, proclaiming that his administration would protect the weak and safeguard human security. But this seemed to be window dressing. The core of the speech was the conventional prescription. It appeared to signal a reduced role for government

---

* After the war, both Currie and Harry Dexter White paid the penalty for having been right. Congressional un-American hunters drove Currie abroad and hounded White to a fatal heart attack.

and reliance on natural forces to end the new slump and the underlying Depression.

The speech, said Eccles later, "made me wonder whether the New Deal was just a political slogan or if Roosevelt really knew what the New Deal implied."

But the Roosevelt who edited and approved Morgenthau's speech was a complex man. FDR signaled to Eccles and his supporters that he had not been deaf to their message. "It now seems clear," Eccles said, "that the President assented to two contradictory policy approaches within the space of a few hours."[55] Alice's Red Queen would have applauded. She said, "Why, sometimes I've believed as many as six impossible things before breakfast."

The President had privately shown Morgenthau he was not convinced by his Treasury Secretary's speech. What was it that business really wanted, or asked? An assurance that Roosevelt would balance the budget, the Treasury Secretary replied. The President said dismissively, that "old record" again. Morgenthau's speech was a last spin of that "old record."[56]

The slump deepened. About 1.8 million more workers lost jobs between September and December alone.[57] In February of 1938, Keynes sent FDR a letter urging large-scale public works and more government-created credit.[58] But FDR, still debating with himself, turned Keynes's message over to Morgenthau for a reply. FDR told his aides that Keynes's prescription was appropriate for 1933, not now. In 1933, the water was at the bottom of the well, FDR said, implying that pump priming was then in order. But now the water was 25 to 30 percent from the top. Pump priming was inappropriate. Keynes had earlier dismissed Roosevelt as an economic illiterate:[59] the President's parable would not convince him that much progress had been made. In fact, Roosevelt was working his way toward a Keyne-sian, or at least a New Deal, answer.

By early March, FDR agreed with his Duchess County friend, who said the President was treading water, still looking for a solution. On March 25, shares took another nose dive and Roosevelt plunged in. The upcoming autumn congressional elections may have sharpened his economic understanding. In the next few days, the President met privately with expansion-minded advisers: Harry Hopkins, the head of WPA; Leon Henderson; Aubrey Williams, deputy to Hopkins; Beardsley Ruml, an imaginative businessman in the Eccles mold. They came up with a package that ignored the deficit and strengthened de-mand, increasing spending and credit. They proposed $2 bil-lion in extra outlays for the WPA—"ammunition of the highest grade for attack on recession," Roosevelt called it[60]—and other relief agencies; an extra $950 million in loans, mostly to the Public Works Administration, and more credit for banks by reducing the reserves they were compelled to keep idle at the Federal Reserve. Highways, housing, flood control, and Fed-eral buildings all got more money. The President had no prob-lem finding projects once he put his mind to it.

Even so, the program was only half that proposed by his advisers. Ruml had calculated that national income must rise from $56 billion to $86 billion to employ all the jobless. The water was barely above the well's mid-level. Ruml said that the needed $30 billion increase could be gained by adding $10 billion in outlays; the magic of the multiplier would do the rest. If $4 billion came from private business, the government must increase its outlays by $6 billion.[61] But Roosevelt, still cautious, split this total in half. As a result, the first genuine New Deal program to attack slump produced a marked but incomplete recovery. When World War II broke out in August 1939, output and employment still had not reached the peak levels of mid-1937.

Nevertheless, five years after FDR's first inaugural, he finally set in motion a New Deal for the economy. At long last, he was directly attacking depression, unemployment, lower output, and shrunken incomes.

FDR called in Morgenthau in April 10 to show off his handiwork. "You will have to hurry to catch up," the President said kindly. "Mr. President, maybe I never can catch up," Morgenthau replied in some pain.[62] His policy overturned, the Treasury Secretary told FDR he wanted to resign. But Roosevelt, apparently fearful of a conservative campaign against his proposals, pleaded with Morgenthau to stay. Essentially a simple man with limited personal ambition, Morgenthau agreed. He sacrificed his deeply held economic prejudices to his friendship with FDR.

Twenty years later, after rearmament and war proved the expansionists were right, Morgenthau could still say he was sorry that his approach had not been tried longer. His limited understanding of the economy remained invincible.

Eccles, who had orchestrated the great turn, stayed on as head of the central bank until 1951. In his last years, he showed a rare consistency. With the postwar economy near full employment, he successfully struggled to free the Federal Reserve from the Treasury's grip and so reestablish the central bank as a deflationary force. Eccles was no mindless deficit spender but a man who saw that right policy depends on circumstances.

Roosevelt brought his expansionary program to Congress on April 14 and revealed that he was now a convinced partisan of compensatory fiscal policy. He called attention to the unbalanced economy, not the unbalanced budget. The national income had reached $80 billion in 1928, he said. It fell below $40 billion in 1932. Then it climbed to $68 billion in 1937, but it had been falling for six months and now stood at only $58 billion. We must increase national income and employment, FDR said, but "we suffer from a failure of consumer demand."

This was the decisive phrase and it required the government to act. The economy was stumbling because of a lack of aggregate demand; only the government could supply the missing purchasing power. The private sector could but would not respond until government demand increased. Let us lift national income to the 1928 level, to $80 billion, said Roosevelt. Let us seek to rise above $100 billion in a decade.[63] (By 1948, output of goods and services, allowing for price changes, actually reached $144.8 billion.[64]) As the incomes of citizens rise, the President explained, government spending for relief and other measures drops automatically; at the same time, receipts from taxes on higher incomes must rise. That is how the budget will be balanced, not on the backs of more unemployed but from the greater wealth in the nation. At last, FDR had reversed the order: A balanced budget, as Morgenthau would have it, could not restore prosperity. Eccles was right. Prosperity made a balanced budget possible.

Like other converts, FDR was a hot gospeler, an impassioned preacher for his new cause. He told the Congressmen, "The Federal debt . . . can only be paid if the Nation obtains a vastly increased citizen income." The latest slump that began in the spring of 1937, he said, can be traced to an overly rapid cutback in public works coupled with the depressing effect of the new Social Security taxes. The recovery that came before the slump was "due to a number of factors. Among the more important was the fact that government expenditures in providing employment and purchasing power had been greatly increased."[65]

In January 1939, a confident FDR asserted that by "resuming government activities last spring, we reversed a recession and started the new rising tide of prosperity and national income." If government spending is maintained, we will reach the $80 billion income level.[66]

History does not disclose its alternatives. We cannot know whether FDR could have maintained this course in the face of the massed opposition of business, banking, the press, and almost everyone that mattered. There are, after all, some advantages in unemployment for the well-fixed. Militant union leaders tend to lose their members when the competition for work is stiff. Managing a plant is considerably easier when there are men outside clamoring for work. Business control of public policy is more difficult in a peacetime economy at high employment.

In the event, the question did not arise. Preparing for war lifted the economy rapidly. Unemployment was still 9.5 million in 1939,[67] more than one in six. But it melted under the outlays for weapons. Weapons and war underlined the ability of governments to counter inadequate demand, to put men and resources to work.

Later administrations paid renewed obeisance to the virtues of a balanced budget. But this was lip service for the most part. Herbert Stein[68] wrote that no government would ever again attempt to balance its budget, to increase taxes or cut expenditures in a depression. No government would repeat the catastrophic policies of Hoover or the five-year paralysis of FDR.

NOTES

1. Samuel I. Rosenman, *Working with Roosevelt* (New York: Da Capo Press, 1972), p. 87.

2. Franklin D. Roosevelt, *The Public Papers and Addresses of Franklin D. Roosevelt*, vol. 5 (New York: Random House, 1938), p. 19.

3. *Historical Statistics of the United States, Colonial Times to 1970: Bicentennial Edition* (U.S. Department of Commerce, 1975), p. 135.

4. Lester Chandler, *America's Greatest Depression 1929–1941* (New York: Harper & Row, 1970), p. 3.

5. Herbert Stein, *The Fiscal Revolution in America* (Chicago: University of Chicago Press, 1969), pp. 107–8; Barton J. Bernstein, "The Conservative Achievements of Liberal Reform," in *Towards a New Past*, edited by Barton J. Berstein (New York: Pantheon Books, 1968), p. 272.

6. Harvard Sitkoff, ed., *Fifty Years Later: The New Deal Evaluated* (Philadelphia: Temple University Press, 1985), p. 485.

7. David Burner, *Herbert Hoover: A Public Life* (New York: Alfred A. Knopf, 1979), p. 239.

8. *Ibid.*, p. 244.

9. Herbert Hoover, *The Memoirs of Herbert Hoover: The Great Depression, 1929–1941* (New York: Macmillan, 1952), p. 30.

10. William J. Barber, *From New Era to New Deal* (Cambridge: Cambridge University Press, 1985), p. 18.

11. *Ibid.*, p. 22.

12. James Stuart Olson, *Herbert Hoover and the Reconstruction Finance Corporation, 1931–33* (Ames, Iowa: Iowa State University Press, 1977), p. 59.

13. Hoover, *The Memoirs of Herbert Hoover*, p. 54.

14. *Ibid.*, p. 56.

15. Burner, *Herbert Hoover*, p. 252.

16. Barber, *From New Era to New Deal*, p. 54.

17. Harris G. Warren, *Herbert Hoover and the Great Depression* (New York: Oxford University Press, 1959), p. 91.

18. Hoover, *The Memoirs of Herbert Hoover*, pp. 291–2.

19. Milton Friedman and Anna Schwartz, *A Monetary History of the United States 1867–1960* (Princeton: Princeton University Press, 1963), pp. 376–7.

20. Albert U. Romasco, *The Politics of Recovery* (New York: Oxford University Press), p. 233.

21. Stein, *The Fiscal Revolution*, p. 32; Chandler, *American Monetary Policy*, p. 125.

22. Barber, *From New Era to New Deal*, p. 124.

23. Friedman and Schwartz, *Monetary History*, p. 407.

24. *Ibid.*, p. 409.

25. *Ibid.*, p. 299.

26. *Ibid.*, p. 301.

27. John Kenneth Galbraith, *The Great Crash—1929* (Boston: Houghton Mifflin Co., 1954), p. 190.

28. Romasco, *The Politics of Recovery*, p. 87.

29. Lester Chandler, *American Monetary Policy, 1928–1941* (New York: Harper & Row, 1971), pp. 7, 59.

30. Bernard Bellush, *The Failure of the NRA* (New York: W.W. Norton, 1975), p. 27.

31. *Historical Statistics of the United States, Colonial Times to 1970: Bicentennial Edition*, p. 135.

32. Chandler, *American Monetary Policy*, p. 59.

33. Chandler, *America's Greatest Depression*, p. 4.

34. Roosevelt, *Public Papers and Addresses*, p. 21.

35. Sitkoff, *Fifty Years Later*, p. 4.

36. Stein, *The Fiscal Revolution*, p. 73.

37. Roosevelt, *Public Papers and Addresses*, p. 654.

38. *Historical Statistics of the United States*, p. 135.

39. United States Federal Reserve Board, *Federal Reserve Bulletin* (Washington, D.C.: U.S. Government Printing Office, May 1937), p. 474.

40. Franklin D. Roosevelt, *The Public Papers and Addresses of Franklin D. Roosevelt*, vol. 6 (New York: Random House, 1938), pp. 1–14.

41. Dean L. May, *From New Deal to New Economics* (New York: Garland, 1981), p. 4.

42. United States Federal Reserve Board, *Federal Reserve Bulletin* (Washington D.C.: U.S. Government Printing Office, January 1938), p. 44; United States Bureau of Labor Statistics, *Monthly Labor Review* (Washington D.C.: U.S. Government Printing Office, January 1938), p. 224.

43. Eleanor Roosevelt in Preface to John Morton Blum, *From the Morgenthau Diaries* (Boston: Houghton Mifflin, 1959).

44. For further biographical information on Henry Morgenthau, see John Morton Blum, *From the Morgenthau Diaries*.

45. May, *From New Deal to New Economics*, p. 102.

46. Blum, *From the Morgenthau Diaries*, p. 389.

47. See Sidney Hyman, *Marriner Eccles* (Stanford University, California: Graduate School of Business, 1976).

48. Hyman, *Marriner Eccles*, p. 77.

49. Arthur M. Schlesinger, Jr., *The Crisis of the Old Order* (Boston: Houghton Mifflin, 1957), p. 136.

50. John Maynard Keynes, *Treatise on Money*, vol. I (New York: Harcourt, Brace, 1930), p. 178.

51. Hyman, *Marriner Eccles*, p. 96.

52. May, *From New Deal to New Economics*, p. 83.

53. Stein, *The Fiscal Revolution*, p. 148.

54. Hyman, *Marriner Eccles*, p. 240.

55. *Ibid.*, p. 241.

56. Blum, *From the Morgenthau Diaries*, p. 392.

57. *Ibid.*, p. 398.

58. Stein, *The Fiscal Revolution*, p. 108.

59. Thomas K. McCraw, "The New Deal and the Mixed Economy," in Sitkoff, *Fifty Years Later*, p. 43.

60. Franklin D. Roosevelt, *The Public Papers and Addresses of Franklin D. Roosevelt*, vol. 7 (New York: Random House, 1938), p. 227.

61. Stein, *The Fiscal Revolution*, p. 111.

62. Blum, *From the Morgenthau Diaries*, p. 420.

63. Roosevelt, *Public Papers and Addresses*, vol. 7, p. 226.

64. *Economic Report of the President* (Washington D.C.: U.S. Government Printing Office, 1950), pp. 149, 169.

65. Roosevelt, *Public Papers and Addresses*, vol. 7, pp. 230–4.

66. Franklin D. Roosevelt, *The Public Papers and Addresses of Franklin D. Roosevelt*, vol. 8 (New York: Random House, 1938), p. 10.

67. *Historical Statistics of the United States*, p. 135.

68. Stein, *The Fiscal Revolution*, p. 54.

II

The War Solution

Despite Roosevelt's belated conversion to the doctrine of aggregate demand, the New Deal failed to end the Great Depression. The new beliefs were not backed with enough money; Federal outlays fell far short of what was required. "Fiscal policy then, seems to have been an unsuccessful recovery device in the 'thirties." said E. Carey Brown, "not because it did not work, but because it was not tried."[1]

Roosevelt's enlarged spending program in 1938 finally raised the economy above the 1929 benchmark. But it was still operating at nearly 25 percent below its potential, what it could produce if all workers able to work were employed and all plants producing. By 1940, orders were coming in from a Europe at war and mobilization began at home. Total output reached $100 billion. After allowing for the Depression's deflation in prices, this was 9 percent above the gross national product in the last boom year.[2] Unemployment remained grim, however. Nine million were jobless in 1939 and eight million, more than one in seven, a year later.[3]

An expert in the New Deal Treasury, Sherwood M. Fine, estimated Roosevelt's 1938 stimulus at $4.5 billion of spending and lending. But, largely agreeing with Ruml, Fine said that more than twice that, $10 to $15 billion, was needed to reach full employment.[4] Such a figure was beyond political reality. FDR may have discovered the virtue of spending and deficit to overcome deficient demand, but Congress was populated with traditional budget balancers.

World War II brought the Depression to an end. What the New Deal had failed to do, create enough extra demand to make up for the deficiency of private businessmen, farmers, and consumers, the war compelled Roosevelt to do. It called forth history's greatest expenditure on public works: rifles, guns, tanks, ships, planes, and all the supporting ordnance to defeat the Germans and the Japanese. The military demand for soldiers alone was enough to absorb all the 8 million unemployed. The armed forces increased by 11 million from 1941 to 1945.[5] Despite this drain, the civilian labor force barely diminished. Women, older men, youngsters who would otherwise have been in school, the disabled who could not find peacetime jobs, all were sucked into munitions plants, drawn by high wages, excitement, and patriotism.

The steep rise in the military and the civilian labor force showed that unemployment in the Depression had been grossly understated. Millions who should have been counted as jobless were left out of the statistics because they were too discouraged to seek work. With the genuine prospect of a job, they would have applied. The war held out that prospect.

How government spending absorbed unemployment shows up clearly in the table on page 35 constructed by Robert Heilbroner and Aaron Singer.[6]

Just before the war, Federal spending was $6 billion and 8 million were jobless. A year later, war outlays tripled U.S. purchases and the jobless rolls fell below 6 million. By 1944, war spending had expanded government outlays nearly 14 times; unemployment was under one million, perhaps less than the

	Federal Purchases ($ billions)	GNP ($ billions)	Unemployment (millions)
1940	6.2	100.6	8.1
1941	19.9	125.8	5.6
1942	52.0	159.1	2.7
1943	81.2	192.5	1.1
1944	89.0	211.4	.7
1945	74.8	213.4	1.0

number simply between jobs, a condition of overfull employment.

The effect of government spending on the nation's total output was just as spectacular. In 1939, before foreign nations began filling their arsenals with U.S. goods and before the first tentative steps to mobilize in the U.S., the government bought $13.1 billion worth of goods and services. Total national output was only $91.3 billion, still below 1929. By 1944, the government was spending $96.5 billion, more than all the output in 1939, and national product had reached $211.4 billion.[7]

Workers, now in demand after years of futile job hunting, enjoyed high wages, even if they couldn't find everything they wanted to buy. But many businessmen refused to believe what they saw. They knew that the nation could not spend its way out of a depression, that government could only hinder not help the economy. A common view held that the war bubble would burst. Many businessmen simply refused to enlarge their plants to meet the new demand. Eleven years of slump had scarred the corporate psyche. So the government had to coax. Businessmen got fast tax write-offs for new plants and tools; they won contracts to cover all their costs and guarantee profits. They were allowed to lease plants built by the government to produce synthetic rubber; they transported oil through a huge government-built pipeline.

This treatment transformed many corporate leaders, even those who mouthed the old slogans. Businessmen learned that government can be an accommodating partner, a profitable partner, a source of power and income. The animal spirits and entrepreneurial innovation that Joseph Schumpeter associated with classical capitalists had long since been tamed in many corporate bureaucracies. Government bureaucracies were much the same, only not as well paid. The alliance of businessmen and Federal government formed in the war has remained unbroken. The rise of corporate executives to the inmost circles of government, on occasion to dominate government, was, with full employment, one of the war's unexpected creations. Between 1940 and 1944, corporate profits rose nearly 60 percent, from $6.1 billion to $9.6 billion.[8]

In some ways, the war's most remarkable effect was on home-front living standards. There was little. Goods and services for noncombatants never decreased. This was an economy of guns and butter. Home-front consumers felt the pinch of shortages only because their incomes had risen rapidly, because they had more purchasing power. But by the end of the war in 1945, output per person for civilians was only one percent less than in 1939.[9]

It is unlikely that any other fighting nation enjoyed so easy a war but then few other nations had suffered so heavily in idle men and plant before the war. This reservoir of unemployed produced the butter and guns. In Britain, output per head for consumers had fallen 30 percent by the end of the war; in the Soviet Union, the cut was 31 percent[10]even though the population had been reduced brutally.

The U.S. economy enjoyed another special advantage. Output for soldiers and civilians was never interrupted by bombing or invasion, the common experience of other nations at war. Actually, bombing need not reduce and can actually increase war production by compelling more rational management. This happened in Germany. Nevertheless, it is unlikely that civilian output gains from enemy bomber strikes. Their absence from U.S. skies helped prevent a drop in home-front standards.

The long war boom brought unprecedented prosperity. Measured in dollars of 1958 purchasing power, income per head rose more than 50 percent above the benchmark 1929 level. It climbed from $1671 to $2538. This more than doubled the $1126 at the bottom of the slump in 1933.[11] But the statistics are incomplete for they do not disclose how the gains were divided. Nearly half of the families in the U.S. still earned less than $3000 a year,[12] the government's minimum standard for a decent living for a family of four.

Among workers, the organized did best, those in the new CIO unions in the mass-production industries—autos, steel, rubber—and those in the old AFL craft unions—building trades, teamsters, machinists, printers. Trade-union membership soared. Anti-union employers took on hands at any price; union workers no longer needed to fear vengeful bosses. The Roosevelt administration encouraged union membership and union rolls grew from 8.7 million in 1940 to 14.3 million in 1945. Outside farming, a third of the labor force held union cards.[13] Vice President Henry Wallace said, "When men begin to hunt for jobs, the bargaining power of labor begins to weaken and union funds begin to melt away."[14] Conversely, plenty of jobs built up union strength and union funds.

Despite differences within and between classes, the war boom was in stark contrast with the pervasive misery of the 1930s. What had happened was clear, at least at the time. A depression had been cured by the massive spending of government for goods and services, by the acceptance of huge budget deficits that absorbed idle men and plants.

But what would happen after the war when military demand would shrink, when war plants would release millions of unwanted workers, when the military would discharge millions of GIs? The more ebullient New Dealers and businessmen were convinced that slumps were a thing of the past, that the war had disclosed the secret of perpetual prosperity. But many others doubted and feared. Conservative businessmen and their trade-union allies, mostly in the old American Federation of Labor, expected and perhaps welcomed a postwar slump. The old orthodoxies had made life agreeable for the traditional chiefs of labor and business corporations. It was far from clear that their interest would be served by a world in which radical industrial unions and Federal officials made crucial decisions about wages, taxes, and public contracts. These conservatives predicted a great economic crash after the war. They would survive, they knew, and government and the radicals would then shrink to their proper size. Other citizens, uninfluenced by interest, were puzzled and worried too. They feared that the government's demand would disappear with peace. They expected a slump that would bring down prices, just like the Great Depression. They backed their beliefs by clinging to their money. The velocity of money, the speed with which a dollar bill travels from hand to hand, matched or fell below Depression levels during the war.[15] This unexpected phenomenon powerfully restrained inflation.

Within the corporate establishment, there were dissenters to the prevailing gloom. *Fortune* Magazine polled some businessmen and found 51.2 percent thought business would be better after the war than before.[16] This was exceptional. The more traditional National Association of Manufacturers had questioned economists in the American Economic Association at the start of the war and 80 percent thought a depression was coming. Only one economist in 25 thought this slump could be eased by appropriate actions.[17] Experience and Keynes had not yet touched everybody.*

William Green, president of the American Federation of Labor, told the Senate, "we are going to be faced with a degree, and I think a large degree, of unemployment."[18] His chief economist, Boris Shiskin, foresaw at least 4 million unemployed at the war's end, those that "cannot be absorbed anywhere," and warned that the jobless level could rise to 20 million. Leo Cherne, a popular postwar publicist and an early television pundit, refined Shiskin a bit. He predicted unemployment of 19 million.[19]

Even at the bottom of the Depression, unemployment had been 12.8 million, far less.[20]

The corporate right and its academic and union allies went too far. Their gloomy forecasts probably strengthened the popular conviction that this must not happen. It created a political climate in which the Republican presidential candidate and a conservative House were ultimately compelled to endorse maximum employment.

Gloomy forecasts were not the exclusive property of the right.

---

* Even after the war in 1946–47 at a prominent college like Dartmouth, *Keynes*, the *multiplier, consumption function, compensatory*, and *countercyclical policy* were words and phrases from a foreign language. The theory side of the economics department was run by Bruce Knight, a less famous brother of Frank Knight, a Chicago economist for whom Keynes and all his work were an illusion.

Many New Deal Keynesians feared the government would not act decisively enough to avert slump. Their warnings intensified the demand for action. Seymour Harris of Harvard said in 1945 that a cut of perhaps $75 billion in Federal spending would produce a "downward spiral from which the system would never recover." The government, not consumers, could fill the gap, but in any event, "the volume of unemployment may be considerable."[21]

Donald Nelson, chairman of the War Production Board, urged an early start on civilian output, even before the war ended. That, he said, might allay some concern. "What gives workers and others 'cutback jitters' is the fear that they will find themselves thrust into a plan-less and chaotic economic state of affairs as soon as war orders fall on a large scale, becoming worse when peace comes." He worried that the Army wanted to "protect war production" from civilian competition "by the simple means of creating pools of unemployment."[22]

In a careful study of the war economy, the Budget Bureau said that government planners recognized there was a postwar danger of either inflation or slump. On the whole it feared slump was likelier. Alvin Hansen, reporting to another governmental agency, said: "Businessmen, wage-earners, white collar employees, professional people, farmers—all alike expect and fear a post-war collapse. Demobilization of armies, shutdowns in defense industries, unemployment, deflation, bankruptcy, hard times."[23] Even Henry Wallace, the visionary Vice President in Roosevelt's third term, who insisted that there could be 60 million postwar jobs, shared the general pessimism. "I hope the postwar slump will not be so big when it finally comes," he told a Los Angeles audience in 1944.[24] A *New York Times* headline on August 12, 1945, two days after victory over Japan, announced "5,000,000 expected to lose arms jobs."[25]

Against the fear of disaster, another current was running. Many Americans had made the connection between government spending and prosperity, between government demand and jobs. They had no interest in perpetuating prewar arrangements. They insisted that wartime prosperity must continue.

Another *Fortune* poll in the fall of 1944 asked whether the Federal government should provide jobs for all those willing to work. Two-thirds said yes.[26] This was significant. It meant that there was a widespread belief that the government was capable of creating jobs, was not merely an economic referee or idle bystander at impersonal markets. It meant many wanted the government to do in peace what it had done in war, assure full employment.

Some New Dealers seized on this mood. "Unemployment and idle plants in the midst of unsatisfied wants represents an intolerable, undesirable and inexcusable condition," said a forceful young economist, Robert R. Nathan.[27] "We have seen the last of our great depressions," Chester Bowles, the price controller, wrote Wallace. "For the simple reason that the public [is] wise enough to know it doesn't have to stand for one."[28]

At the White House, Roosevelt had said he had replaced "Dr. New Deal" with "Dr. Win the War,"[29] putting aside social and economic reform for the duration, subordinating everything to maximum production for victory. He was inviting businessmen to believe that they no longer had anything to fear from his government, that they were welcome to share in power. Even so, New Dealers continued to man outposts in the capacious bureaucracy. One was the National Resources Planning Board, a White House think tank run by the President's uncle Frederic

A. Delano. It was here that Alvin Hansen recited the war's lessons for sustaining prosperity. Hansen was a Harvard economist and the most eloquent Keynesian in the U.S.* He wrote: "We have seen how it is possible to mobilize the productive capacities of the country for war. We can also mobilize them for peace . . . we cannot afford idleness." The $90 billion spent annually on war will disappear with peace. This leaves a gap in demand that must be filled. Consumers, Hansen said, will use their accumulated war savings to buy autos, washing machines, and refrigerators they can't get in wartime. That won't be enough. We must repeal war taxes; expand Federal welfare programs; promote highways, slum clearance and other public works; provide loans to rebuild war-damaged nations and help "backward" countries.[30]

The Hansen program was so prescient that Congress soon after abolished the National Resources Planning Board. It had a socialist flavor. But the damage had been done. The ideas were loose. Full employment was not only practical but became a popular political slogan. Everybody rushed to get on the bandwagon. On his way to a fourth term, FDR declared in his 1943 State of the Union message that veterans "will have the right to expect full employment . . . for themselves and for all able-bodied men and women in America who want to work."[31] By the election year of 1944, Roosevelt was urging a new Bill of Rights which began with "the right to a useful and remunerative job."[32] The Democratic program boasted that FDR's administration had guaranteed full employment.

---

* One of Harvard's intellectual treats after the war was the money and banking course for graduate economics students. Hansen took the first semester and gave a brilliant exposition of Keynes's *General Theory*, a compelling demonstration of its logic. Canny John Williams, an adviser to the Federal Reserve, lectured the second semester, casting grave doubt on nearly every point Hansen had raised.

The Republicans were not far behind. The platform drafters tried to fudge the issue to please those banking and corporate chiefs who were still appalled at the government's new, central role. The platform said, "We shall promote the fullest stable employment *through private enterprise*"[33] (my italics). But the Republican presidential candidate knew that was not what voters wanted to hear. In his acceptance speech Thomas E. Dewey said, "This must be a land where every man and woman has a fair chance to work and get ahead. Never again must free Americans face the specter of long-continued mass unemployment."[34] To clear up ambiguities in the platform, Dewey said that if private enterprise could not provide work for all, "then government can and must create additional job opportunities."[35]

In three years, the war had built bipartisan allegiance for the notion that the Federal government should underwrite a stable economy to assure high employment. In government, the New Deal economists, encouraged by Hansen, quietly came together to turn the wartime practice of compensatory fiscal policy into law. The band included Gerhard Colm of the Budget Bureau, Richard Gilbert and Walter Salant of the Office of Price Administration, Louis Bean of the Agriculture Department, and Leon Keyserling, a lawyer who later became chairman of Truman's Council of Economic Advisers. The group tried to make permanent the revolution wrought by depression and war, to compel future administrations to support full employment. Under American law, no administration can bind its successors without a constitutional amendment. But in the enthusiasm of wartime prosperity, this did not deter the Keynesians.

They drafted an ingenious "Full Employment Act" and found Senator James Murray, a liberal Democrat from Montana, to sponsor it. The bill required the President to make an annual assessment of the economy, to determine whether the economy would fall short of creating full employment or produce too much demand. The President must then map a program of expanded or reduced investment to correct any shortfall or excess.

The economics were as curious as the politics. Read literally, the bill would rely exclusively on Federal spending and ignore taxes or monetary policy. Nevertheless the measure got through the Senate. It carried the blessing of a new President, Harry Truman, who realized Democrats faced an election in 1946 with little else to combat the massive postwar unemployment most people feared. A conservative House of Representatives, however, was less easily stampeded. It worked its will and heavily altered the Murray bill.

In the end, however, the conservatives had to acknowledge the force of public opinion. The Keynesian New Dealers got the essence of what they had sought, a Congressional commitment to the proposition that the government can and should promote jobs. The final version was styled The Employment Act of 1946. The word "Full" had been dropped as a modifier for "Employment" and conservatives thought this was a major triumph. The presidential forecast and investment program were also deleted. Instead the act simply stated: "The Congress hereby declares that it is the continuing policy and responsibility of the Federal Government to use all practicable means . . . to promote maximum employment, production and purchasing power."[36] What this lacked in compulsory investment planning it gained in simplicity. Successive governments in the United States and later in western Europe made similar commitments to maximum employment, the heart of economic policy until about 1980. Then, a new breed of conservatives took power in Britain, the United States, and West Germany, and the pledge to maintain jobs was quietly killed.

Even in 1945 and 1946, not everyone thought high employment was a good idea. Several businessmen extolled the value of jobless men. Carlyle Fraser of the Atlanta Chamber of Commerce insisted that capitalism requires a "floating pool of unemployed." Ralph Blodgett, another witness before the Senate Banking Committee, hoped depressions would never be abolished because they offered opportunities for "smart folks."[37] In 1945 and 1946, however, these were not popular policies.

As it happened, the conversion from war to peace was far smoother than the framers of the Employment Act had expected. The cries of postwar disaster were confounded. *Fortune*'s businessmen, at least the narrow majority, got it right. Unemployment stood at an irreducible minimum of 830,000 in August 1945. Despite the joblessness forced on men and women moving from one life to another, unemployment rose only to 2.7 million in 1946.[38] This was half the forecast implied by the *New York Times* and about one-seventh the volume predicted by Shiskin of the AFL or Leo Cherne. There had been some deliberate strengthening of demand by the government, notably a tax cut, and that had helped. But a force largely unexpected, outside the models of the Keynesian policy makers, made the feared conversion to peace almost painless, sustaining aggregate demand, easing the shift of returned soldiers and released defense workers to new peacetime work.

So many had been so wrong because they had missed a critical fact: workers and businessmen had built up huge savings during the war, forced savings generated by the explosion of incomes in the war. The wartime output of consumer goods was higher than the Depression levels but wasn't nearly large enough to absorb the huge increase in demand created by putting the jobless to work and rapidly expanding paychecks. Makers of autos, refrigerators, and washing machines had turned to producing tanks, planes, and ships. Construction workers, those not in the Army, built war plants instead of civilian factories or homes, so consumers almost tripled their liquid savings, their holdings of bank deposits and government bonds. These soared from $48 billion to $146 billion from 1940 to the war's end. The liquid holdings of business rose even faster, from $22 billion to $80 billion. Here was a huge reservoir of effective demand, waiting to be spent when peace came. Before the war, those with incomes saved less than $5 of every $100 earned; during the war, this skyrocketed to $24.10 and from much larger incomes.[39]

With peace, the dam broke and this huge reservoir of demand poured across a rapidly retooling American industry. Savings in 1945 were at a peak of $19.20 in every $100. Then they plunged to $8.20 in 1946, $3.10 in 1947 and $5.90 in 1948.[40] This reflected a buying binge of mammoth proportions. Citizens were spending income faster than they earned it. Lester V. Chandler calculated that for every added dollar of income in 1945, people spent $2.80. The next year, this rose to $3.53 and fell back only part way to $1.38 in 1947.[41] This was a remarkable reversal of the normal order of things, a flat contradiction of Keynes's consumption function. He held that people save a growing fraction of extra income, spend relatively less as incomes rise. Both common-sense observation and the consumption function, valid in normal times, were tossed overboard. American consumers went on a postwar spree, drawing down their huge accumulation of wartime savings.

The widely predicted hump in unemployment never took place. In fact, jobs rose by 7 million in the first postwar year to

58 million. Unemployment at 2 million was 3.3 percent, near the minimum possible.[42] (There is always some unemployment since people shifting from one job to another are counted as unemployed. Many discharged veterans and dismissed war workers fell into this class briefly.)

Hoover and Roosevelt had vetoed bonuses for World War I veterans, deepening the Depression. This time, politicians competed to give veterans benefits. The GI bill sent 800,000 to college right after the war and provided training for about half of 15.6 million veterans.[43] Besides enlarging skills, the measure sharply reduced the demand for jobs. That is what it was supposed to do, and also support the colleges. Some 2.2 million women left war plants and the labor force to go back to school or make homes for returning veterans.[44] By the fall of 1945, war jobs had shrunk by the five million that the *Times* had forecast. But this brought no hardship. War plants became civilian factories and hired many who were laid off. Others stopped working of their own accord.

The government was not a passive spectator. The new Truman administration shared the common fear of a postwar slump and made a contribution to shore up demand. There was a tax cut of $6 billion in 1945 and it reflected "the fear of deflation and unemployment," Chandler wrote.[45] Reliance on a tax cut was, moreover, something of a departure. The New Deal's Keynesian planners had concentrated on expanding government outlays to enlarge demand. They rarely discussed tax cuts, putting money directly in the hands of taxpayers. Before the war, tax cuts would have benefited directly only a relative few, the rich who paid taxes. But the tax net had widened more than tenfold during the war, from 4 million taxpayers in 1940 to 42 million by 1945.[46] Now, most households would gain purchasing power from a tax cut.

In terms of economic stimulus, there is little to choose between cutting taxes and increased spending, although tax cuts can enlarge incomes more quickly. Conservatives prefer them because they expand individual choice, give people more discretion over how any extra income is to be spent. Economists like Keynes and John Kenneth Galbraith, those who argue that a selfish capitalism starves public, social goods—the arts, housing, cleansing the environment, roads, recreation—urged added increments of spending for public works. Bureaucrats and union leaders also prefer public works because they enhance their power. But the economic consequences are largely the same: added spending or tax reduction enlarges income when resources are idle; reduced spending and tax increases shrink income.

Despite the ease of conversion, the depth of the national commitment to the new policy of high employment was untested. The postwar economy was bedeviled more by inflation than deflation, by rising prices rather than falling jobs. Truman was neither psychologically nor politically prepared to deal with the first postwar recession late in 1948. So Truman's response was tepid despite his earlier tactical support for Murray's full employment bill. Indeed, he had shown he was a reluctant convert to countercyclical policy—deliberate spending or tax cutting to offset a slump—in his first major message to Congress in August 1945.

The new President said he wanted "a national reassertion of the right to work" and "a declaration of the ultimate duty of Government to use its own resources." But government should be invoked only if "all other methods should fail to prevent prolonged unemployment."[47] In other words, the government is a last resort and intervenes only when unemployment lasts a long time. This largely passive position was common to Truman and Eisenhower. Both were willing to accept the deficits created automatically by a slump, a fall in taxes collected, a rise in outlays for unemployment compensation. But they were reluctant to increase the deficit by active measures to fight recession vigorously.

Early in 1949, with the recession already underway, Truman actually sought a $4 billion tax increase. It was "essential," he said, to balance the budget.[48] That revived the discredited policy of Hoover and the language of the first-term Roosevelt. Of course, Truman's tax call came when the short, shallow slump had barely begun. A reporter asked the President if he wanted the tax increase even in a recession. Truman replied that it was "just as advisable then as now for the simple reason that it doesn't affect the expenses of the government and we are trying to avoid a deficit."[49] If this means anything it means that Truman thought he could fight a slump simply by maintaining government outlays, that what he did with taxes was irrelevant. Clearly, understanding of aggregate demand had not reached all corners of the White House. *

Anyway, Truman's performance was better than his words. Six months after his plea for a tax increase, Truman announced he no longer wanted the measure. By doing nothing, by letting tax receipts fall and spending like unemployment benefits rise, Truman had fought off the slump. The budget had been in surplus at a $3.8 billion yearly rate in the fourth quarter of 1948. The automatic stabilizers, particularly the broad-based, progressive income tax, produced a deficit of $3.9 billion in the spring

---

* Presidents are often better dealing with economic ideas in writing than off the cuff. Truman's 1950 Economic Report pointed out that "an expanding economy" is the best course toward a balanced budget and "In the long run, the Government's fiscal position depends upon the health of the national economy."[50] This hints at the nice distinction between a deficit caused by inadequate demand, a cyclical deficit, and one caused by inadequate taxes or excessive spending, a structural deficit.

of 1949.[51] The switch from surplus to deficit gave the economy a stimulus of $7.7 billion, enough to end the slump. Truman, moreover, was clearly uneasy about the dip that had taken place. "The downturn brought anxiety and suffering to millions who became unemployed and to their families," Truman wrote.[52] In fact, unemployment had averaged 3.4 million or 5 percent.[53] This is lower than the jobless rates more recent presidents have celebrated as the product of unmatched prosperity.

One reason for the smooth transition from war to peace was that peace in fact never came completely. Instead, World War was replaced by Cold War, a conflict of feint and maneuver that sustained arms and aid spending on a generous scale, expanding total demand. Among government and private élites, there was a common view that the Soviet Union was determined on world domination and this challenge must be met by a robust U.S. response. Among other things, the response meant rebuilding the economies of friendly nations in Western Europe, Greece, and Turkey with large loans and gifts. These were claims on American resources, an increment of added demand. A robust response also meant reversing the precipitous drop in American spending on soldiers and arms, reconstructing the nation's armed might, further expanding Federal demand.

During the war, Sherwood Fine, the Treasury expert, said, "Defense expenditures and subsequent war outlays are, in a sense, carrying to fruition the expansionist spending doctrines expressed during the 1930s. The enormous war-spending program is achieving what peacetime relief and recovery outlays failed to accomplish." He shrewdly forecast that after the war, "We shall attempt to avoid the dislocating impact of swift demobilization upon our domestic economy."[54]

The more sophisticated government officials knew they must avoid the dislocation of swift demobilization, find something to match at least part of the war spending that had brought prosperity.

One way of reducing dislocation was to enlarge exports, sales to foreigners. A war-ravaged Europe and Japan were hungry for U.S. food, tools, plants, consumer goods, everything they could not yet produce. They lacked the dollars to pay for the goods, however. So the U.S. gave them gifts and loans, paying American exporters the currency their foreign customers did not have. The motives for all this were mixed. The U.S. was genuinely concerned about suffering abroad; it wanted to win Europeans from communism and carve out an expanding share in world markets. But as Chandler wrote, a major reason for U.S. generosity was "the desire to avoid depression and unemployment here." Chandler doubted that "we needed an export surplus to avoid depression but this seems to have been an important though not the dominant consideration."[55]

Between 1946 and 1948, the years of reconversion, exports totaled an impressive $25.4 billion. About 60 percent of this was paid by the Marshall plan or European Recovery Program and other government grant and loan schemes. This must be kept in scale, however. Exports in the period never ran above 5 percent of total output, virtually the same as the current share.[56]

President Truman and his officials were sensitive to aid's contribution to postwar American recovery. Truman's first Economic Report in 1947 observed, "Intense demand of foreign countries for goods available only or chiefly in this country has been one of the factors accounting for a high level of employment, production and purchasing power in the United States during 1946."[57]

Six months later, the President was citing an "unprecedented rise of exports" and noting that half the trade surplus had been financed by U.S. aid and loans. The surplus in turn accounted for half the increase in the gross national product in the first six months of 1947. Truman said that exports employed 2.5 million Americans.[58]

The President's midyear 1950 report noted that increased spending for foreign aid and arms made up nearly half of the Federal stimulus in 1949, a stimulus that pulled the nation out of its brief slump. This was buried in a sea of soggy prose, but the thrust was clear. The government had discovered a relatively painless form of compensatory spending, aid and arms, money for geopolitics. A chart pictured the surplus of exports over imports from 1946 through 1949. The legend said, "All of the export surplus was financed by ERP (European Recovery Program) or other Government aid."[59]

But Truman was clearly uneasy at pointing up economic advantages from the Cold War. He said. "Outlays for national defense and international affairs are higher than they would be in a more peaceful world but the fact must be accepted that their present level is determined by security reasons."[60] His final report was franker: "Our prosperity has of course been accompanied and stimulated by high and rising defense spending."[61]

Wars notoriously breed inflation. They are rarely if ever paid for by taxes. Instead, governments borrow or print money to cover their expenses. At the same time, more workers are hired at higher wages to build weapons. Since the offsetting stream of civilian goods is not large enough to absorb these expanding incomes, war workers and managers have two choices: they may squirrel away what they can't spend now for a binge after the war, or they bid up prices on the spot.

In the War of 1812, wholesale prices rose 40 percent; they leaped 120 percent in the Civil War and 170 percent during World War I. Despite an enormous outpouring of civilian goods and well-enforced controls, wholesale prices more than doubled in World War II, rising 115 percent from September 1939 through August 1948.[62] To be sure, this span includes the climb in prices during Europe's mobilization and the three postwar years when suppressed inflation emerged. Two-thirds of this increase took place after the war, when controls unraveled.

In the six years after the U.S. mobilization began in June 1940, the government spent $383.4 billion, mostly on men and arms. It taxed back $196.7 billion, a remarkable performance but not good enough. That left a deficit of $186.7 billion.[63] This money—payments to soldiers, sailors, airmen, builders of aircraft and their workmen, to widows, government clerks, and all the other recipients of Federal wartime dollars—built up savings accounts. That was the pent-up demand that would drown any postwar unemployment threat. There were efforts to narrow the gap. In 1942, for example, a presidential committee recommended $11.6 billion in new taxes. The Roosevelt administration thought $7.6 billion was more realistic. Congress shaved this to $3.6 billion, less than a third of the original proposal.[64]

Nevertheless, inflation had been well contained during the war. Between 1940 and 1945, consumer prices rose only 28 percent.[65] Comprehensive controls over prices and wages, strict rationing of scarce goods, and the allocation of materials held buyers back. Thousands of volunteers manned price control boards, a contribution to the war that made controlling prices a neighborhood concern.

With peace, this elaborate apparatus disappeared and prices soared. In the first three years after Japan's surrender, consumer prices climbed 35 percent and wholesale prices 61 percent.[66] Truman pleaded for continued controls but Congress, responding to a nation that was tired of restraints and wanted a party, stripped them away. To its credit, the administration quickly saw that inflation and not deflation would be its chief problem although at times its trumpets sounded uncertain.

As early as October, 1945, two months after the Japanese surrender, Fred M. Vinson, Truman's Treasury Secretary, told the House Ways and Means Committee: "We should have adequate demand" to cope with deflation. But "We shall continue to be faced with inflationary pressures. There is an enormous pent-up demand . . . the budgetary deficit will be large."[67] That same month, however, Truman was still saying he favored reasonable wage increases "to sustain adequate purchasing power."[68] This no doubt pleased unions; it also fueled inflationary fires. A month later, however, the message got through. Truman acknowledged that the threat of inflation was far greater than that of deflation. Nevertheless, the administration was not prepared to do much about it. It called for no tax increases, curiously, until boom had turned to slump. It did not curb the buildup in exports or arms, although both enlarged demand. Fiscal policy was still an untried tool.

It is not clear how much if any of the postwar inflation could have been contained. The wartime gap between spending and taxing meant price increases had been delayed or suppressed by controls. Perhaps continued controls might have slowed the pace. No one can say with certainty how buyers or sellers will respond in such a climate. It certainly would have been difficult to mobilize in peace the patriotic spirit that made controls a neighborhood affair in war. In 1948, the spree had more or less run its course and Truman was skillfully exploiting at the polls Congress's failure to keep controls. But his willingness to wage a determined fight against rising prices was handicapped by his populist Missouri roots, his dislike of high interest rates. Truman refused for six years to use the great arm of monetary policy, money supply and interest rates, to restrain inflation.

In effect, Truman had idled one of the two great engines for driving the economy. The other is fiscal policy, the combination of taxes and spending to inject or withdraw purchasing power. Monetary policy, the technique Truman forswore, is the power to add to or subtract from the volume of cash and credit and so raise or lower the price of money. New Dealers tended to focus mainly on spending and secondarily on taxes, ignoring the money supply. In part, this was because money supply had done little to cure the Great Depression. Interest rates had been driven down close to zero and nothing had happened. No businessman will borrow for a new venture, no matter how cheap the cost, if there are no customers. William McChesney Martin, the chairman of the Federal Reserve, frequently said that you can't push on a string. Monetary policy, it appeared, could not cure a deep slump. The New Dealers also paid little attention to credit policy because it lacked glamour and power. To revive an economy by spending for a dam, the relief of the unemployed, or a network of roads was a great enterprise. It was a tangible manifestation of imagination at work. It also spawned a bureaucratic agency that gave someone power of appointment, power to fix contracts. Impersonal monetary policy, more abundant and cheaper credit, was drab. The New Deal bias was reflected in the first version of the Full Employment Act, which spoke only of government investment—spending—as an antidote to recession. But the neglected monetary weapon became a focus of attention when it was clear that inflation, not slump, would engage postwar policy makers.

The central bank, the Federal Reserve, could move quickly against rising prices, much more quickly than a tax increase or spending cut. The Federal Reserve could at a stroke reduce the reserves of commercial banks, thereby reducing their volume of loans. The less credit, the higher the price of money, or interest rate. Thus businessmen could be discouraged from borrowing, from adding to an inflationary demand, in two ways: they would find less credit on offer from their banks and what they did find would cost more. Evidently, you can pull if you can't push on a string.

Here then was a splendid machine to curb inflation. The trouble was it had been locked up and Truman wanted to throw away the key. The Federal Reserve had been compelled to serve the government during the war and surrender its notorious independence. The government wanted to pay as little as possible for the billions it borrowed, a long-term interest rate near 2 percent. The central bank was ordered to peg the bond rate, to stand ready as a purchaser of last resort, to buy any Treasury bonds that went unsold at the low, guaranteed rate. This may have been necessary in wartime; however, it left the Fed impotent to control the supply of money. Interest rates were fixed and the volume of credit in the land depended on what the Treasury needed.

With the end of the war, the central bank struggled to shake off its bonds. It wanted to curb inflation. It also sought power. As a Treasury agent, the central bank was powerless. If independence could be regained, the Fed, fixing credit volumes, would again be a great power in the land.

Right-thinking bankers supported the Fed. Bankers, with some justification, see the central bank as their representative in government. Both regard inflation as far more pernicious than unemployment. Right-thinking economists also backed the Fed, fearful that an unchecked Democratic administration was an engine of inflation.

One such was Paul Douglas, a distinguished professor at the University of Chicago. Chicago was and is a citadel of belief that money drives an economy for good or ill. Douglas had become a U.S. Senator and ran a subcommittee that published the Fed's cry for independence.[69] Marriner Eccles, the Fed chairman who had been instrumental in converting Roosevelt to fiscal expansion, now showed his intellectual mettle. The present problem was too much, not too little demand, Eccles said. The Fed must be freed from its obligation to support Treasury bonds. If the central bank, said Eccles, "expected to survive as an agency with any independence whatsoever [it] should exercise some independence."[70]

Harry Truman was not impressed. He refused to reappoint Eccles as chairman and instead put in Thomas B. McCabe. "I hope the [Federal Reserve] Board will recognize its responsibilities," Truman said, "and not allow the bottom to drop from under our securities. If that happens, that is exactly what Mr. Stalin wants."[71]

Truman spoke with feeling as a debtor whose business had gone bankrupt from a lack of credit. He knew bankers are biased toward tight money, slump or boom, and are not to be trusted. He remembered that he had bought Liberty Bonds after World War I for $100 each. But their price in the market fell to $80 because the banks drove up interest rates.[72] Treasury Secretary John W. Snyder, who evidently welcomed the low cost of Treasury borrowing, supported Truman, and there matters rested. But the Korean War and the inflationary pressures it touched off changed things dramatically. Inflation was now a source of vast public concern. Negotiations began with the Fed. Truman was comforted because a fellow Missourian, Assistant Secretary William McChesney Martin, represented the Treasury. Martin, however, had long since left Missouri behind and was known as the boy wonder who had headed the New York Stock Exchange at thirty-one. The Treasury-Fed talks reached a foregone conclusion. In the spring of 1951, the Fed pulled the plug.

It let long-term interest rates rise for the first time in ten years. Monetary policy had been freed to fight inflation or deflation.

No doubt the bankers and others in the business establishment were right to back the Fed against Truman. Money as well as spending and taxes should be enlisted in the war against inflation. Whether an agency totally uncontrolled by elected officials should determine matters so vital as credit volumes and interest rates is another issue. The Fed, after all, perversely tightened money in the Depression to satisfy the gold requirements of the Bank of England. But after the war, the question was put almost exclusively in terms of the need to revive money policy against inflation. That was an argument the bankers could not lose.

If Truman had been an uncertain student of the war's lesson for slump, he had paid extremely close attention to its consequences for inflation. Perhaps his experience as a debtor made him at bottom a sound-money man. The episode with the Fed did not mean he disliked sound money, although debtors understandably prefer cheap dollars. It was bankers he didn't trust.

An any rate, he told the nation three months after the Korean hostilities broke out, "We should pay . . . as we go out of taxes."[73] This was the route FDR had failed to follow in World War II. Congress was balky, and Truman urged "very much more" than Congress would approve. "Much higher taxes" should be paid by individuals and corporations, he said. In the end, he wrested three bills increasing taxes from the legislators. They had a remarkable effect. By the end of 1952, the war's third year, he could report that the budget, measured in terms of cash flowing in and out, was in surplus by $5.5 billion. Taxes were taking a larger share of national income than at any other time in history.[74] The effect on prices was just as remarkable.

The price index rose only 1.3 percent from November 1951 to November 1952.[75]

However, Truman did not rely on fiscal and monetary policy alone. He had revived the price and wage controls Congress hastily scrapped after World War II. Further, Korean War spending was nothing like that in the earlier war. World War II ate up four times as much of the gross national product as Korea.

There was an inflationary spurt during Korea but it was a mistake. With the outbreak of the conflict in June 1950, consumers, remembering shortages in the Second World War, went on a spree. There were no shortages in fact, but before Truman got his tax increases and price controls from Congress, scare buying had pushed up consumer prices briskly. In the first eight months of the war, they climbed at a yearly pace of 12 percent.

Even so, the record is remarkable. Among other things, Korea demonstrated that Keynesian compensatory policy was symmetrical. If a relaxed fiscal and monetary policy can cure slump, then tighter fiscal and money policies will master inflation.

World War II and its aftermath brought a revolution in economic policy making for advanced industrial states. Now governments could no longer escape responsibility for the material well-being of their citizens. All had learned that, even in a society devoted to private property, only modern government can determine whether this property shall be used fruitfully or lie idle. There could be quarrel over details—whether to cut taxes or expand spending against a slump, whether to raise interest rates or taxes in an overheated boom—but the broad lines were clear. Fiscal and monetary policy, spending, taxing, and credit fixed by the central government, will determine whether men work or go jobless, whether incomes rise or fall.

At the end of an almost painless conversion to a civilian economy, the U.S. was launched on a quarter century of prosperity. There were recessions; but they were short and mild and incomes rose with a growing economy. Employment was high, sometimes near the full employment that the House had been reluctant to make a stated policy goal. Prices rose, but at a moderate rate. The goals of the Employment Act were met, by and large, and successive administrations knew how to meet them. In some degree, this prosperity was supported by geopolitical expenditures, aid or subsidies for exports, arms or subsidies for the aerospace industry. The rapid emergence of the Cold War and the Korean War left untested the proposition that Keynesian affluence can be maintained without a military budget. Nevertheless, the war and its aftermath made it appear that men through their governments could now master their material fate. The Great Depression and World War II exacted a heavy price for this lesson. But for twenty-five years after the war citizens enjoyed the dividends of those terrible experiences.

NOTES

1. E. Carey Brown quoted in Robert Lekachman, *The Age of Keynes* (London: Allen Lane, Penguin Press, 1967), p. 121.

2. Lester Chandler, *America's Greatest Depression 1929–1941* (New York: Harper & Row, 1970), p. 4.

3. *Historical Statistics of the United States, Colonial Times to 1970: Bicentennial Edition* (U.S. Department of Commerce, 1975), p. 135.

4. Sherwood M. Fine, *Public Spending and Postwar Economic Policy* (New York: Columbia University Press, 1944), pp. 117–18.

5. Seymour E. Harris, *The Economics of Mobilization and Inflation* (New York: W.W. Norton, 1951), p. 110.

6. Robert L. Heilbroner and Aaron Singer, *The Economic Transformation of America: 1600 to the Present* (New York: Harcourt Brace Jovanovich, 1977), p. 314.

7. Lester Chandler, *Inflation in the United States 1940–1948* (New York: Harper and Brothers, 1951), p. 19.

8. *The Economic Report of the President* (Washington, D.C.: U.S. Government Printing Office, 1989), p. 322.

9. Simon Kuznets, *Postwar Economic Growth* (Cambridge: Harvard University Press, 1964), pp. 91–2.

10. *Ibid.*, pp. 91–2.

11. Peter Fearon, *War, Prosperity and Depression: The U.S. Economy 1917–45* (Oxford: Philip Allan, 1987), p. 273.

12. *Historical Statistics of the United States*, p. 289.

13. Harold G. Vatter, *The United States Economy in World War II* (New York: Columbia University Press, 1985), p. 120.

14. Henry Wallace, *Democracy Reborn*, selected from public papers and edited by Russell Lord (New York: Reynal & Hitchcock, 1944), p. 18.

15. Chandler, *Inflation in the United States*, p. 42.

16. Jack Stokes Ballard, *The Shock of Peace: Military and Economic Demobilization after World War II* (Washington, D.C.: University Press of America, 1983), p. 22.

17. *Ibid.*, p. 18.

18. William Green quoted in *ibid.*, p. 15.

19. Boris Shiskin's and Leo Cherne's predictions in *ibid.*, pp. 17–18.

20. *Historical Statistics of the United States*, p. 135.

21. Seymour E. Harris, "Introduction" to *Economic Reconstruction*, edited by Seymour E. Harris (New York: McGraw-Hill, 1945), p. 3.

22. Donald M. Nelson quoted in Richard Polenberg, *War and Society: The United States 1941–1945* (Philadelphia: J.B. Lippincott, 1972), p. 229.

23. Alvin H. Hansen, *After the War—Full Employment* (National Resources Planning Board, 1943), pp. 1–6.

24. Wallace, *Democracy Reborn*, p. 21.

25. Robert J. Donovan, *Conflict and Crisis: The Presidency of Harry S. Truman 1945–48* (New York: W.W. Norton, 1977), p. 108.

26. Herbert Stein, *The Fiscal Revolution in America* (Chicago: University of Chicago Press, 1969), p. 174.

27. Robert R. Nathan, *Mobilizing for Abundance* (New York: McGraw-Hill, 1944), p. 9.

28. Chester Bowles quoted in Richard Polenberg, *War and Society: The United States 1941–1945* (Philadelphia: J.B. Lippincott, 1972), p. 95.

29. *Ibid.*, p. 73.

30. Alvin Hansen, *After the War*, p. 6.

31. FDR's 1943 State of the Union address in Stephen Bailey, *Congress*

Makes a Law: The Story Behind the Employment Act of 1946 (New York: Columbia University Press, 1950), p. 41.

32. Ballard, *The Shock of Peace*, p. 125.

33. Republican platform in Bailey, *Congress Makes a Law*, p. 41.

34. "Text of Dewey's Acceptance Speech," *New York Times*, June 29, 1944, p. 10.

35. Dewey quoted in Stephen Bailey, *Congress Makes a Law*, p. 42.

36. Employment Act of 1946 in Barton J. Bernstein and Allen Matusow, editors, *The Truman Administration: A Documentary History* (New York: Harper & Row, 1966), pp. 47–8.

37. Ralph Blodgett and Carlyle Fraser cited in "Assuring Full Employment," *Report from the Committee on Banking and Commerce*, Senate Report No. 583, 79th Cong., 1st Session 9–22–1945, p. 23.

38. Unemployment statistics in Ballard, *The Shock of Peace*, p. 130.

39. *Ibid.*, p. 166.

40. Chandler, *Inflation in the United States*, p. 35.

41. *Ibid.*, p. 38.

42. Employment statistics in Ballard, *The Shock of Peace*, p. 131.

43. *Ibid.*, p. 131; Vatter, *The United States Economy*, p. 136.

44. Ballard, *The Shock of Peace*, p. 131.

45. Chandler, *Inflation in the United States*, p. 254.

46. *Ibid.*, p. 84.

47. Bernstein and Matusow, *The Truman Administration*, p. 91.

48. Truman's State of the Union Message in *ibid.*, p. 155.

49. Truman's reply to reporters quoted in Stein, *The Fiscal Revolution*, p. 238.

50. *The Economic Report of the President* (Washington, D.C.: U.S. Government Printing Office, 1950), p. 11.

51. Stein, *The Fiscal Revolution*, p. 239.

52. *Economic Report of the President*, p. 2.

53. Unemployment statistic in *ibid.*, p. 3.

54. Fine, *Public Spending and Postwar Economic Policy*, p. 123.

55. Chandler, *Inflation in the United States*, p. 228.

56. *Ibid.*, pp. 228–9.

57. *The Economic Report of the President* (Washington, D.C.: U.S. Government Printing Office, 1947), p. 17.

58. *Mid-year Economic Report of the President* (Washington, D.C.: U.S. Government Printing Office, July 1947), p. 45.

59. *Economic Report of the President*, p. 54.

60. *Ibid.*, p. 104.

61. *The Economic Report of the President* (Washington D.C.: U.S. Government Printing Office, 1953), p. 23.

62. Chandler, *Inflation in the United States*, p. 1.

63. *Ibid.*, p. 384.

64. Bureau of the Budget, *The United States at War* (Washington, D.C.: U.S. Government Printing Office, 1946), pp. 258–9.

65. *Historical Statistics of the United States*, p. 210.

66. Chandler, *Inflation in the United States*, p. 216.

67. Fred M. Vinson quoted in Bernstein and Matusow, *The Truman Administration*, p. 50.

68. Truman quoted in Donovan, *Conflict and Crisis*, p. 120.

69. Stein, *The Fiscal Revolution*, pp. 257–8.

70. Eccles quoted in Robert J. Donovan, *Tumultuous Years: The Presidency of Harry S. Truman, 1949–53* (New York: W.W. Norton, 1982), p. 329.

71. Truman quoted in *ibid.*, p. 330.

72. Stein, *The Fiscal Revolution*, pp. 271–2.

73. Truman quoted in Donovan, *Tumultuous Years*, p. 325.

74. *Economic Report of the President*, p. 78.

75. *Ibid.*, p. 39.

III

Fat Years

A largely uninterrupted tide of prosperity governed the economy from Eisenhower through Johnson. It was a time of steady increase in material well-being. Output rose on average 3.7 percent a year. Employment climbed and the jobless rate was 4.9 percent, never rising above 6.7 percent for a full year. Price inflation was largely contained until the disastrous failure to suppress excess demand from the Vietnam War. The yearly increase in the consumer price index averaged about 2 percent.[1] All Americans shared in the gains, even the poorest, although the best-off invariably did better.

Income for the median family, one in the middle of a ladder stretching from richest to poorest, rose 56 percent. After subtracting price increases, this meant a rise in real income of $200 every year and in dollars of 1967 purchasing power.[2]

Some escaped from poverty; others bought bigger houses, newer cars, college for children, longer vacations. All enjoyed a measure of economic security never reached before in American life. Memories of the Great Depression faded. Young men and women expected to get jobs as a matter of course.

Alvin Hansen said that the period "shows a degree of stability and growth rarely if ever matched, at any time in our history."*[3] But like other Keynesian celebrations at the time, this was exaggerated. Robert Aaron Gordon of California compared the fat years of 1949–69, with the two decades from 1889 to 1909, the first wave of American imperialism. In the earlier period, output grew 4.25 percent a year, slightly faster than in the fat years; prices on average were unchanged and unemployment at 5.4 percent was only slightly higher.[4] To be sure, a great deal of joblessness at the turn of the century was hidden on the farm. When times were hard in Iowa City, young men went back to the family farm. There they were probably underemployed but were not counted as jobless. Even so, it was clear that the fat years were prosperous but not unique.

Except in one respect. The 1889–1909 period had been scarred by two panics or depressions, in 1893 and 1907. The good years had been very good indeed, but they were punctuated by severe slump. The great triumph in the fat years after World War II was the avoidance of deep or prolonged slump.

After the Truman recession of 1948–49, there were three more dips, all under Eisenhower in 1953–54, 1957–58, and 1960–61. All, as Paul Samuelson said, were "short and mild."[5] The longest, in 1953–54, ran only four quarters. In the most severe, 1957–58, total output fell just 4.3 percent. The heaviest unemployment came in 1960–61 and did not reach 7 percent in any month.[6]

The succession of brief, moderate slumps was genuinely new. Their mildness appeared to owe something to policy makers who had absorbed the lessons of the Great Depression and the war. Government seemed able to reverse a drop in output with considerable speed and reduce the misery of prolonged unem-

* Hansen was describing the years 1948–63.

ployment. Whether or not government was responsible for this happy state of affairs, one thing was clear. The fat years enriched citizens not because of explosive gains but because losses from slumps were contained. In the middle 1960s, before Vietnam and inflation struck, economics and economists in government won a new respect.

In fact, the successful performance owed something to the hard-won wisdom of economists but far more to the profound and accidental transformation of the economy in World War II. The biggest source of stability in the fat years and in the leaner years that followed was the enormous expansion of government demand. Neither Republicans nor Democrats tried seriously to shrink the huge outlays for goods and services thrown up by the war.

In 1929, the government accounted for one dollar in every twelve spent in the economy, 8.5 percent of goods and services. In 1987, under a radical regime devoted to private enterprise, government spent one dollar in every five, more than 20 percent.[7] The government's share in a far larger economy had risen two and a half times.

It is this huge force, unaffected by changes in private demand, spending, and investing according to bureaucratic and political imperatives, that provides a solid base for aggregate demand and prevents long slides or deep ones.

Moreover, this huge demand acts unguided to turn slumps into recoveries and cool off an overheated economy. The thermostat consists of two built-in stabilizers of great power. The strongest is the progressive income tax. This arrangement increases tax rates as a citizen's income rises. So when the economy slumps and incomes before taxes fall, the impact is softened. Incomes after taxes don't fall as much or perhaps not at all. Citizens simply fall into lower, less onerous tax brackets.

In a slump, citizens may put off buying autos but, if their after-tax income is protected by progressive gradients, much of their buying will be sustained. A progressive tax structure builds a floor under incomes and under consumer spending. It is reinforced by another stabilizer, jobless benefits. They mount as unemployment increases. On the upswing, taxes and benefits work in reverse, withdrawing buying power from citizens, curbing demand. As long as policy makers leave unchanged huge levels of government spending and do not tamper with the stabilizers, no disaster can happen.

This does not mean that policy made no difference. Typically, however, government programs to counter slump were too little and too late. They modestly reinforced an upturn rather than reversed the direction of an economy that had turned itself.

Perhaps the most important thing government did in the Truman-Johnson period was get out of the way. None of these administrations tried to crack the base of aggregate demand by shrinking the government's enlarged share in the economy. Not until Reagan, who weakened the progressive income tax, was any effort made to tamper with a stabilizer.

The power of stabilizers to turn an economy around and the lesser role played by government decision has been measured by Wilfred Lewis of the Brookings Institution.[8] He asked what part stabilizers play in converting a budget surplus to a deficit, in stimulating demand. For the four slumps of the Truman-Johnson period, he found that the shift from surplus to deficit totaled $26.8 billion. Of this sum, all but $1 billion came from the reduced take of progressive taxes and increased spending for jobless benefits. The stabilizers were overwhelmingly important. No discretion was involved and government policy decisions were of minor consequence—less than 4 percent of the recovery force.

The major exception was the Kennedy tax cut, and Lewis's findings provided a rationale for it. He discovered that the stabilizers were so strong that they aborted recoveries during periods of upswing. The tax cut successfully released the brake, making the stabilizers bite later, closer to full employment.

But government attempts to smooth the business cycle are events of the second order. The crucial fact in the modern U.S. economy is World War II and its heritage of a great volume of government demand for welfare and war. It is this rather than the wisdom of economists and politicians that has given American capitalism and its cousins in Western Europe a unique stability.

When he took office, Dwight Eisenhower wrote in his diary that he was "offering myself as a political leader to unseat the New Deal–Fair Deal bureaucracy."[9] This sentiment had surfaced in the 1952 election campaign and led the innocent to think that Republicans in power might reconvert the transformed American economy. But a recession their first year in office made quick students of the new team.

Eisenhower's first Economic Report declared that "Government must use its vast power to help maintain employment and purchasing power as well as to maintain reasonably stable prices."[10]

This was critical. It meant that Republicans, in power for the first time in twenty years, would accept and not try to overcome deficits in a slump, would permit the stabilizing forces embedded in the Federal budget to lift the economy. It even hinted at a willingness to enlarge demand with extra government spending in a recession, a policy that must have pleased the New Deal–Fair Deal bureaucrats Eisenhower thought he was unseating.

Indeed, Arthur F. Burns, the head of Eisenhower's Council of Economic Advisers, wrote later that the annual budget balance was as dead as the dodo. "No serious attempt was made to resurrect it," he said, "even during the Republican regime of the fifties."[11] Seymour Harris, another Keynesian voice at Harvard, was reassured. "In 1952, I was fearful," Harris wrote, "that an administration that would operate on the economic and ideological principles enunciated in the 1952 campaign would wreck our economy and destroy our welfare programs. But this has not happened. In fact, the years 1952–60 were on the whole prosperous years."[12]

The bipartisan agreement announced by candidate Dewey in the war had been put in practice by the first Republican president in the postwar era. A Republican White House might not attack a recession vigorously, particularly if it was neither deep nor long. But a Republican president like a Democrat would not worsen a slump by lowering the spending stream.

Even so, there were conflicting impulses in Eisenhower's economics and they were embodied in Burns, the chief economist, and George M. Humphrey, the Treasury Secretary. Vigorous, self-confident, opinionated, they were too shrewd to clash face to face. Eisenhower expected his staff to sort out their differences before coming to the commander. But Burns and Humphrey knew that each had only part of Eisenhower's attention, that neither could be sole mentor to a remarkable soldier-politician despite his scant knowledge of business, finance, and economics. All during his eight years, Eisenhower wavered between Burns, an undoctrinaire conservative who believed government could and should halt slump, and Humphrey, a rich corporate executive who would have been at home in the primitive Treasury of Andrew Mellon.

Sherman Adams, Eisenhower's trusted aide, described the awful impression Burns made on the President's cabinet of millionaire businessmen. The new chairman of the economic advisers had "a glassy stare through thick lenses peering out from under a canopy of unruly hair parted in the middle, a large pipe with carved stem: the very incarnation of all the externals that were such anathema to Republican businessmen and politicians."[13] Even worse, although Adams, the friend of Bernard Goldfine, was too polite to say so, Burns was Jewish.

He had been born Burnseig or Burnzeig in a part of Austria later taken by the Soviet Union. His father, a house painter, had brought him to Bayonne, New Jersey, as a child, and he early displayed precocity, translating the Talmud into German at the age of six. He went to Columbia on a scholarship, did brilliantly, and found as his patron Wesley C. Mitchell, a pioneer student of the business cycle. At Mitchell's National Bureau for Economic Research, scholars measured the rise and fall of the economy and its constituents, splendid training for a presidential adviser. In time, Burns became a professor at Columbia and succeeded Mitchell at the National Bureau. Burns was eclectic in doctrine, conservative, thoughtful, and strong-minded in manner.

In the Eisenhower cabinet, Burns began with no friends, no support, and little standing. He could convince only by his own powers of persuasion. Adams remembered how Burns succeeded. "In discussions at the White House, the expression 'counter-cyclical' became a familiar term. In the language of Arthur Burns, upswings and downswings in the economy were cycles, and measures to counteract them were counter-cyclical. As anxious as he was to keep enterprise free from the govern-

71

ment, the President was ready to take extraordinary steps to keep the country out of a depression, had that actually threatened."[14]

Burns then had reached the President. If a slump was deep enough or lasted long enough, Eisenhower would act. In fact, he acted only modestly in the three recessions during his time in office. But these were brief, modest affairs. Moreover, there was Humphrey, a power in the inner circle. He spoke for a constituency Eisenhower admired, successful businessmen. He reflected Eisenhower's inner convictions and no professor could shake them. Humphrey was sound.

A ruddy-faced man who enjoyed riding on his 150-acre estate near Cleveland, Humphrey was the son of a comfortable lawyer from Saginaw, Michigan. He studied law and, at twenty-eight, became general counsel to the M. A. Hanna Company, a shipping concern and the creature of Mark Hanna, the Republican boss in the McKinley era. Humphrey displayed great skill at agglomerating companies, at combining bits of paper to build giants. The shipping company became in time a major producer of steel, coal, a banker, found its way into rayon, plastics, natural gas. Humphrey was a vestryman in the Episcopalian Church. He was a member of the New York Jockey Club, Links, and the Dusquesne in Pittsburgh, clubs inhospitable to Jews.

He knew a lot about business but little about the economy, a trait common to business leaders. He tended to believe that any government spending was always inflationary, always tainted. When Burns proposed reducing taxes or increased spending to counter slump, Humphrey said: "I will contest a tax cut out of deficits as long as I am able . . . I think it would start a downward spiral that would be serious . . . I don't think you can spend yourself rich." He embarrassed Eisenhower when he presented the fiscal 1958 accounts. He invited Congress to slash the budget he was supposed to defend and warned, even as the economy was sliding downhill, that unless cuts were made, "I will predict that you will have a depression that will curl your hair."[15]

It was naïve analysis and absurd prediction. But apart from Hamilton and Gallatin, the office of Treasury Secretary has rarely been filled by anyone with much knowledge of the larger world.

This odd pair, Burns and Humphrey, put Eisenhower to the test in his first year at the White House. The new President had fulfilled his pledge and quickly settled the Korean War. Generals sometimes understand better than civilians what can't be won on the ground won't be won at the negotiating table. The end of the war brought a sharp drop in military orders. Spending for military goods and services was running at a brisk yearly pace of $54.3 billion in the spring of 1953. Fifteen months later, it had sagged to $42.1 billion, a steep drop of $12.2 billion.[16]

With nothing to replace the Pentagon's demand, with the fall in military orders exerting a multiplied effect as arms suppliers and their workers cut their spending, a recession was inevitable. Total output, the gross national product, slumped $14.4 billion, from $369.9 billion to $355.5 billion between the second quarter of 1953 and the third quarter of 1954.[17] Would Eisenhower become the first genuinely Keynesian President and cement bipartisan support for countercyclical action? Would he revert to the Republican form of 1930, fret over an increasingly unbalanced budget and worsen the slump by increasing taxes and cutting more expenditures?

Of course he did neither and chose a middle way. As early as September 1953, Burns regularly lectured Eisenhower and the cabinet on the declining economy and rising unemployment. Burns drew up lists of projects the government might launch.

Eisenhower and the cabinet urged Burns to keep them informed but were in no hurry to act. Burns lectured so skillfully that after one meeting Eisenhower proffered his highest praise. "You would have made a fine chief of staff overseas during the war," the General said.[18]

On the other side, there is no record that Humphrey turned Hooverite and sought to close the growing deficit in the budget. Quite the contrary, he was induced to get out of the way of a fortuitous cut in taxes. At the end of the Korean War, Chairman Dan Reed of the House Ways and Means Committee urged an early end to wartime taxes on individuals and corporations. Reed, an old-fashioned Republican, could hardly be described as a countercyclical congressman, but he at least sensed that the end-of-war spending was an opportunity for tax relief.

In the spring of 1953, before the recession began, Eisenhower opposed Reed's plans. Eisenhower wanted all the revenue he could get to cover a disturbing deficit. By May, still before the slump started, the President agreed that personal taxes could be cut as scheduled on the first of the year. There could be no advance on this date, however. On the very eve of the recession, the President persuaded Congress to delay a scheduled cut in corporate taxes, also until the end of the year. This meant that taxes for individuals and business would fall on January 1, right in the middle of the recession. It was sheer accident, unconnected with any anti-slump policy. If anything, Eisenhower had delayed the tax cut and its countercyclical force.

That curious history did not stop partisan activists from claiming later that Eisenhower had acted with sagacity, foresight, and Keynesian wisdom. Even Eisenhower forgot how things actually went and implied that he had cut taxes in a timely, anti-recession fashion. In his memoirs, he claimed that "the government reduced taxes" in the recession. But he also acknowledged that "most of the administration's major legislative proposals did not become law until the recession had evaporated."[19] Again, "as early as September 1953, I had decided that because the danger of immediate inflation had given way to the possibility of recession, the administration would not oppose the tax reductions already scheduled to take effect on the next New Year's Day."[20] In fact, of course, the decision was taken in July, well before any sign of slump.

More important, perhaps, Eisenhower knew what he must not do. His memoirs observed that the Federal government had "drastically increased taxes" in 1932, 1934, 1935, and 1936, when the country was mired in Depression. But "tax increases hobbled the spending power of individuals and business."[21] Burns had gotten through.

Burns also implied that modern Republicans reversed the slump. At the Economic Club in Detroit in 1954, Burns said: "Late in September 1953 when it seemed plain that an economic decline had already begun but when unemployment figures still continued to move downward for seasonal reasons, the Government announced that it would make sizable tax cuts for individuals and corporations effective in January 1954 so that people would have more money to spend or invest."[22]

This was a splendid piece of literal truth and substantive falsehood, the game of government everywhere. Burns was suggesting that the tax cuts were made in response to slump; in reality, they had been reluctantly accepted before the downturn.

In the Economic Report for 1955, Burns crowed that the successful emergence from the recession reflected government monetary and fiscal policy. "The growing confidence of people in their Government's ability to moderate economic fluctuations is desirable and not misplaced," he said.*[23] In fact, the Eisenhower administration had done little apart from applauding the central bank's increase in the supply of money.

Recovery actually began when the automatic stabilizers took hold, when taxes stopped shrinking and enlarged spendable incomes, when jobless benefits began swelling demand. The huge volume of government spending unlinked to the Korean War had ensured that the slump was mild.

But the post-recession boasts by Eisenhower, Burns, and others are important. Republicans not only accepted but were proud of the fact that government decisions over taxes and spending could and should steer an economy out of trouble. This bipartisan accord guaranteed against a 1929 for nearly half a century and probably beyond.

In May 1954, with the slump in its trough, the Eisenhower administration began speeding up Federal orders for projects that had already won appropriations. Orders were placed earlier and in larger amounts than scheduled. On a big enough scale, such measures could encourage a temporary spurt, although they would lead to a slowdown later. This was Eisenhower's favorite technique because it appeared to affect spending totals the least.

The amount involved in the 1954 speed-up was small, about $545 million. But it was significant for one reason. More than 70 percent of the accelerated orders came from the Pentagon.[25]

It was the clearest case so far of military outlays as a coun-

---

* In time, Democrats found it useful to broadcast this story. President Johnson, eager to rally support for the Kennedy tax cut, claimed that "in 1954, the bipartisan character of expansionary fiscal policies were established for the first time as . . . President Eisenhower adopted measures that had been previously linked to the New Deal and Keynesian economics."[24]

tercyclical device, an economic prop, a Keynesian weapon. The fact that it was small, about $400 million, and late is not the point. The general whose farewell address warned of the military-industrial complex turned to weapons spending as the outlay of choice against recession.

This was irony rather than hypocrisy. Eisenhower almost alone of postwar presidents strenuously wrestled with the Pentagon's generals. Better than most, he knew the fantasy built into their demands. His turn to military orders reflected the character of his cabinet. Businessmen tend to accept government outlays for arms and oppose them for anything else unless it directly subsidizes their own concerns.

After the 1953–54 slump, Eisenhower presided over the first recovery since the Crash that had no links to war or war preparation.[26] He actually sliced $1 billion from defense spending at the end of 1957.[27]

As it happened, his timing was wrong. The economy was sliding into its third postwar slump and the leading characters had changed in Eisenhower's team. Humphrey had been replaced at the Treasury by Robert B. Anderson, a lawyer from Texas. Eisenhower admired Anderson so much he wanted him to succeed to the White House in 1960. Anderson, an old-fashioned budget balancer, appeared to be a man of unyielding rectitude and high principle. He was in fact one of the great confidence men of modern times. He had arranged a million-dollar capital gain for himself that depended heavily on his own decision to curb imported oil. He ultimately went to jail for defrauding private clients. But in 1957 he was widely admired as rich, devout, and bright. His was the decisive voice in the second term. Pitted against him was Raymond J. Saulnier, a Barnard economist and a pale shadow of the self-assured Burns.

The change in men had little effect on policy. Eisenhower

characteristically resisted pleas from Vice President Nixon and Nixon's ally Labor Secretary James Mitchell for a tax cut to end the 1958 slump. Burns urged a tax cut too. But he was now a professor again and advisers lose their magic when they leave the White House. Eisenhower wrote to Burns, "I am against vast and unwise public works programs (they would need some years to get truly underway) as well as the slash-bang kinds of tax-cutting from which the proponents want nothing so much as immediate political advantage."[28] Humphrey would have liked that.

The administration at first relied exclusively on the automatic stabilizers to turn things around. As the recession worsened—it was the deepest in the fat years—the administration unbent. The trick learned in 1953–54 was given another run. Defense orders were accelerated and, initially, Pentagon spending was scheduled to rise by $1.4 billion. Some orders for public works were speeded up. Jobless workers were paid an extra $390 million in benefits. All this, however, was modest compared to the drop in total demand of $12.6 billion.[29]

But conveniently, the Russians orbited Sputnik in October 1957, the first satellite in space. This was something that had to be answered and with billions (although Sherman Adams had first dismissed Sputnik as an "outer space basketball game").[30] Now there was a tripling in contracts for big arms projects, from $2.2 billion in the third quarter of 1957 to $6.1 billion in the second quarter of 1958. The President's Economic Report for 1959 said bluntly, "the rise in defense contracting in the first half of 1958 . . . had a significantly stimulative effect on the economy."[31] The fear of Sputnik and the desire to halt the economy's steep slide tempted Eisenhower to forswear abstinence. He relied on the Pentagon again for countercyclical spending.

The recovery did not last long, a mere eight months. By September, the economy was turning down; unemployment was rising.[32] Eisenhower, prodded by Anderson, had created the first recession deliberately made by government. Perhaps it was made bearable by the fact that it was Nixon, not Eisenhower, who would pay the political price.

The Eisenhower-Anderson slump was undertaken to fight an intractable inflation. In the previous downturn of 1957–58, prices had behaved in a most curious fashion. They had risen instead of falling, climbing despite a drop in demand. The textbooks argue otherwise. When demand falls, prices should fall. In fact, consumer costs rose 3 percent from June 1957 to June 1958.[33] If prices rise when demand falls, defying laws of economic gravity, they threatened to climb even faster in recovery. The administration believed that brakes must be slammed on to halt this pernicious state of affairs.

Something else troubled Eisenhower and his Treasury Secretary. The balance of payments, the difference between dollars earned and spent abroad, was in deficit. The U.S. was losing gold. By squeezing the domestic economy, fewer imports would come in and less gold would go out, or so Anderson and Eisenhower reasoned.

They cut back Federal spending with unusual severity. A budget in deficit had been contributing $11 billion a year to total output in mid-1958. By the first quarter of 1960, this deficit had been converted to a surplus of $6 billion.[34] In effect, $17 billion had been amputated from aggregate demand. Since a dollar spent or withheld yields a multiple of itself in demand, the economy was shrunk by about 7 percent.[35]

Gabriel Hauge, another of Eisenhower's economic advisers, had warned the President against so swift a turnaround. But Eisenhower listened to Anderson, Saulnier, and Chairman

William McChesney Martin of the Federal Reserve. The President later wrote, "I believe that we were engaged then in a battle against an inflationary psychology . . . if wages and prices could *increase* during a recession, we could get into real inflationary troubles in time of prosperity."[36]

The Federal Reserve added to the fiscal squeeze, tightening its credit screws. Ever since its accord with the Treasury had ended and the central bank had won its freedom, it had behaved with great circumspection. Typically, the Fed supported the administration, easing credit in a recession, tightening when recovery was assured. Now the central bank shared the Eisenhower-Anderson worries.

It was not hard to see what would happen, and Burns hastened to his friend Nixon in March 1960. Nixon has told the tale: "In January, virtually all the economists in the country had been bullish about the prospects for the economy throughout 1960. But when Burns came to see me in March, he expressed great concern about the way the economy was acting . . . Burns' conclusion was unless some decisive governmental action were taken, and taken soon, we were heading for another economic dip in October, just before the elections. He urged strongly that everything possible be done to avert this development. He urgently recommended that two steps be taken immediately: by loosening up on credit and, where justifiable, by increasing spending for national security."[37]

Nixon persuaded Eisenhower to put the issue before the cabinet. But there, others, presumably led by Anderson, argued that the pessimism was overdone.

"Unfortunately, Arthur Burns turned out to be a good prophet," Nixon wrote in *Six Crises*. Unemployment increased in October by 452,000. "All the speeches, television broadcasts, and precinct work in the world could not counteract that one hard

bold enough to win the title of "New Economics." Most daring, Kennedy wanted to cut taxes even though the budget was in deficit and the slump was over.

Despite the publicists, this was not new economics. It simply built on the insights of Keynes and his followers, drew lessons from the Great Depression and the Second World War, and brought to politics the practical techniques that had been dissected and polished in graduate seminars for a generation.

What was fresh was Kennedy's goal. Truman and Eisenhower were persuaded that government must act in deep slump and high inflation. But they aimed chiefly at smoothing the business cycle, cooling down an overheated expansion, or reviving faded production. They tried to keep the economy on an unaltered path.

Kennedy was more ambitious. His advisers calculated that a growing American economy, free of slump, was still producing well below its capacity. Even when output increased, there was enormous waste. Idle men and women sought jobs vainly. There were unused plants that could have been turning out goods. Policy must now aim at ending waste, at putting all these resources to work. That meant raising actual output nearer to the potential through the familiar devices, government spending or taxes, supported by the money supply. Government should no longer act merely as traffic cop, arresting slump and inflation, but as engineer, lifting output indefinitely.

The postwar experience, good as it was, inspired the new approach. Each recovery, no matter how mild the slump, had left more unemployed behind. In the four years before the 1954 recession, the jobless rate was 4 percent; in the four years before the next trough in 1958, the rate climbed to 5 percent. Most recently, in the four years before 1962, unemployment rose to 6 percent.[47] To be sure, output had increased and living standards of most Americans improved. But each cycle also left behind more misery, more jobless men. Conservative economists insisted these were structurally unemployable, unfit for modern labor; liberals retorted that most were victims of the business cycle, and an aggressive high-employment policy would put them to work. At any rate, the idle jobless had deprived the nation of goods and services.

At the start of his presidency, Kennedy said that the 1946 Employment Act "registered the consensus of the American people that this Nation will not countenance the suffering, frustration and injustice of unemployment, or let the vast potential of the world's leading economy run to waste in idle manpower, silent machinery and empty plants."[48]

His advisers took this seriously. Unlike earlier administrations, the Kennedy regime was not divided by significant differences over the broad lines of economic policy. Walter Heller, the forty-six-year-old chairman of the Council of Economic Advisers, was an engaging figure with a knack for explaining abstruse economic ideas in lively language without vulgarizing his material. Heller, from the University of Minnesota, had been urged on Kennedy by Governor Orville Freeman of Minnesota and they hit it off quickly. Heller was supported by a rising star in economics, James Tobin of Yale, who won a Nobel Prize in 1981.* From Cambridge, Mass., Paul Samuelson, a Nobelist in 1970, sent in a stream of proposals. All had been graduate students when Keynes's *General Theory* transformed economics in the universities.

They had some feel for the way theory and practice must be

---

* Tobin was reluctant to accept Kennedy's invitation and told him, "I'm afraid you've got the wrong guy, Mr. President. I'm an ivory tower economist." Kennedy replied with a laugh, "That's the best kind. I'll be an ivory tower President."[49]

joined, for the politics of an economic issue. This they shared with Burns. Their natural opponent, the Treasury Secretary, was, in most matters, a cautious ally. C. Douglas Dillon was a sophisticated New York investment banker, comfortable with ideas, art, and fine wine as well as money.

Dillon did not hold the simple-minded views of his predecessors who saw peril lurking in every dollar of a Federal deficit or every government outlay. He was sensitive to the concerns of the New York financial community, of the rich, and he was unlikely to get in the way of tax cuts that reduced levies on the wealthy and their corporations.

Kennedy himself had taken a Cambridge crash course in economics when he was running for President. At Harvard, Seymour Harris, one of the strongest Keynesian voices, tutored him at length. So did John Kenneth Galbraith, eclectic, independent, a staunch believer in government intervention and controls. Paul Samuelson of MIT was also on the personal faculty.

No President was better prepared in modern economics. It was all the more surprising that Kennedy almost failed his first test, proposing to cover his Berlin crisis spending with a tax increase, a move that would have aborted the recovery.

At the central bank, William McChesney Martin was perhaps the least convinced. But he had mastered the essential political lesson. The Federal Reserve cannot fly in the face of an administration determined to execute policy.

The new administration relied on three linked ideas to promote full employment. There was the gap between actual and potential output. Potential output measured what the gross national product would have been at a high level of employment, with only 4 percent idle. This calculated level of production was compared with actual output, the gross national product the nation had registered in any period. The difference between potential and actual output was the gap. The gap was the volume of lost goods and services in an economy running with more than 4 percent jobless. In 1962, the gap was estimated at $23 billion,[50] billions that were wasted, lost.

There was no magic in 4 percent unemployment. It was always described as an "interim target," and rates had been lower. But 4 percent, it was thought, was a plausible target that need not create inflationary strain. At the end of 1962, unemployment was well above the 4 percent target, 40 percent higher, at 5.6 percent.[51] "That is not *maximum employment*," Kennedy wrote,[52] using italics for emphasis. He would do something about it.

The Kennedy economists observed that the economy's growth, the rate at which output increased each year, had been falling while unemployment rose. From 1947 to 1955, output had gained 4.5 percent a year; from 1955 to 1962, output rose only 3.5 percent a year.[53] In an economy of $575 billion, the 1962 level,[54] each 1 percent represented a loss of $6 billion. (The Kennedy people seldom noticed that fast growth was closely linked to the Korean War.)

Growth, it was thought, had slowed because of fiscal drag. This was the second central notion. The stabilizing Federal budget was applying the brakes too early in a recovery. Before high employment could be restored, progressive income taxes suppressed too much aggregate demand, reducing the income stream below the level needed to give jobs to all. The fiscal burden, the tax and spending mix, had to be changed.

The last key idea was a brilliant rhetorical device. What mattered, Kennedy said, was not the budget balance at every level of the economy; what mattered was budget balance at high employment, at 4 percent unemployment. If the budget balanced with unemployment at 5 percent, it would generate a crushing, deflating surplus when more were at work and paying taxes. Conversely, a deficit at 4 percent was likely to push up prices. Then there would not be enough idle resources to produce goods to offset the stream of higher incomes. So, the message went, we are not interested in balancing the budget for its own sake; we are balancing the economy and seek budget balance at our high employment target.* "Recessions and slack generate deficits," the economic advisers said; "prosperity and growth balance budgets."[55]

In his famous speech at Yale in 1962, Kennedy said: "The myth persists that federal deficits create inflation and budget surpluses prevent it . . . sizable budget surpluses after the war did not prevent inflation and persistent deficits for the last several years have not upset our basic price stability."[56] What counts is where the budget is balanced, above or below high employment.

The three linked ideas of gap or waste, fiscal drag, and balanced budgets at high employment were the legs on which Kennedy's tax reform rested. The gap could be closed and fiscal drag released either by increased Federal spending or by a tax cut. Which method was used depended on values, on politics. The Kennedy advisers came down strongly in favor of increased spending. They had been influenced by Galbraith's best seller *The Affluent Society*. He argued that the world's richest nation wasted its substance on chromium-plated cars with metal tail fins and neglected schools, hospitals, low-cost housing. "The

---

* In fact, the budget balance is never the critical issue, as Tobin observed. The goal is a budget that matches the savings generated at high employment with the level of private investment demand from an economy growing at its potential rate. An excess of savings would bring deflation; an excess of investment, inflation. Those skilled teachers on the Heller Council wisely did not try to promote this notion for popular understanding.

council consistently pushed the expenditure side of the budget," Tobin recalled. "But the political limits to deficit spending in that guise were even more stringent than the obstacles to tax reductions. The effective alternative was not a larger expenditure budget, but continuing fiscal drag, with every prospect that the recovery, like the previous upswing in 1960, would be aborted short of full employment."[57]

For Kennedy, the choice was clear. His plan to stimulate the economy when the budget was in deficit and output increasing enraged conventional conservative opinion. Arthur Burns was not enraged, but nevertheless called it "a radical departure in economic policy making."[58]

Businessmen anyway were suspicious of Democrats, particularly so young a one, and Catholic, too. They had even been hostile to Kennedy's earlier gift, faster tax write-offs for their plants and tools and a tax credit that reduced the price of any new investment by 7 percent. These loopholes had been opened on the excuse that they would spur added investment. This ignored the rule that business invests to meet expected demand, not because taxes make tools cheaper.

The businessmen had looked at Kennedy's tax gifts with suspicion. They turned positively hostile in the spring of 1962 when Kennedy denounced an increase in steel prices and damned businessmen generally. Clearly, something lavish was required to heal the breach with business. It was inevitable, then, that Kennedy would turn to a tax cut rather than repairing a neglected public sector. Moreover, he provided a cut well suited to business tastes. His proposed $11 billion reduction[59] would bring down rates for the richest from 91 to 65 percent. The bottom bracket would drop from 20 to 14 percent, with slices for each bracket in between. He also urged Congress to cut the corporate rate from 52 percent to 47 percent, a move rich in symbolism as well as money.[60] Now the government would no longer take more than half of a company's profits.

Some businessmen and Congressmen still loathed Kennedy's second and greater gift. How could taxes be cut without a budget surplus and why tinker with an economy that was advancing? But most got the point. The Chamber of Commerce is a representative institution, run by large corporations with a membership from the ranks of modest concerns. Its president, Ladd Plumley, greeted Kennedy's scheme by saying: "The tax cut must be substantial . . . recessions cost money too. The 1957–8 recession resulted in a deficit of $12.5 billion." If Kennedy's tax cut worked, Plumley said, "this could be by far the least costly way to combat this problem." Senator Harry F. Byrd, the Virginia Democrat who ruled the Senate's Finance Committee, accused Plumley of "fiscal irresponsibility."*[61]

Kennedy went to the heart of Eisenhower's constituency, seeking business support for his tax cut from the Economic Club of New York. There he said his measure would strengthen business investment. He promised to cut the government's spending on things other than arms and pledged allegiance to the idea of balanced budgets. Galbraith called it "the most Republican speech since McKinley."[63]

Whatever the economics, Kennedy got the politics right. The economics, moreover, worked as forecast. After Kennedy's assassination, Lyndon Johnson embraced the tax cut and quickly got it through a docile Congress. The rates were very close to those Kennedy had sought, with a top bracket of 70 percent for

---

* Former president Eisenhower, who had so often resisted Burns's plea for a tax cut in a recession, was baffled at a tax cut in prosperity: "A tax cut alone is only half the equation," he said. "Without a commensurate curtailment of Federal expenditures a tax reduction by itself is a cruel illusion; what is given to the taxpayer in one hand is more than taken away from the other by cheapening his money and increasing his burden of public debt."[62] He no longer understood.

individuals and 48 percent for corporations. The fresh injection of purchasing power expanded demand, output, and jobs. Between the middle of 1964 and the middle of 1965, the unemployment rate fell from 5.4 percent to 4.7 percent,[64] total output rose $30 billion,[65] nearly 6 percent, and consumer prices advanced only 2 percent.[66]

For a brief, heady moment economists, particularly the new breed, were the toast of the country.

Tobin exulted over "the triumph of Keynesian ideas" and the consensus that a "steadily growing, fully employed economy is both desirable and attainable; that government fiscal and monetary powers can contribute greatly to achieving full employment, steady growth and price stability."[67]

Walter Heller gave the Godkin lectures at Harvard and announced, "Economics has come of age in the 1960s. Two Presidents have recognized and drawn on modern economics as a source of national strength." We have, he said, finally accepted the Employment Act of 1946, completed the Keynesian revolution and "put the political economist at the President's elbow."[68]

"The tax cut has opened minds and let new ideas in. It has led to a growing consensus—a higher level of understanding— on the active use of government tools to manage prosperity . . . the level of economic debate and hence the quality of economic decisions has been permanently raised."[69]

Even then, Johnson's burst of Vietnam spending was bringing the fat years to a close. Heller's works have an eerie ring now, like Irving Fisher's claim that shares had reached a permanent high plateau on the eve of the Great Crash. But at the time there was remarkably little dissent. A tax cut and rising demand suited unions and corporations, whatever they may have thought of gap, drag, and high-employment budget balancing. There were a few complaints from the right, and a sharp one came from George Terborgh, an economist for the Machinery and Allied Products Institute. An unemployment rate of 3.5 to 4 percent is incompatible with stable prices, he warned.[70] The target must be higher or aggressive unions will demand wage increases that lead to a price spiral. The new economics, like Prohibition, Terborgh warned, had been oversold.

While historians have focused on Kennedy's tax cut, his boldest economic venture lay well outside the Keynesian tradition. He was the first president to employ incomes policy, a radical new approach for curbing inflation.

Kennedy asserted that the law of supply and demand, the ten commandments of economics, had been at least partially repealed by the power of giant corporations and large unions. Free to some extent of market restraints, these powerful entities enjoyed a measure of discretion in setting wages and prices that most textbooks ignored. *

Ordinary citizens, untainted by economic theory, knew that General Motors raised car prices in good times and bad, that a local carpenters' union raised wages even when its members were jobless. But most economists and government policy makers could not fit these anomalies into their scheme and so the implications were ignored.

Even before Kennedy, the Eisenhower administration was made keenly aware that something was wrong. In the 1957–58 slump, prices generally rose, not fell. Eisenhower was venturesome enough to identify the culprit as the "exercise of economic

---

* As early as 1929, William Chamberlin had written *Monopolistic Competition* and Joan Robinson a year later published *Imperfect Competition*. Both described the theory of the competition of the few but neither work affected mainstream economics or public policy. Their ideas were regarded as awkward, sports.

power."[71] But the President had only the vaguest notion about what to do with his alarming discovery. Sherman Adams, his confidant, said Eisenhower wanted to appeal to the patriotism and sense of fair play of union and corporate leaders to restrain their appetites. But, Adams related, the cabinet's seasoned millionaires told the President he couldn't stop men from making money. Eisenhower did make a direct appeal to unions, which have "great power" to limit wage gains to productivity increases. He said nothing about the far greater power of business. More to the point, he choked off recovery from the slump, curbing spending and plugging the economy into still another recession that helped Kennedy win the White House.

When Kennedy took office, there was a substantial body of empirical inquiry dealing with the phenomenon of pricing power. What little theory existed had been developed by an original New Deal economist, Gardiner Means. Investigations into the auto, steel, drug, and other industries to support Means's work had been carried out by a lonely Senator, Estes Kefauver of Tennessee. His economist, John Blair, represented a dying breed. Blair believed in unfettered classical competition and could not be persuaded that it was identical with the competition of the giant few. Kefauver and Blair were among the most tenacious investigators on Capitol Hill. Their antitrust and monopoly subcommittee documented the fact that in industries dominated by a handful of firms prices were higher and output lower than they would be in markets of many competitors. Because they dealt with important matter in a serious, careful fashion, their work was largely ignored by the media. Because it didn't fit economists' preconceptions, it received scant attention from the profession. The Kennedy economists at least recognized a fact, the threat of corporate pricing power. However, they too ignored the unfashionable Means, Blair, and Kefauver.

Indeed, pricing power could undermine all policies aimed at restoring high employment and speeding up growth. Any increase in demand generated by a tax cut or spending increase might evaporate in price increases. There would be little or no gain for jobs, incomes, and output. If corporations and unions could defy the market, inflationary price increases would multiply as the economy used up its slack.

Means, who had been struck by the failure of big corporations to lower prices despite shrunken demand in the Great Depression, did not argue that large corporations were entirely immune from competition. One product can be substituted for another, so more coal was used when the OPEC cartel forced oil prices to breathtaking levels. Imports can check prices, unless they are curbed. So the handful of competitors in steel and autos have crippled or outlawed foreign competition. The point is that the competition of a few, of the handful of competitors making computers, cars, or electrical machinery, is very different from the competition of the many. The neighborhood stationery store has too many competitors to affect the price and supply of the newspapers it sells. If there are only two or three dailies in a city, they set their prices for ads and papers with a careful eye on each other. Even without illegal collusion, they can tacitly agree that one is the price leader for classified ads, another for retail ads, and all can push up rates without fear of undercutting. Similarly, a union that can halt production in a plant may push up wages even when layoffs take place.

Means identified the steelmakers as the single biggest source of inflation in the 1950s. Between 1953 and 1959, steel prices rose 36 percent; less than half that, 15 percent, would have covered all increased costs. The rest simply widened profits. As a result, the steelmakers could make a profit even with two-thirds of their plant shut down. What Means called "administered pricing" gave steel masters a mechanism to slash output and jobs while speeding up inflation.[72]

The new Kennedy administration seized on Means's theory, which had been reinforced by Kefauver's inquiry into the industry. The White House used its considerable influence—Labor Secretary Arthur J. Goldberg had been the steel union's chief counsel—to urge restraint in wage bargaining. But the industry, led by U.S. Steel, responded with a large price increase of $6 a ton, 3.5 percent. The President exploded, denouncing a "wholly unjustifiable and irresponsible defiance of the public interest,"[73] and ordered an antitrust inquiry. The steel makers retreated under the assault and rolled back their increase, at least for the time being. An entirely new weapon had been forged for economic policy makers.

This was incomes policy, arraying "the power of public opinion and Presidential persuasion," as Walter Heller put it, "against the market power of strong unions and strong business." It was an effort, Heller said, "to bring to the bargaining table and board rooms where wage and price decisions are made a sense of the public interest in noninflationary wage and price behavior."[74]

Kennedy set the tone early in his administration. He said, "Where both companies and unions possess substantial market power, the interplay of price and wage decisions could set off a movement towards higher price levels."[75] "Market power" was the language of Blair and Means. A conservative president had employed it and it would remain part of the public vocabulary until it was banished by Reagan.

The Heller council erected guideposts for wage and price decision making in industries where firms exercised market power. In general, the guideposts held that unions should limit wage increases to the national average gain in productivity, efficiency, or output per hour. If productivity gains were 3 percent a year, workers could win 3 percent wage increases without forcing any increase in price. This would permit a 3 percent rise in profits and leave the shares of workers and owners unchanged in a growing economy. The guideposts allowed for appropriate exceptions. In efficient industries where productivity exceeded the national average, a 3 percent wage gain would allow price cuts; in less efficient industries, the 3 percent standard would require price increases. On average, the price level should hold steady.

The real if unacknowledged thrust of the guideposts was to restrain wages. Many business observers believe that large corporations seek a fixed-target rate of return on investment, that prices are raised chiefly to cover rising costs and maintain a profit rate. In this view, prices are set passively in response to wages. It is a view belied by steel and other industries. They frequently seek to raise their rates of return, their profits, by raising prices faster than costs increase. But in industries where firms seek an unchanged standard rate of return and in which unions observe the guideposts, no price increases need take place. Large corporations could earn their target return and pay for higher wages from increased output per man-hour. Inflation then evaporates.

Galbraith, who had mocked Kennedy's rationale for a tax cut, called incomes policy Kennedy's "most important innovation."[76]

He was right. Circumstance forced Kennedy to address a critical area, market power, that Keynes and other mainstream economists had largely ignored. The President, a tempered conservative, had responded cautiously. He never tried to impose or enforce his guideposts; he sought voluntary assent, backed by public opinion. It was Nixon who later enacted guideposts into law, creating peacetime wage and price controls. The Kennedy guideposts, moreover, implicitly rejected the trustbusters who wanted to pulverize corporations, breaking them down into classical competitors. Such a course had been urged on Roosevelt who borrowed the rhetoric but largely ignored the substance. Kennedy kept the structure of corporations and unions intact; he sought instead to influence their decisions.

On the surface, Kennedy was successful. Consumer prices rose only 3.6 percent from 1960 through 1963,[77] little more than 1 percent a year. But unemployment averaged 5.8 percent each year[78] and this raised a crucial question. Did guideposts work only when there was great slack in the economy, when unions and corporations were reluctant to push their market power? Would they break down when the economy reached the high employment Kennedy's tax cut sought? Arthur Burns, a Republican realist who saw some utility in incomes policy, thought so. Guideposts, he said, helped hold prices down, "but far more important . . . has been the moderate slack of industrial capacity and the moderately large unemployment of recent years."[79] In the three years after the tax cut, and propelled by spending for Vietnam, unemployment fell just under the Kennedy target, to 3.9 percent. But consumer prices rose 8 percent and the price gains were accelerating.[80]

Business and labor can't be expected to act against interest, Burns said. They won't follow guidelines if all the slack is used up. In 1970, he wrote that current inflation reflects "especially the commitment to maintain high levels of employment and rapid economic growth."[81] This was shrewd. Like Terborgh, it anticipated Ronald Reagan's solution, deliberate slack.

After Kennedy, however, no policy maker seeking both high employment and stable prices could neglect corporate power and some policy to contain it. But after Kennedy, it was equally clear that reliance on voluntary restraint must fail when a high-employment economy is propelled by excessive spending.

This happened after the huge jump in outlays for the war in Vietnam. President Johnson maintained the guideposts, even refined them by declaring 3.2 percent as the appropriate limit for wage increases.[82] But prices rose rapidly under the force of the war's demand, 3.4 percent from start to finish in 1966, 3 percent in 1967,[83] 4.7 percent in 1968.[84] The guideposts splintered. Fewer corporations and unions listened to appeals for restraint. No union would accept a 3.2 percent limit, impose cuts in real income on members whose services were in demand. No corporation willingly permits profits to wither by refraining from price increases to cover costs. "The idea of excess demand could not be talked down," said Arthur Okun,[85] council chairman for Johnson.

The Johnson government quietly stopped urging adherence to guideposts, gave up asking unions to limit wage increases to the rise in the trend of national productivity. Instead, there were vaguer appeals for restraint.

The big jump in Vietnam spending destroyed more than Kennedy's innovative incomes policy. The resulting surge in prices helped erode the long generation of postwar prosperity, turned fat years into lean, and left the nation with new, reduced expectations of how the economy could perform. Other forces later finished off postwar prosperity: dollar depreciation and the oil shocks. But the end of the fat years began with President Johnson's refusal to pay for an expanded war when there was little slack in the economy. Nineteen sixty-five was not 1940. Then war demand put armies of unemployed workers and their idle plants back to work. But in mid-1965, the unemployment rate was 4.7 percent and falling, within sight of the target.[86] A big war demand was bound to spill over into prices unless

Johnson cut spending for his Great Society welfare programs or increased taxes to shrink private demand. From the second to the fourth quarter of 1965, military buying rose $3.4 billion.[87] The Pentagon bought weapons at a yearly rate of $48.4 billion in the first quarter of 1965;[88] by the end of 1967, this had risen to $74.3 billion, an enormous increase of more than 50 percent.[89] The budget, computed for national income accounts, showed a yearly surplus of $3.5 billion in the first half of 1965. The Federal government was restraining prices by taking more from aggregate demand than it was putting in. In the second half, Vietnam turned this into a deficit of $2.5 billion.[90] Now the government was swelling the demand stream.

The big surge in demand was not eaten up entirely by prices. Unemployment fell swiftly, from 4.5 percent in 1965 to 3.8 percent in 1966 and 3.6 percent in 1968. As Johnson left office, unemployment dropped to 3.3 percent.[91] Thanks to the war, Kennedy's temporary goal, 4 percent, had been reached and exceeded. But the consequence for prices was dismal. The extra demand pulled consumer prices up 1.9 percent in 1965. By 1969, prices were rising at a 6.1 percent rate.[92] Inflation was rampant; it no longer could be traced to the market power of corporations and unions.

Curiously, this folly, unlike the Great Depression or the first stagflation recession of 1957, was well understood and accurately forecast, in and out of government. At the start of the war buildup in December 1965, Gardner Ackley, chairman of Johnson's economic advisers, wrote the President, "There is little question in my mind that a significant tax increase will be needed to prevent an intolerable degree of inflationary pressure." A few days later, Ackley underlined his message. Taxes should be increased "as soon as possible."[93]

Johnson was not moved. He feared Congress would insist instead on cutting back his Great Society programs. He was probably right. Many congressmen would have preferred to slash programs for the poor rather than raise taxes for a peculiar war. In addition, a plea for more taxes would have invited a debate on the war itself. Johnson feared that and invented statistics to disguise the war's cost. His budget for the year ending June 30, 1967 proposed $60.5 billion in defense spending; it actually came to $70.1 billion. Ackley said, "We knew damned well that neither of these figures [budget and defense] was in the least bit relevant."[94] At the Federal Reserve, there was outright contempt. The central bank's internal statistical summary, the Green Book, was compelled to quote Johnson's estimate for Vietnam spending. Some wag wrote, "For internal use only, but dangerous if swallowed."[95] With no help from Johnson's fiscal power, the Federal Reserve cracked down hard on credit and drove up borrowing rates. Johnson was annoyed.

William Moyers, his close aide, described Johnson's refusal to heed Ackley and other advisers as "the single most devastating decision in the Johnson administration. It was the beginning of the end . . . a time when he lost control of the administration, lost control of events."[96]

More than a year and a half later, Johnson turned around and asked for a 6 percent increase in all income taxes.[97] It took still another year before a suspicious Congress delivered. But it was too late. An era of stable prices had ended. Businessmen, consumers, labor, everybody now made plans in the expectation of ever-rising prices. This belief, partly self-reinforcing and partly reinforced by fact, was destroyed only when the Federal Reserve Bank imposed a long and painful recession in 1980–82.

The war spending also hastened the end of the dollar's supremacy in global transactions, a major element in postwar prosperity. The flow of dollars abroad for troops and weapons and the increased imports sucked in by the economy's artificial boom made the dollar increasingly less desirable. When Johnson began his buildup in 1965, the world monetary system was more or less stable. The rates at which currencies exchanged for each other were largely fixed and all were fixed against the dollar. But a world flooded with dollars would not use the American currency as a reserve or an ultimate measure of value. The outflow of dollars destroyed the postwar monetary system. To stanch the hemorrhage, Johnson curbed spending by U.S. corporations abroad. On the eve of his Vietnam splurge, he announced, "There can be no question of our capacity and determination to maintain the gold value of the dollar at $35 an ounce."[98] As late as 1968, he proclaimed, "The dollar will continue to be as good or better than gold."[99] But the trade surplus under Johnson fell steadily, from $8.4 billion in 1965 to $3.7 billion in 1968.[100] The war sped dollars abroad and sucked in foreign goods.

For the first time since World War II, the U.S. became aware of economic constraints on its political power. General Charles de Gaulle, the French President, had a sovereign's contempt for economics but a tactician's eye for leverage. Sooner than most, he understood that U.S. foreign policy rested, among other things, on the dollar's privilege. He detested the American war—France had lost its Indochinese colonies in the fifties—and he found a way to help end it.

De Gaulle simply exercised France's right to swap dollars for gold. As dollars flowed to the French central bank, they were sent back to Washington, where the Federal Reserve earmarked more gold bars for the French account in New York. De Gaulle hoped the Germans and Japanese would do the same, but as defeated former enemies they were timid. While the U.S. stock of gold shrank, that of France and others mounted. At last, even the Germans began to cash in some dollars. Now the finite limit was felt. In February 1968, General William Westmoreland, the U.S. commander in Vietnam, asked for 206,000 more troops.[101] Johnson rejected the plea, a turning point in the war and the start of the slow American withdrawal. A major reason for Johnson's decision was his well-founded fear that a stepped-up war would speed the outflow of gold, and a brief buying panic took place when Westmoreland's request leaked out. The European and Japanese dollar holders rightly reasoned that a bigger war meant a bigger deficit that would ultimately force the U.S. to devalue the dollar.

De Gaulle can't claim credit for driving the U.S. from Vietnam; that was the doing of the North Vietnamese and a mounting domestic opposition. But the French President did succeed in helping halt an expansion of the war. He used gold and dollars far more skillfully than anyone else to bring about a decisive turn in Johnson's policy.

Under Johnson, the U.S. was fast losing its privileged purchasing power over foreign goods. Under Nixon, it would disappear entirely. The Vietnam War took its casualties in the most unexpected places.

NOTES

1. *Historical Statistics of the United States, Colonial Times to 1970: Bicentennial Edition* (U.S. Department of Commerce, 1975)—average annual percentage rates of change in the GNP, pp. 226–7, unemployment, p. 135, CPI, p. 210.

2. *Ibid.*, p. 297.

3. Alvin Hansen, *The Post-War American Economy* (New York: W.W. Norton, 1964), p. 5.

4. Robert Aaron Gordon, *Economic Instability and Growth* (New York: Harper & Row, 1974), p. 12.

5. Paul A. Samuelson, *Stability and Growth in the American Economy* (Stockholm, Sweden: Almquist & Wicksell, 1961), p. 29.

6. *Historical Statistics of the United States*, p. 135.

7. *Economic Report of the President* (Washington D.C.: U.S. Government Printing Office, 1989), pp. 308–9.

8. Wilfred Lewis, *Federal Fiscal Policy in Post-War Recessions* (Washington, D.C.: The Brookings Institution, 1962), pp. 15–16.

9. Dwight Eisenhower, *The Eisenhower Diaries*, edited by Robert H. Ferrell (New York: W.W. Norton, 1981), p. 231.

10. *Economic Report of the President* (Washington, D.C.: U.S. Government Printing Office, 1954), p. iv.

11. Arthur F. Burns, *The Management of Prosperity* (New York: Columbia University Press, 1966), p. 15.

12. Seymour Harris, *The Economics of Political Parties* (New York: Macmillan, 1962), p. vii.

13. Sherman Adams, *Firsthand Report: The Story of the Eisenhower Administration* (New York: Harper & Brothers, 1961), p. 156.

14. *Ibid.*, p. 162.

15. *Ibid.*, p. 366.

16. *Economic Report of the President* (Washington D.C.: U.S. Government Printing Office, 1955), p. 137.

17. *Ibid.*, p. 37.

18. Adams, *Firsthand Report*, p. 156.

19. Dwight Eisenhower, *Mandate for Change 1953–56* (Garden City, New York: Doubleday, 1963), p. 307.

20. *Ibid.*, p. 297.

21. *Ibid.*, p. 487.

22. Burns quoted in E. Cary Brown, "Federal Fiscal Policy in the Postwar Period," in Ralph E. Freeman, editor, *Postwar Economic Trends in the United States* (New York: Harper & Brothers, 1960), p. 168.

23. *Economic Report of the President*, 1955, p. 66.

24. *Economic Report of the President* (Washington D.C.: U.S. Government Printing Office, 1966), p. 173.

25. Lewis, *Federal Fiscal Policy*, p. 178.

26. *Ibid.*, p. 194.

27. Bert G. Hickman, *Growth and Stability of the Postwar Economy* (Washington, D.C.: The Brookings Institution, 1960), p. 151.

28. Dwight Eisenhower, *Waging Peace, 1956–1961* (Garden City, New York: Doubleday, 1965), p. 309.

29. *Economic Report of the President* (Washington D.C.: U.S. Government Printing Office, 1959), p. 40.

30. Adams, *Firsthand Report*, p. 415.

31. *Economic Report of the President*, 1959, p. 41.

32. *Business Conditions Digest* (U.S. Department of Commerce, January 1988), p. 104.

33. *Economic Report of the President*, 1959, p. 184.

34. Lewis, *Federal Fiscal Policy*, p. 237.

35. *Ibid.*, p. 237.

36. Eisenhower, *Waging Peace: 1956–1961*, pp. 461–2.

37. Richard M. Nixon, *Six Crises* (Garden City, New York: Doubleday, 1962), pp. 309–310.

38. *Ibid.*, p. 310.

39. Anderson quoted in *The Eisenhower Diaries*, p. 382.

40. *Economic Report of the President* (Washington, D.C.: U.S. Government Printing Office, 1961), p. 59.

41. *Ibid.*, p. 60.

42. *Economic Report of the President* (Washington, D.C.: U.S. Government Printing Office, 1962), p. 4.

43. James Tobin, *The Intellectual Revolution in United States Economic Policy-Making* (London: Longsman, Green, 1966), p. 10.

44. Lewis, *Federal Fiscal Policy*, p. 262.

45. *Economic Report of the President*, 1962, p. 207.

46. Lewis, *Federal Fiscal Policy*, p. 274.

47. Herbert Stein, *The Fiscal Revolution in America* (Chicago, Illinois: University of Chicago Press, 1969), p. 455.

48. *Economic Report of the President*, 1962, p. 3.

49. William Breit and Roger W. Spencer, editors, *Lives of the Laureates: Seven Nobel Economists* (Cambridge, Massachusetts: MIT Press, 1988), p. 131.

50. *Economic Report of the President*, 1962, pp. 51–3.

51. *Economic Report of the President* (Washington, D.C.: U.S. Government Printing Office, 1963), p. ix.

52. *Economic Report of the President*, 1963, p. xii.

53. *Ibid.*, p. 42.

54. *Economic Report of the President*, 1989, p. 308.

55. *Economic Report of the President*, 1963, p. 74.

56. Kennedy quoted in Robert Lekachman, *Inflation: The Permanent Problem of Boom and Bust* (New York: Random House, 1973), p. 16.

57. James Tobin, *The New Economics One Decade Older* (Princeton: Princeton University Press, 1974), p. 25.

58. Arthur F. Burns and Paul A. Samuelson, *Full-Employment, Guideposts and Economic Stability* (Washington, D.C.: American Enterprise Institute for Public Policy Research, 1967), p. 16.

59. Stein, *Fiscal Revolution*, p. 435.

60. Jim F. Heath, *John Kennedy and the Business Community* (Chicago: University of Chicago Press, 1969), p. 121.

61. Stein, *Fiscal Revolution*, pp. 417–18.

62. Eisenhower quoted in Robert Aaron Gordon, *The Goal of Full-Employment* (New York: Wiley, 1967), pp. 15–16.

63. Galbraith quoted in Stein, *Fiscal Revolution*, p. 421.

64. *Economic Report of the President*, 1966, p. 235.

65. *Ibid.*, p. 209.

66. *Ibid.*, pp. 257–60.

67. Tobin, *The Intellectual Revolution*, p. 2.

68. Walter W. Heller, *New Dimensions of Political Economy* (New York: W.W. Norton, 1967), pp. 1–2.

69. *Ibid.*, pp. 40–41.

70. George Terborgh, *The New Economics* (Washington, D.C.: Machinery and Allied Products Institute, 1968), p. 194.

71. *Economic Report of the President* (Washington D.C.: U.S. Government Printing Office, 1958), p. 4.

72. Gardiner C. Means, *Pricing Power and the Public Interest: A Study Based on Steel* (New York: Harper & Brothers, 1962), p. 149.

73. Heath, *John F. Kennedy and the Business Community*, pp. 68–9.

74. Heller, *New Dimensions of Political Economy*, p. 43.

75. *Economic Report of the President* (Washington, D.C.: U.S. Government Printing Office, 1962), p. 16.

76. John Kenneth Galbraith, *The New Industrial State* (Boston: Houghton Mifflin Company), p. 256.

77. *Historical Statistics*, p. 210.

78. *Ibid.*, p. 135.

79. Burns, *The Management of Prosperity*, p. 26.

80. *Historical Statistics*, p. 135.

81. Arthur F. Burns, *Reflections of an Economic Policy Maker: Speeches and Congressional Statements, 1969–1978* (Washington, D.C.: American Enterprise Institute for Public Policy Research, 1978), p. 92.

82. *Economic Report of the President*, 1966, p. 78.

83. *Economic Report of the President* (Washington, D.C.: U.S. Government Printing Office, 1968), p. 261.

84. *Economic Report of the President* (Washington, D.C.: U.S. Government Printing Office, 1969), p. 269.

85. Arthur Okun, *The Political Economy of Prosperity* (Washington, D.C.: The Brookings Institution, 1970), p. 77.

86. *Economic Report of the President*, 1966.

87. *Economic Report of the President* (Washington D.C.: U.S. Government Printing Office, 1967), p. 213.

88. *Ibid.*, p. 213.

89. *Economic Report of the President*, 1968, p. 207.

90. *Economic Report of the President*, 1966, p. 52.

91. *Economic Report of the President* (Washington, D.C.: U.S. Government Printing Office, 1970).

92. *Economic Report of the President*, 1969, p. 378.

93. Gardner Ackley quoted in James E. Anderson and Jared E. Hazelton, *Managing Macroeconomic Policy: The Johnson Presidency* (Austin: University of Texas Press, 1986), p. 35.

94. *Ibid.*, p. 58.

95. *Ibid.*, p. 124.

96. William Moyers quoted in Robert A. Divine, *The Johnson Years, Volume Two* (Lawrence, Kansas: University Press of Kansas, 1987), p. 54.

97. *Economic Report of the President*, 1967, p. 9.

98. *Economic Report of the President*, 1965, p. 7.

99. *Economic Report of the President*, 1968, p. 16.

100. *Economic Report of the President*, 1989, p. 424.

101. Townsend Hoopes, *The Limits of Intervention* (New York: David-McKay, 1973), p. 161.

IV

Lean Years

The long skein of postwar prosperity unraveled rapidly in the 1970s. The Vietnam legacy, a stubborn inflation built by excessive demand, was never erased. Now the nation fell into something new and nastier: stagflation. The awkward word describes an unpleasant set of facts. Prices continued to rise although the economy slumped; inflation mounted even when demand fell. Moreover, when demand expanded, few new jobs were created. More strikingly, prices shot ahead at a faster rate. The nation was in the grip of simultaneous unemployment and inflation, the worst of both worlds.

This condition was not entirely new although the word was freshly minted. In the 1957–58 recession, Eisenhower officials had noted with alarm that prices had increased although experience and theory said they should fall. The Eisenhower response, severely curbing demand early in a recovery, foreshadowed the policy of the 1970s. Eisenhower and Treasury Secretary Anderson deliberately created a recession, called by Europeans a "policy recession," to tame prices. It worked, but at a fearful cost in jobs. The Kennedy administration, more sophisticated in these matters, concluded that prices were rising not because demand was excessive, but because of the power of large corporations and unions. So the Kennedy team turned to incomes policy, guideposts, jawboning, public pressure to persuade price and wage decision makers to restrain their power.

In the 1970s, the experience gained in the Eisenhower and Kennedy years was briefly exploited but quickly abandoned. Unexpected economic events, nearly all of them hurtful, outsped government's ability to cope. President Ford, a decent if unimaginative man, summed up the confusion: "Conventional economic theory held that when you had high inflation, unemployment was low. That may have been true in the past, but it wasn't true any longer."[1] Ford bobbed like a cork in rough water, first urging a tax increase to halt inflation, then calling for a tax cut to stem unemployment.

The Carter administration was just as confused, unable to decide whether the problem was inflation, deflation, or both. When a goal was fixed, Charles Schultze, the chief economic adviser, said, "We were always, in terms of an anti-inflationary program, six months to a year behind the game."[2]

Bizarre economics invaded the loftiest circles. At a Paris conference aimed at holding down the price of oil, Secretary of State Henry Kissinger actually insisted on an agreement among consumer nations to put a floor under oil prices.[3] Otherwise, Kissinger contended, the new investment that consuming nations sought to expand oil supplies would become profitless. This is roughly the economic equivalent of destroying the city to preserve the city.

The end of prosperity shattered the confidence of the Keynesian managers. Inflation was something the Keynesian prescription could treat, although Keynes said little about it in a book written in the depths of the Great Depression. But the simultaneous combination of slump and inflation was in no one's text.

Nevertheless, economists linked to the University of Chicago, particularly Milton Friedman, thought they had an answer. These thinkers argued there could be no price increases if the Federal Reserve didn't print the money, didn't expand bank monetary reserves, didn't create the basis for more loans. This was true but unhelpful. As a policy guide it was of limited use because the level of prices depends not only on the volume of money but also on the speed or velocity with which it circulates from hand to hand. A Friedmanite trying to cure inflation by cutting the money supply can be confounded by an equal and offsetting rise in velocity, a force that can't be managed or predicted. Monetarist policy claps with one hand, influencing only one of two critical factors.

Which way to turn baffled policy makers to a degree unseen since Roosevelt's first five years. Then, at least, the same players could be found on the same side of the fence from one month to the next. Those favoring reflation, those for expansion, and those for trust busting were more or less unchanged. But in the dismal 1970s, when jobs, incomes, and certainty vanished at a frightening rate, the players hopped all over the lot.

Nixon, the most radical president since the second-term Roosevelt, set the style. He first decided to deal with Johnson's Vietnam inflation before it could damage his reelection. Nixon quickly scrapped the Kennedy and Johnson experiments with incomes policy, guideposts, and standards. He wrote in his memoirs: "The major theme of my economic policy in 1969 and 1970 was the rejection of government 'jawboning' of business and labor as a way of restraining inflation."[4] Instead, he turned to the method that Eisenhower had used in 1960, monetary and fiscal restraint, which had cost Vice President Nixon the election.

Nixon promoted a policy recession his first year in office, a deliberate attempt to force down the rate of price increase by curbing the supply of money and limiting government spending. "The basic strategy," wrote Philip Cagan, a thoughtful monetarist, "was to fight inflation with a mild dose of excess productive capacity,"[5] a modest increase in idle men and idle plants.

Nixon got his recession. Output fell and unemployment climbed from 3.5 percent in 1969 to 5 percent by May of 1970.[6] But prices kept right on rising at ever faster rates, to 6 percent by the first half of 1970.[7] Interest rates in 1969 were the highest in a century,[8] although the Federal Reserve drove them higher in later anti-inflation crusades.

Nixon's policies failed just as Eisenhower's did in 1960 because this was no longer an inflation propelled by excess demand. It was a cost-push inflation, an inflation stemming from the price and wage power of large corporate actors.

Nixon, however, did not let dogma interfere with politics, and he changed course with breathtaking speed. He knew he must stimulate the economy, bring down unemployment in 1972, his election year. But how could he do that without worsening inflation? The answer was the ultimate incomes policy, mandatory price controls. Nixon slapped a lid on prices as he had learned as a lawyer at OPA in World War II. Now he could revive output and jobs with a tax cut and spending, unworried about inflation.

This still left a nagging problem, however. His expansion in demand threatened to wipe out the nation's diminishing gold stock, shrinking exports because of higher prices, attracting lower-priced imports. But Nixon had the answer for that too. He stopped selling gold to foreigners, repudiating a U.S. pledge and tearing up the postwar international monetary system. He forced a devaluation of the dollar with consequences barely perceived at the time.

Nixon's stunning about-face, lubricated with easy money supplied by his friend Arthur Burns, now chairman of the Federal Reserve, worked brilliantly. A speedup in spending, notably by the Pentagon, also helped. So in 1972, prices rose only 4 percent,[9] the unemployment rate fell from 5.9 percent to 5.6 percent[10] and total output rose a brisk 5.7 percent.[11] Nixon's remarkable switch made him the last fully successful economic manager in the postwar period. He was rewarded with a landslide triumph over George McGovern despite his failure to end the war in Vietnam.

Gerald Ford had to be just as nimble, undoing one day what he had pledged the day before. But he was not nearly so lucky. Ford inherited from Nixon what was then the worst slump since 1938, the deep recession of 1974–75. On his first day in office, however, Ford's aides reassured him. The jobless rate would reach only 6 percent, they forecast. (It climbed to 9 percent nine months later.)[12]

The key aides were Alan Greenspan, chairman of the Council of Economic Advisers, and William Simon, the Treasury Secretary. Both had made careers in Wall Street, where concern for the value of bondholders' assets tends to be more common than fear of unemployment. Ford proclaimed that "inflation was domestic public enemy number one."[13]

With consumer prices racing ahead at a rate of 12 percent a year,[14] Ford, urged on by Greenspan and Simon, first demanded a tax increase. But unemployment had already climbed above 7 percent[15] and, at the Federal Reserve, Burns insisted that slump, not boom, was the enemy. By January, the President agreed with Burns, abandoned his plea for a tax increase, and called for a $16 billion tax cut. Congress enlarged it by $7 billion[16]—Simon wanted Ford to veto such recklessness—and gave the economy an extra stimulus it badly needed.

Although Burns urged the tax cut on Ford, the Federal Reserve chief had not covered himself with glory. In the worst of the slump, the central bank tightened money, thereby ensuring that the massive increases in oil and food prices would push down jobs and output. If Burns had eased credit, oil and food would have caused a one-time worsening of inflation but employment and production would have been saved. From the first quarter of 1974 to the first quarter of 1975, the supply of money—after correcting for price increases—actually fell by 7 percent,[17] with a devastating effect on housing and financial markets that rippled throughout the economy. A generous judgment by Alan Blinder of Princeton does not blame the Fed entirely for the slump's severity. Burns' bank, Blinder said, was "guilty of contributory negligence, not of first degree murder."[18] At its worst, from the end of 1973 to the end of 1974, output plunged 5 percent.[19] While Burns, Greenspan, and Simon were not solely responsible for this calamity, their names are indelibly stamped on the event. As is so often the case in American life, error on a truly grand scale assured all three a public reputation for extreme wisdom.

The gyrations between repressive tax increases and stimulating tax cuts were painful. Governments and politicians like to pretend they are consistent. Violent swings in policy are not only an embarrassing confession of failed judgment; they have economic consequences. Business firms and individuals have trouble planning their own outlays, their own investment, when they do not know from one month to the next whether they will endure a tax increase or enjoy a reduction, whether government spending will rise or fall, whether prices and wages will be determined by corporate and union power or the power of government.

After the high confidence of economists and the largely successful economic policy in the Kennedy administration, the antics of the 1970s were a shock. In real terms, incomes no longer grew except for the wealthiest. The income for the median household, allowing for inflation, was $23,565 in 1980. In 1970, it had been $24,662, 4.7 percent higher.[20] Recessions were no longer brief and mild. The slump of 1974–75 lasted five quarters, longer than previous postwar recessions.[21] The 4.8 percent loss in output markedly exceeded the 3.2 percent of 1957–58.[22] Clearly, something important and disturbing had overtaken the American economy.

"Now I am a Keynesian,"[23] said President Nixon in 1971 after announcing that his deficit budget would balance only at high levels of employment.* He meant that he was no longer wedded to traditional conservative belief in the sanctity of annual balanced budgets. More, he was proclaiming his faith in the modern view, that government money, spending, and tax policies could assure bigger output, fewer jobless, and only moderately rising prices.

Even as he spoke, Nixon was the last of a line of Keynesians in the White House, at least acknowledged ones.

Ford never could decide whether a budget deficit was good or bad in a recession. "The budget deficit is likely to remain excessively large in fiscal 1977," his advisers had him say at the bottom of an awesome slump.[25] Ford even pressed for excise taxes on oil and other products to undo some of his demand stimuli. This was the economics of Janus. Even stranger, Greenspan discovered a matter of great importance that argued for even deeper budget deficits. Greenspan found that stagfla-

---

* He was paraphrasing Milton Friedman, who had declared in 1965, "We are all Keynesians now and nobody is any longer a Keynesian."[24] Friedman meant that every literate economist had absorbed and drawn on Keynes's teachings but also relied on fresher ideas.

tion exerted a peculiarly perverse effect.[26] It had converted the progressive tax system from a stabilizer, resisting slump, into a powerful destabilizer, deepening slump.

Greenspan saw that inflation threw taxpayers into higher brackets without enlarging their real incomes. A man earning $20,000 a year might pay 24 percent on the last slice of his income. But rising prices could lift his dollar income to $28,000 and push him into a 27 percent bracket. After subtracting inflation, his income was unchanged before taxes. After taxes, however, he suffered a real cut. A larger slice had been taxed away from the same real income. His purchasing power had fallen and so would his demand. Throughout the nation, this was happening to millions. The economy was slumping but the tax system no longer fed income to citizens; instead, it seized a larger share of their pay, depressing demand. Inflation had converted the tax system into a big unlegislated increase in taxes. So about half of Ford's tax cut added nothing to demand, provided no stimulus. It was eaten up by the high tax levies from larger dollar incomes created by inflation.

All this was reason for an even more expansive budget. At least Congress had seen the point in 1975 and had increased Ford's tax reduction.

The most radical turn was made by the conservative Carter. In his first year in office he echoed Democratic doctrine and promised he would not attempt to cure inflation with high unemployment and slow growth. "The human tragedy and waste of resources associated with policies of slow growth are intolerable," he said.[27]

By the time he left office, the "human tragedy" of unemployment had been subordinated to the perils of higher prices. In the election year of 1980, he announced, "Our economy is likely to undergo a mild recession early this year."[28] But instead of disclosing how he would stop it, he let his Council of Economic Advisers say that it wasn't deep enough. "Only sharply restrictive monetary and fiscal policies, which strengthen the forces leading to recession, can prevent an increase in the underlying inflation rate." If that wasn't harsh enough, the council added, "While recessionary forces came into play in 1974 and 1980, the slackening of aggregate demand was not sufficient to avoid another upward ratcheting of the inflation rate."[29]

Behind the scenes, an odd switch took place. Carter's economists warned him of the awful political consequences he faced if he persisted. "He overruled all his economic advisers in terms of having a contingency tax cut,"[30] Schultze said.

Instead, Carter became a flagellant and sternly backed Federal Reserve monetary curbs that plunged the nation into an even worse slump than that suffered by Ford. Clearly, some of the punishment had to be endured. From 1976 through 1979, the money supply had climbed rapidly, 29 percent.[31] Prices had risen a disturbing 27 percent[32] during this span and a brake was necessary. But there is little reason to believe that it needed to be as harsh and as abrupt as the one sanctioned by Carter and imposed by Paul Volcker, the Fed's chairman.

There is something almost heroic in Carter's political suicide, like the charge of the Light Brigade. A weak echo of the New Deal, a hortatory bill from Senator Hubert Humphrey of Minnesota and Representative Augustus Hawkins of California, called on the government to announce its plans for reaching 4 percent unemployment and 3 percent inflation in 1983. No chance, said Carter. Four percent unemployment in 1983 meant more inflation; put it off until 1985. There is equally no hope of reaching the inflation goal until 1988. This was brave but it was neither politics nor economics. Moreover, it overthrew a tradition since Roosevelt that the President's first economic task is to stop slump and reduce unemployment. Carter's turn opened the way for new men who would claim that government had no power over output, jobs, and prices. Until this posture was upended, it seemed for a while that nobody was a Keynesian.

The eclipse of Keynes followed the economy's downhill path. Starting in 1973, there was a sharp break in the major indexes of material well-being. Except for brief periods of slump, output did not actually fall but it grew less rapidly. Inflation did not turn into runaway price increases but prices rose more rapidly. Unemployment never reached the depths of the 1930s but the jobless rate stuck at high levels.

The sudden discontinuity in the economic series after 1973 —the sharp downward plunge in the principal economic indicators—is widely attributed to a fall in productivity, the efficiency of workers, the extra amount a worker can produce in a given period of time.

Prosperity, ever-higher incomes, depends essentially on two things: an expanding labor force and an increasing productivity rate. Either or both add each year to the stream of goods and services. More workers can produce more goods. So can the same number of workers laboring more efficiently.

Clearly something happened to the rate of productivity increase in the age of stagflation. From 1948 to 1966, the period of distinct postwar prosperity, productivity in the American economy increased on average by 3.3 percent a year.[33] That assured brisk growth in output.

But after the Vietnam inflation, from 1966 to 1973, productivity rose only 2.1 percent a year, a full third less. From 1973 through 1976, productivity barely increased, less than 1 percent a year. From 1977 through 1980, the rate actually fell.

This was a sport. Generally, workers were more efficient each year than the one before. There were usually some productivity gains. But they were far smaller than they had been in the past. As a result, the gains in output, income, and wealth were smaller.

But why did productivity fall? Nobody argues that in 1973 American workers everywhere suddenly became slack, lazy, preferred leisure to income. The most common explanation holds that workers were given fewer new tools with which to labor. The ratio of capital or plant and equipment to the labor force dropped steadily. This implies that productivity depends largely on how well workers are equipped. When firms invest more in tools and factories, worker efficiency rises; when investment falls, productivity falls.

As it happens, there is a close link between the course of investment and productivity. In the 1948–66 prosperity era, capital per hour of labor rose 3.1 percent a year. But from 1966 to 1973, capital per labor hour gained only 2.8 percent a year, a fall of 10 percent. From 1973 to 1976, the increase in tools and plants for each hour worked was only 1.7 percent, little more than half the rate of the fat years. [34]

That seems to tidy everything up. But it really raises another question. Why did business cut its investment? Why did the rate at which workers were armed with tools and new plants decline? Economists offer endless answers. But the best, the most plausible, came from the Carter administration. Its economists said: "Much of the low recent growth in productivity may come from the effect which the extreme instability of the economy since 1968 has had on investment." [35]

Economic turmoil, the switch back and forth from expansionary to restrictive policies, the dilemma of stagflation made corporations cautious. They were much less willing to put money into new factories and machines; tomorrow the govern-

117

ment might decide inflation was the chief problem and create another policy recession. Investment is likelier to increase steadily when the government ensures demand, when high employment is the goal. Then a firm is confident that there will be customers for the extra products coming from the new factories and tools. If markets are damaged by governments that blow hot and cold, urging tax increase one quarter and tax cut the next, investment will dry up.

The economy bent and corroded in 1973 because productivity took a nose dive. Productivity fell because new investment was curbed. Investment was held back because demand was no longer assured, because the postwar pledge of high employment had been revoked.

Stagflation brought about the repeal. The two-front struggle with rising prices and rising unemployment bewildered governments. When the promise to maintain high employment was kept, an accelerating spiral of prices threatened. If prices were checked, unemployment worsened. Stagflation had caused government to stumble, lurch, contradict its solemn pronouncements. Stagflation chilled the postwar expectation of ever higher incomes.

The stagflation that gripped the United States and Europe in the 1970s began with the failure to subdue the inflation generated by Vietnam by a tax increase or a cut in civilian spending. But the immediate cause was the disintegration of the world monetary system, Nixon's destruction of the rules governing the rates at which currencies exchanged. In August 1971, it is unlikely that Nixon gave much thought to the notion that he was making history, sweeping aside the careful arrangements elaborated at Bretton Woods, New Hampshire, in 1944. His memoirs barely mention the episode. As always, he thought in direct, practical terms. The British ambassador wanted to cash in

$3 billion for U.S. gold.[36] How could Nixon preserve the gold stock? What could he do to spare the nation and his election prospects from a drastic deflation? How could he preserve his freedom of action in Vietnam? How could he meet the demands on a dwindling U.S. gold stock? His decision, bold and imaginative, achieved all three objectives brilliantly. His package—a domestic stimulus, a freeze on wages and prices, and the closing of the gold window—was even hailed by sophisticated Democrats. Otto Eckstein said: "The President's program substantially improves the outlook for the U.S. economy . . . the measures are a triumph of common sense and modern economics and contain the promise of extricating the U.S. economy from its current impasse."[37]

Neither he nor Nixon nor perhaps anybody else understood that Nixon's improvised solution must undermine a major prop of postwar U.S. prosperity.

Like most new economic institutions, postwar monetary arrangements were created to meet pressing immediate needs. The U.S. was the only major industrial power to emerge from the war with its capital, plant, and machinery intact. Indeed, the U.S. had greatly enlarged its productive capacity. Europe and Japan hungered for goods; only the U.S. could supply them. At the same time, American authorities were determined to revive the Japanese and German economies, to build them as bulwarks against what was thought to be aggressive, expanding communism. These two forces, the unique economic position of the U.S. and the decision to rebuild the defeated enemies, dictated the monetary order. It must be centered on the dollar. All other currencies were expressed at a fixed rate with the dollar, a pound at $2.80 or a franc at 20 cents. The British and French could adjust these rates but only when they were in extreme difficulties.

The system meant that the U.S. bought without hindrance all the goods the Europeans and Japan could produce. They happily received dollars for these goods, the world's safest currency, the currency banks put away in their vaults with gold. The U.S. had one obligation. It must supply an ounce of gold whenever foreigners presented $35. That was easy. The U.S. came out of the war with most of the world's gold. Anyway, who wanted gold that earned nothing when he could hold dollars in the form of Treasury bills earning 2 or 3 percent?

The arrangements endowed war-damaged nations with a critical advantage in foreign trade. The Germans and the Japanese particularly exploited this advantage. Their currencies were undervalued,[38] trading for fewer dollars than they would earn in a free market. So the mark was fixed near 25 cents but might fetch 50 cents in an open market; the yen was established at a third of a cent and could have have earned two-thirds of a cent.

The Germans and the Japanese did not complain. Their undervalued currencies let them penetrate foreign markets, particularly the U.S., with great ease. It meant the goods they were beginning to produce—coal, steel, tools—were far cheaper than any competitor's. A German wrench might sell for 100 marks. Thanks to the devalued currency, it would cost $25 in New York; a more realistic rate might have lifted the price to $50 and hurt sales. So German and Japanese prosperity began and remained linked to exports. Export-led prosperity was the cry. Commentators spoke of miracles, the glory of free markets, German and Japanese willingness to work. Less was said of the critical role played by undervalued currencies.*

---

* Nor was much said of the other great factor in the miracles, the migration of peasants to factories, from a less productive to a more productive sector. The process had been completed in Britain and the U.S. generations earlier.

The system—gold exchange, dollar-based, fixed but adjust-able rates—worked brilliantly in the 1950s. Europe, especially Germany and Japan, recovered and surpassed prewar levels of output and income. The U.S. prospered. The dollar was wel-come everywhere. But recovery and prosperity abroad changed foreign views of the dollar. The undervalued rate meant that Germans and Japanese were making bad bargains, giving up products embodying labor that could earn $50 in the United States for only $25 worth of American goods. The U.S. ability to send unchecked dollars abroad meant that Americans could buy up European companies cheaply and at no exchange cost. The system meant that Europeans must finance American ad-venture in Vietnam or anywhere else around the globe. The U.S. didn't need to worry about spending abroad for weapons, barracks, communications, buildings, food, anything. The dol-lar was as good as gold.

This could not last. Early on, the system's fragility impressed the Eisenhower administration, when imports began exceeding exports.[39] Between 1953 and 1962, the U.S. share of world exports fell from 22 percent to 17 percent, a measure of com-petitors' growing strength.[40] As his term ran out in November 1960, Eisenhower sent Treasury Secretary Anderson to Bonn on perhaps the most humiliating mission in the postwar era. Anderson asked Chancellor Adenauer to strengthen the dollar by paying for U.S. troops in West Germany. Adenauer was too shrewd to give a lame-duck president anything. But the mis-sion, a bizarre attempt to offer Hessians to Hessians, signaled the end of dollar supremacy even before Vietnam.

An international monetary system designed to assure Euro-pean and American leadership had done the first part of its job so well it was destroying the second. The rise and fall, or at least relative decline, of American power depended on no inherent

121

law of history but on a built-in contradiction in the global monetary order. The revival of Europe and Japan ended the supremacy of the dollar, and an international system built around it had to collapse.

All during the 1960s, finance ministers and central bankers labored quietly to revamp Bretton Woods. They finally brought forth an interesting addition to the monetary armory, a new reserve unit, Special Drawing Rights. But the system's essential structure and the problem it created remained.

Midway in Nixon's first term, it became evident that another global monetary crisis was in the making. The difference between the outflow of dollars and the inflow of foreign currencies, the basic balance, had averaged $700 million between 1960 and 1964. This was manageable. By 1969, the deficit had mounted to $2.9 billion, and to $3 billion in 1970. But in the first nine months of 1971, the deficit skyrocketed to $10 billion and this could not go on. Late in 1971, foreign central banks owned $45 billion in dollars, more than four times the total amount of U.S. gold. Something had to give.[41]

Under the dollar-based system, a nation confronted with a huge outflow of reserves could deflate drastically, impose severe unemployment on its people, ruthlessly suppressing the demand for imports and making its exports cheap. But Nixon would not do that, and no reasonable economist could then urge such a course.

The U.S. could have withdrawn immediately from Vietnam, saving huge expenditures overseas, and giving foreigners fewer dollars to cash in for gold. But nobody surrenders power so abjectly except at the point of a gun.

Instead, Nixon shut down the gold window. He simply refused to pay out any more gold for dollars. He even imposed a temporary tariff or tax on imports of 10 percent.[42] This was roughly the same as devaluing the dollar by 10 percent.

It was a bold and ingenious answer. But there were some obvious costs. Paul Volcker, then an Under Secretary of the Treasury and a central figure in the deliberations leading to the decision, dryly observed that the Bretton Woods system "has permitted the United States to carry out heavy overseas military expenditures and to undertake other foreign commitments and to retain substantial flexibility in domestic economic policy."[43] Those days were over.

In the next year and a half, the finance ministers fumbled for new agreements to refix currency exchange rates. Happily, they never succeeded. After the first such pact, the deal made at the Smithsonian Institution in 1972, Nixon claimed the agreement on rates was "the most significant monetary agreement in the history of the world."[44] It lasted six months, not even long enough for Nixon to use in the 1972 election.

Market forces overpowered the finance ministers. A system of fixed rates would have put nations in a terrible straitjacket when the Arabs lifted oil prices and might very well have converted a severe slump into another Great Depression. Instead, the world drifted into a system of floating rates. The price of the dollar, franc, lira, and all the rest are determined daily by supply and demand, nudged up and down by central banks. No currency is king, although the dollar, pound, mark, and yen are the most important.

The consequences for American prosperity, as well as American political power, were far greater than expected. The dollar was devalued about 20 percent in the two years after the closing of the gold window. That is it lost about 20 percent of its ability to buy a bundle of foreign currencies. This meant a stiff rise in the prices of raw materials everywhere in the world, not only oil. The terms of trade, the relationship between what exports bring and imports cost, shifted dramatically against industrial nations like the U.S. and in favor of the Third World. The inflation segment of stagflation was thereby given another upward twist. Alan Blinder has calculated that dollar depreciation added two percentage points to the rocketing inflation between mid-1972 and 1973,[45] about a quarter of all the increase in prices.

Perhaps the single biggest continuing consequence of the new order was the loss of the huge American advantage. With an overvalued currency, the reciprocal of undervaluation in other nations, the U.S. had enjoyed a permanent bargain sale. An American worker might labor ten hours to produce a tool that he could exchange for fifteen hours of a German worker's time. The American tool sold for more marks than a free-market rate would yield; the German product earned fewer dollars than it should. But once exchange rates floated, escaped from the fixed system, these disparities were corrected. There was a permanent loss of income for Americans, a permanent gain for Germans, Japanese, and everyone else. Along with Vietnam, the closing of the gold window is another major reason for the changed state of American prosperity.

There is still another malign consequence that has done immeasurable damage and promises more. The end of Bretton Woods doomed the system of open trade. With the U.S. as the leader, the postwar world had steadily bargained down the tariffs or import taxes used to protect domestic industries. Progress was remarkable and the barriers were vanishing everywhere. The U.S. had deliberately permitted one great exception. The European Common Market countries were allowed to discriminate against the goods of Americans and other nonmembers. But that was essentially a political arrangement. *

Even so, the trade barriers erected by the Common Market were brought down in negotiations, especially in the round named for President Kennedy at Geneva. Everybody benefited from the lower barriers against trade. It meant that goods were cheaper everywhere, that nations tended to produce the things that they were comparatively best fitted to make. Economists frequently quarrel but until recently it was difficult to find an independent one who did not believe that free trade is a blessing.

Free trade, however, depends on fixed exchange rates. Floating rates not only wipe out existing trade barriers but create new ones. If the dollar falls 10 percent against the mark, all German goods become about 10 percent more expensive in New York. The dollar's downward float is the same as a new U.S. tariff. Conversely, the cheaper dollar means American goods are less costly in Frankfurt. Any tariff protection put up by the Germans is eroded. If the Germans and the rest of the Common Market have given a trade concession to reduce a U.S. tariff, the deal is stripped of its value.

Under the floating-rate regime, the U.S. soon invented orderly marketing agreements, a cartel-like device to carve up markets. The Common Market responded in kind. So-called voluntary export restraints further curbed trade. Foreign competition was again suppressed by charges of dumping. A whole

* The U.S. swallowed a clever argument perfected by Continental statesmen. They contended that the Community could hold West Germany against the blandishments of the East only by political attraction buttressed by economic integration. Integration, in turn, it was argued, depended on a common tariff against outsiders, discrimination, and preserving agricultural markets for French and German farmers. The Common Market, of course, has almost no political weight, although its individual members certainly do. As a group, the Community is not, as advertised, a political force against Russia. It does enjoy protected markets. This protection against U.S. and other foreign goods is likely to increase in 1992 when the Community adopts its "single market" rules.

new wave of protectionist devices entangled world trade in autos, steel, semiconductors, shoes, textiles, television sets, and more. These arrangements, moreover, do not lend themselves easily to the trade negotiations that brought down tariffs. Floating rates have reduced the benefits from trade everywhere. This is a loss suffered by all nations as well as the U.S.

There is no sign that Nixon or anyone else foresaw that this would flow from the decision to abandon fixed rates and Bretton Woods. Indeed, it is still not well understood. Some politicians like Ronald Reagan continued to proclaim their allegiance to free markets while multiplying dumping charges and other curbs on trade.

The devalued dollar and Vietnam inflation that transformed the American economy were largely products of conscious policy. They were not happenings visited by a wrathful God or unreliable foreigners but the outcome of political decision in Washington. The first two postwar presidents, Truman and Eisenhower, sought to rebuild Europe and Japan as bulwarks against communism. They deliberately opened U.S. markets to Japanese, German, and other European products. There was little choice if the war-ravaged states were to revive. But the process had a limiting point, the volume of dollars foreigners would accept and the finite quantity of gold the U.S. had amassed. Whether they knew it or not, Truman and Eisenhower also willed an ultimate devaluation and an end to the system that had given the U.S. such political and economic advantage.

In the same way, Lyndon Johnson implicitly willed the end of stable prices. His conscious decision to permit excess demand, to promote bigger military outlays at high levels of employment without imposing offsetting taxes or cutting civilian spending, ensured that stable prices must end. Nixon adjusted with skill to both phenomena, cutting loose from fixed exchange rates, directly controlling wages and prices. That left him free to stimulate output and jobs with tax cuts and extra spending.

But two unexpected events, only remotely connected with Washington, made stagflation an enduring feature of the 1970s. Between 1972 and 1974, the world was struck by bad weather in many regions and that produced the worst explosion in food prices in half a century. The Soviet Union's grain crop was a failure. In the 1972–73 crop year, the Russians had to buy abroad 19.6 million metric tons, sixteen times as much as they had purchased the year before.[46] A wet spring drowned U.S. soybeans; a summer drought and then early frost killed corn. Unlike the concentrated computer and steel industries, there are many farmers and they labor in markets that are largely competitive, apart from government efforts to put a floor under prices. A drastic drop in supply is promptly translated into a drastic increase in price. In the U.S., consumer food prices rose only 4.3 percent in 1972, but more than 14 percent, three times as much, in 1973 and 1974.[47] They raised the level of consumer prices generally about two percentage points in 1973 and 1974, a major force in the 18 percent rise.[48]

The crop failures struck directly at the struggle to contain inflation. But at least much of the high-priced produce enriched American farmers. The food explosion barely touched national income. Instead, it shifted income from food consumers to producers.

In the fall of 1973, as a desperate Nixon was trying to hold his crumbling administration together, a U.S. airlift of arms saved Israel from defeat and perhaps destruction at the hands of Syria and Egypt. This last gasp of Nixonian foreign policy enraged Arabs, producers of most of the oil that is sold abroad. Inspired by Libya's price increases beginning in 1970, Saudi Arabia and other states exploited the October war to drive the price of oil skyward. Oil had sold for $1.62 a barrel at the start of 1973. It doubled to $3.15 in October and then doubled again to $7.11 in 1974.[49]

For many years, oil prices had been fixed by seven great Western companies, the Seven Sisters: Exxon, Royal Dutch Shell, British Petroleum, Gulf, Texaco, Mobil, and Standard of California. In the 1960s, the Middle East nations who leased their oil lands to the Sisters assumed more and more control. They called themselves a cartel, but they never really achieved that status. A cartel fixes production quotas for its members and punishes transgressors. The Organization of Petroleum Exporting Countries, or OPEC, could only urge but never command entities that regarded themselves as sovereign. Moreover, OPEC has always depended heavily on the Sisters to produce and distribute the oil. If the private companies had been fully in control, however, it is unlikely that they would have consented to the reckless price policy on which the oil-bearing states embarked after the October war. The Sisters knew that if oil was pushed up too far too fast, it would only encourage discovery of this abundant fossil resource outside cartel control. It would encourage substitution of coal and nuclear power. It would even stimulate saving on energy, a demand curve shifting to the left. In time, of course, all these things happened, OPEC was reduced to squabbling impotence, and the real price of oil, allowing for inflation, fell back sharply.[50]

But while the OPEC show lasted, it had a dramatic and devastating effect.

The quadrupled price of oil, coupled with the jump in food prices, drove inflation in the West and Japan into double digits, over 10 percent a year. The nine European Common Market nations, plus Canada, the U.S., and Japan, suffered consumer price increases of 4.4 percent in 1972. The next year, largely because of food, this rose to 7.5 percent. In 1974, it was a shocking 13.2 percent and retreated only to 11.1 percent in 1975.[51]

What was not well understood was that the oil-price increase was a two-edged scimitar. It spurred inflation and deflation simultaneously. It epitomized stagflation. The price rise acted like a massive excise tax. But this was not a tax collected by the oil-consuming governments of Germany, the U.S., or Japan. It went to the Arabs. Again, income was transferred from consumers to producers, but these producers were foreigners who put back little into the demand of consuming nations. The oil excise slashed the demand of industrial nations.

Unless this massive deflation was offset, perhaps by cutting domestic excise taxes on cigarettes, clothing, whiskey, and even gasoline—cuts that never happened—domestic demand had to be flattened. It was. The Common Market, U.S., Canada, and Japan had enjoyed a 6.1 percent rise in output in 1973, perhaps overly exuberant. But then output fell 0.4 percent in 1974 and another 1.8 percent in 1975.[52] The U.S. suffered the most severe recession since the Great Depression. Unlike the last two slumps, this was unplanned, no policy recession. It was created by oil, with an assist from food, not by policy makers in Washington.

Otto Eckstein, the leading student of the 1974–75 decline, concluded that "the energy crisis became the largest single factor in the development of the Great Recession."[53] Without the oil increase, he figured the slump would have lasted only three quarters instead of five; output would have fallen 3.6 percent instead of 7.8 percent.[54] By the end of 1974, oil had added 4.1 percentage points to the consumer price index and a massive 10 percentage points to wholesale prices.[55]

To increase the misery, the U.S. lacked direction. Vice President Gerald Ford had taken over from a disgraced Nixon but Ford was only a caretaker. Even if he had been endowed with more imaginative advisers than Simon and Greenspan, it is unlikely that policy would have much improved. There simply was no precedent for coping with forces that generated inflation and slump together.

Ford's instinct was to grapple with the inflationary consequences. "Republicans," he wrote, "have always considered inflation to be public enemy number one"[56] while Democrats fret more over unemployment. So Ford first urged his tax increase, and then, having discovered the slump, reversed himself to call for a tax cut. A few of the old Keynesians urged the government to absorb the price increases, accept a one-time boost to inflation, and actively counter recession with expansionary policies. Little attention was paid.

The oil states had one more barrel to fire before economics reduced them to size. Iran's new ruler, Ayatollah Khomeini, displayed his contempt for the modern world and its material goods by slashing Iran's oil exports. The other oil governments promptly exploited the reduced supply. They pushed the price from $12 to $32 a barrel,[57] another blow to stable prices and national output. The Carter administration early in 1980 estimated that $200 billion had been added to the world's bill for oil imports. The U.S. share was $45 billion.[58] Like a $45 billion tax increase, this sum was subtracted from national demand. Because of the multiplier, the impact of spending cuts on other spenders, the total depressing effect was about $90 billion.

This dreary fact enabled Carter to predict with confidence

that "mild recession" in 1980, the year of his reelection campaign. Ignoring aides who pleaded for expansionary policies, Carter appeared to listen only to Volcker at the Federal Reserve. In Volcker's view, fiscal policy—taxes and spending—was bankrupt or had abdicated. Stern medicine was needed to cure inflation. A banker, a Republican, a man of towering self-confidence, Volcker was convinced he alone could administer the medicine in the required dosage. With Carter's support, Volcker turned Carter's mild recession into a harsh slump, worse even than the deep recession of 1974–75.

Evidently Volcker believed that high unemployment was a small price to pay for extricating the country from inflation in excess of 10 percent. Nobody told Carter that Reagan would administer the therapy of unemployment continuously. In a world of concentrated markets, there are no once-and-for-all cures for pricing power. It must be dealt with continuously, through some institutional mechanism. Repressed today, pricing power will assert itself tomorrow—unless society will accept a hitherto unseen severity in antitrust that permanently dissolves large corporations and unions.

All three presidents in the 1970s were driven to recognize pricing power and its inflationary force. All three toyed with some form of incomes policy, influencing wage and price decisions. But none gave more than half-hearted support to these efforts. One way or another, they all believed that markets, no matter how distorted, yielded better results than controls, direct or indirect. Unlike Kennedy's robust acceptance of economic fact, the 1970s presidents thought there was something immoral or peculiar in government that urged an appropriate price or wage standard.

When Nixon's attempt at a policy recession in 1969 failed to produce much relief from inflation, he found or rather discovered a way out: first jawboning and then outright controls to curb wages and prices. He had ridiculed jawboning when he took office. At his first news conference, he said you can't expect labor and management to put "what is in the best interests of the nation" above "the interests of the organizations they represent."[59] But his political instincts convinced him otherwise. He would not accept the unpalatable choice, unemployment or inflation.

His friend Arthur Burns and others supported incomes policies on classic grounds. The U.S. in 1970 was not a textbook economy in which competition determined wages and prices; it was an economy of concentrated power, among corporations and unions, and their ability to determine prices must be offset by government influence or controls.

Paul McCracken, chairman of Nixon's economic advisers, said Nixon, a football fan, had no use for the offensive strategy of "four yards and a cloud of dust," small incremental gains.[60] He preferred the bomb, a long scoring forward pass. After a few attempts to bring pressure against steel and other prices,[61] jawboning, Nixon threw an economic bomb. Until his administration, no one had imposed compulsory limits on wages and prices in peacetime. Against all conventional economic wisdom, Nixon's worked well. Price increases were checked, Nixon safely stimulated the economy for his smashing electoral triumph, and then the controls were junked. Controls were popular, said Nixon later, "But in the long run I believe that it was wrong."[62]

The Nixon curbs indicate that the public will accept and corporations will generally comply with controls in periods of stress, even in peacetime. Nixon was liquidating the Vietnam legacy and this appeared to be understood. The sharp stagflationary consequences of food and oil increases might have given controls an extended run. Then the government could have moved to a less rigid incomes policy, one that would again permit prices to allocate resources among their best uses. But government was falling apart in 1973. Gerald Ford, caught in the worst stagflationary episode so far, was in no position to innovate. He denounced a General Motors price increase, but never had a coherent incomes policy.

Carter understood the logic of the inflation-jobless dilemma. He had firmly ruled out unemployment at first. This led him to try incomes policy, and he toyed with several approaches. He attempted "voluntary deceleration,"[63] asking price and wage decision makers to cut increases in 1978 below the average of 1976 and 1977. He proposed no numerical standard, however, and his vague cry went unanswered. Prices on all output rose a worrisome 7.4 percent.[64] Then Carter urged something fresh. He set a standard, a familiar approach: wage increases should not exceed 7 percent. If inflation was greater, Carter would protect workers' buying power with tax credits, and that was new. Those credits would be big enough to match any fall in real pay. In other words, if a worker got a 7 percent increase but prices rose 9 percent, his taxes would be cut enough to make up for the lost two percentage points.

This was the first attempt at TIP, a tax-based incomes policy, an imaginative effort to restrain wages with tax rewards. On paper, a TIP has also been invented for price makers. Most of the TIPs proposed for prices impose a tax penalty for exceeding a price standard rather than giving a reward for meeting one.

None of this impressed Congress. Carter's introduction of TIP, wage insurance, was never passed. Prices rose 8.6 percent in 1979 and a frightening 9.3 percent in 1980.[65] By then, inflation and unemployment, stagflation, was virulent. If the nation was to be spared massive unemployment, a Nixon bomb was required, stiff controls gradually leading to more voluntarist incomes policies. But Carter was no bomb thrower and anyway his earlier belief that unemployment was a human tragedy had faded.

Carter's changed view reflected new attitudes in the country toward the underclass. They were made a scapegoat for inflation. Some conservative economists argued that inflation was caused in part by the postwar concern with high or full employment. This goal, they said, invited government intervention, particularly easy money. Government intervention had an inflationary bias.

Until the 1970s, that was a distinctly minority view. All politicians accepted that unemployment could make or break their electoral fortunes. The memory of the Great Depression, its misery and its threat to democracy, were still sunk deep in the national consciousness. When George Terborgh asserted that the 4 percent jobless target was too low for price stability, few paid much attention.

Stagflation changed all that. Those who sought to bury the Employment Act and raise the level of acceptable unemployment soon had support from the Federal Reserve, the White House, and the country at large. Inflation had become the chief villain.

A more relaxed view of unemployment, it was argued, could restrain inflation in two ways. One was to redefine the jobless target, to make 4.6 or 5 percent the desired level instead of 4 percent. That would take pressure off government to reduce the jobless rolls by expanding demand. Another method was to insist on a purgative, a deep slump that would create enough joblessness to end pressure for wage increases. Corporations, with or without power, would happily accommodate price restraint to this new circumstance.

The Carter administration made a practical contribution to the new thought. It redefined benchmark unemployment, the rate at which so-called high-employment budgets should be calculated, the target for policy. Carter economists decided that 4 percent had been appropriate until 1958 and then became obsolete. Thereafter the benchmark level was raised slowly until it touched 4.9 percent in 1976.[66] All this really meant that the yardstick changed to accommodate unemployment, that government was reducing its responsibility. The Carter approach provided a splendid ramp for Reagan.

At the same time, thoughtful conservatives began preparing opinion for the great purgative, the sharp deflation that launched the 1980s. Milton Friedman argued that there was a "natural rate of unemployment"[67] and it was rising in the U.S., above the old target levels. This was because women, teenagers, and part-timers were a growing fraction of the labor force. They were more mobile than solid male family heads; they shifted jobs more readily. Moreover, the spread of unemployment compensation reduced the pressure to find jobs.

This is pop sociology, not economics. It reflects Friedman's unsupported belief that unemployment is less painful to women, part-timers, and teenagers. It implies, mistakenly, that most women workers are second-income earners. It forgets that part-timers are officially counted as fully employed even when they work part-time involuntarily. In any case, Friedman ignored the lost income and output the nation suffers when unemployment is high among women and youths. A qualified sociologist might measure the social—and ultimately economic—cost of unemployment among youths, especially blacks. But Friedman's view was popular among economists seeking to raise the jobless target.

William Fellner, another respected economist, said it was a

mistake to bring unemployment below 5 percent.[68] That, he said, puts you in a danger zone of tight labor markets. As unemployment rose during the decade, so did Fellner's benchmark. Six years later he said full employment "is now close to 6 percent" and attempts to get it lower breed inflation.[69]

But the most striking shift in what may be called the Pangloss school came from Martin Feldstein. A professor at Harvard, successor to Burns as head of the National Bureau for Economic Research and first chairman of Reagan's Council of Economic Advisers, he could shape and then influence policy. In 1973, Feldstein found Kennedy's temporary 4 percent target too modest. It is realistic, he wrote, to think we can lower permanent unemployment "significantly less than 3 percent."[70] He sounded like a left New Dealer, although he urged policies to improve labor skills rather than expansion to reach his new goal.

By August 1979, however, on the eve of Reagan's victory, Feldstein played a different tune. Unemployment was then nearly 6 percent but that wasn't enough for Feldstein. "Inflation will only be tamed by a consistent policy of tight money," he said. "The record so far this year had been encouraging." Above all, monetary policy must not be eased to shorten the recession the nation was again enduring. "What is needed is a long term commitment by the Fed to pursue the current policy until inflation is eliminated, and enough political courage in the Congress and the administration to let the Fed do it."[71]

Feldstein had forecast Reagan's policy.

Charles Schultze, Carter's adviser, was candid, at least after the fact. "Nobody but nobody was willing to say quite explicitly, yes, we are going to force the unemployment rate up."[72] But that is what policy came to be, he implied.

Some of the Kennedy-Johnson economists dissented. But

they were throwbacks to an earlier era and nobody paid much attention. Arthur Okun contended that inflation with 4 percent unemployment is not a sign of excessive demand.[73] Rather, 5 percent inflation with 4 percent out of work means that competitive forces have lost out, that corporate and labor power impart an inflationary bias to the economy. Curbing demand to cure inflation, the Feldstein-Reagan-Volcker method, is costly. Okun figured that each one percentage point cut in inflation would slash 3 percent from total output.[74] In the 1990 economy of $5 trillion, it costs $150 billion of lost income to shave one point off the inflation index by idling resources.

Abstract numbers describe only one side of the loss from unemployment. Another came from Hyman Minsky, an original economist. "Dignity and independence are best served," he wrote, "by an economic order [providing] compensation for work performed. Permanent dependence on . . . transfer payments that have not been earned is demeaning. . . . Social justice and individual liberty demand . . . an economy of opportunity in which every one . . . earns his or her way. . . . Full employment is a social as well as an economic good."[75]

Stagflation, however, appeared to have doomed prospects of jobs for all. The sources of this stagflation are clear. Vietnam inflation inhibited any stimulus to output. Food and oil price increases not only sharpened inflation but actually reduced demand. The overthrow of the global monetary system stripped Americans of their advantage in the exchange of goods, further depressing demand. Finally, governments set new and higher levels of acceptable and even desirable unemployment, and these imposed a strong curb on spending. In the end, all these limits on demand discouraged business investment, so worker productivity, efficiency, rose at slower and slower rates.

NOTES

1. Gerald R. Ford, *A Time to Heal: The Autobiography of Gerald R. Ford* (New York: Harper & Row, 1979), p. 202.

2. Charles Schultze in Erwin C. Hargrove and Samuel A. Morely, editors, *The President and the Council of Economic Advisors: Interviews with CEA Chairman* (Boulder, Colorado: Westview Press, 1984), p. 479.

3. Lester A. Sobel, editor, *Ford and the Economy* (New York: Facts on File, 1976), p. 207.

4. Richard M. Nixon, *RN: The Memoirs of Richard Nixon* (New York: Grosset & Dunlap, 1978), p. 516.

5. Phillip Cagan et al., *A New Look at Inflation: Economic Policy in the Early 1970's* (Washington, D.C.: American Enterprise Institute for Policy Research, 1973), p. 3.

6. *Economic Report of the President* (Washington, D.C.: U.S. Government Printing Office, 1971), p. 26.

7. *Ibid.*, p. 249.

8. *Historical Statistics of the United States: Colonial Times to 1970: Bicentennial Edition* (U.S. Department of Commerce, 1975), p. 1003.

9. *Economic Report of the President* (Washington D.C.: U.S. Government Printing Office, 1973), p. 244.

10. Sobel, *Ford and the Economy*, p. 2.

11. *Economic Report of the President*, 1973, p. 19.

12. *Economic Report of the President* (Washington, D.C.: U.S. Government Printing Office, 1976), p. 199.

13. Alan S. Blinder, *Economic Policy and the Great Stagflation* (New York: Academic Press, 1979), p. 148.

14. *Economic Report of the President*, 1976, p. 224.

15. *Economic Report of the President* (Washington, D.C.: U.S. Government Printing Office, 1975), p. 57.

16. Blinder, *Economic Policy*, p. 150.

17. *Ibid.*, p. 206.

18. *Ibid.*, p. 201.

19. Otto Eckstein, *The Great Recession: With a Post-script on Stagflation* (New York: North-Holland, 1978), p. 4.

20. United States Census Bureau, *Statistical Abstract*, 1988. p. 422.

21. Blinder, *Economic Policy*, p. 45.

22. Robert J. Gordon, editor, *The American Business Cycle: Continuity and Change* (Chicago: University of Chicago Press, 1986), p. 783.

23. Leonard Silk, *Nixonomics: How the Dismal Science of Free Enterprise Became the Black Art of Controls* (New York: Praeger, 1972), p. 14.

24. Herbert Stein, *Presidential Economics: The Making of Economic Policy from Roosevelt to Reagan and Beyond* (New York: Simon & Schuster, 1988), p. 113.

25. *Economic Report of the President*, 1975, p. 4.

26. *Ibid.*, p. 19.

27. *Economic Report of the President* (Washington, D.C.: U.S. Government Printing Office, 1978), p. 17.

28. *Economic Report of the President* (Washington, D.C.: U.S. Government Printing Office, 1980), p. 5.

29. *Economic Report of the President* (Washington, D.C.: U.S. Government Printing Office, 1981), p. 43.

30. Hargrove and Morely, *The President and the Council*, p. 495.

31. *Economic Report of the President*, 1980, p. 271.

32. *Ibid.*, p. 262.

33. *Economic Report of the President* (Washington, D.C.: U.S. Government Printing Office, 1977), p. 45.

34. *Ibid.*, p. 45.

35. *Economic Report of the President*, 1978, p. 148.

36. Nixon, *Memoirs*, p. 518.

37. Otto Eckstein, editor, *Parameters and Policies in the U.S. Economy* (New York: North-Holland, 1976), p. 331.

38. Joanne Gowa, *Closing the Gold Window: Domestic Politics and the End of Bretton Woods* (Ithaca, New York: Cornell University Press, 1983), p. 45.

39. *Economic Report of the President* (Washington, D.C.: U.S. Government Printing Office, 1989), p. 331.

40. *Ibid.*, p. 331.

41. *Economic Report of the President* (Washington, D.C.: U.S. Government Printing Office, 1972), p. 150.

42. *Ibid.*, p. 164.

43. Gowa, *Closing the Gold Window*, p. 63.

44. Nixon quoted in *Facts on File Year Book* (New York: Facts on File, 1971), p. 987.

45. Blinder, *Economic Policy*, p. 29.

46. Eckstein, *The Great Recession*, p. 63.

47. *Ibid.*, p. 66.

48. *Economic Report of the President*, 1975, p. 300.

49. *Ibid.*, p. 75.

50. *Statistical Abstract of the United States* (Washington, D.C.: Bureau of the Census, U.S. Department of Commerce, 1989), p. 466.

51. Eckstein, *The Great Recession*, p. 96.

52. *Ibid.*, p. 94.

53. *Ibid.*, p. 116.

54. *Ibid.*, p. 117.

55. *Ibid.*, pp. 121–2.

56. Ford, *A Time to Heal*, p. 152.

57. Oil was $12 a barrel in October 1978 and had risen to $32 by mid-1980, according to Ezra Solomon, *Beyond the Turning Point: The United States Economy in the 1980's* (San Francisco: W. H. Freeman, 1981), p. 43.

58. *Economic Report of the President*, 1980, p. 3.

59. Richard Nixon quoted in Craufurd D. Goodwin, editor, *Exhortation and Controls: The Search for a Wage-Price Policy, 1945–71* (Washington, D.C.: Brookings Institution, 1975), p. 299.

60. Paul McCracken in Hargrove and Morely, *The President and the Council*, p. 345.

61. Silk, *Nixonomics*, p. 42.

62. Nixon, *Memoirs*, p. 521.

63. *Economic Report of the President*, 1978, p. 20.

64. *Economic Report of the President*, 1989, p. 378.

65. *Ibid.*, p. 378.

66. *Economic Report of the President*, 1978, pp. 84–5.

67. Milton Freidman, "Inflation and Unemployment," in Martin N. Bailey and Arthur M. Okun, editors, *The Battle Against Unemployment and Inflation* (New York: W.W. Norton, 1982), p. 48.

68. William Fellner in Cagan et al., *A New Look at Inflation*, p. 136.

69. Phillip Cagan, *Persistent Inflation: Historical and Policy Essays* (New York: Columbia University Press, 1979), p. 216.

70. Martin Feldstein in Eckstein, *Parameters and Policies*, p. 180.

71. Martin Feldstein, "Tax Rules and Monetary Policy," in Bailey and Okun, *The Battle Against Unemployment and Inflation*, pp. 122–3.

72. Charles Schultze in Hargrove and Morely, *The President and the Council*, p. 485.

73. Arthur M. Okun, *Economics for Policymaking*, edited by Joseph A. Pechman (Cambridge: MIT Press, 1983), p. 47.

74. Arthur M. Okun, *The Political Economy of Prosperity* (Washington, D.C.: The Brookings Institution, 1970), p. 137.

75. Hyman P. Minsky, *Stabilizing an Unstable Economy*, A Twentieth Century Fund Report (New Haven: Yale University Press, 1986), p. 9.

V

The Economics
of Slack

Leaving office in 1989, President Ronald Reagan pointed proudly to his achievements. He had led a revolution, he said, overthrowing "a 50-year trend of turning to the government for solution." In the Biblical language of Cecil B. De Mille, Reagan proclaimed a "world . . . born anew." By "reducing taxes and regulatory bureaucracy, we have unleashed the creative genius of ordinary Americans and ushered in an unparalleled period of peacetime prosperity."[1]

Reagan contended that he had obliterated the half century reaching back to Roosevelt's second term when government discovered the techniques to end depression and promote jobs and growth. All that, Reagan argued, had been a snare and delusion. He had found the right road. Instead of government guiding the economy through fiscal and monetary measures, he had freed an economy for perfect competition, one described by Adam Smith. As Reagan told it, he had allowed the economy to follow its natural bent, thereby enjoying a golden harvest of market-allocated resources and ever-rising expansion.

Reality differed from the President's vision. Government remained at the center of affairs, bigger than ever. Reagan presided over the first trillion-dollar budgets, twice spending more than $1,000 billion on Federal enterprises. In all, Reagan spent a fifth of the national output on government, much like his predecessors in the troubled 1970s.[2] Reagan had not restored Smith's invisible hand by removing those of bureaucrats. He multiplied them, putting many to work procuring arms.

Like those who preceded him, Reagan countered slump with more or less orthodox measures. He enlarged spending, reduced taxes, and successfully fought for easier credit. To be sure, the character of the instruments changed. Even more than earlier presidents, Reagan relied on arms to bolster aggregate demand. He made heroic cuts in the handful of welfare programs for the most impoverished and politically least interesting. But he preserved and even enlarged the core of the modern welfare state, the pension and health programs for the middle classes, many of them his constituents. He failed to deliver on his promise to get government off business backs. He did reduce Federal rules for broadcasters, airlines, and some others. But far more important, he created the thickest network of protective devices against imports since the Smoot-Hawley tariff of 1931, as William Niskanen, a Reagan economic adviser, has observed.[3] Moreover, Reagan's cartelizing techniques for autos, steel, semiconductors, and other products interfered more strongly with market forces than tariff increases.

Reagan claimed both too much and too little. In his eight years, the economy grew at an annual rate of 2.8 percent, nearly a quarter less than in the fat years and little more than in the stagflation from 1973 to 1981.[4]

A troubling inflation rate that had exceeded 10 percent was cut more than half, the President's most widely acclaimed achievement. But by the end of his term, prices were rising again, nearly 5 percent.[5] In addition, he had led the nation out of its deepest postwar slump, and unemployment had been sharply reduced. But it remained above 5 percent,[6] a level previous administrations had rejected as far too high and more than 25 percent above the temporary target set in the 1960s. The combination of sluggish growth, falling jobless levels, and rising prices suggested that Reagan had found no new magic. His economy was a cousin of the stagflation that had plagued Carter and Ford.

Reagan, however, made distinctly original contributions in two areas. Without fanfare, he abandoned the attempt of eight presidents from Roosevelt through Carter to reach full or high employment. Without notifying Congress, he repealed the 1946 Employment Act, a measure that had embodied the wisdom of the war. He deliberately used unemployment, an economy of slack, to tame workers and check inflation. This was a bold departure.

So too was Reagan's astonishing success in redistributing income. Normally the shares of rich and poor change little in peacetime. Major changes can occur in war when sacrifices are accepted more readily, when heavy taxation to pay for arms falls on the wealthiest. It was Reagan's singular achievement to bring about a significant peacetime shift, one that reversed the direction of the wartime flow from rich to poor. He did it by maintaining high unemployment and with tax and spending measures. This was his revolution.

Rewarding the wealthy, particularly entrepreneurs who saw themselves as self-made, appears to have been a central objective of Reagan's economics. The auto dealers, oil speculators, savings and loan executives, and entertainers in Reagan's personal circle are typical American businessmen, heavily reliant

143

on government. They enjoy federally financed capital from national highways, peculiar tax advantages won by their congressmen, Federal guarantees against disaster or even their own fraud, government allocation of scarce broadcasting channels, and the like. Almost the only genuine self-made entrepreneurs in America, those whose income is not deliberately increased by government intervention, may be engaged in the distribution of illicit goods or services.

To achieve Reagan's goal, a slack economy, one with a strong margin of unused plant and labor, was vital. The reasoning was clear. An adequate level of jobless keeps trade unions weak. Their members are reluctant to strike for higher pay when confronted with the threat of unemployment. Non-union workers are equally docile. Faced with wide unemployment they are unlikely to press for wage increases. Lower wage demands reduce unit labor costs and reduce the pressure to increase prices in the wide array of concentrated industries where corporate executives enjoy considerable discretion over prices. Unemployment helps tame inflation.

David Stockman, Reagan's budget director and a candid witness to some events, told the Chamber of Commerce early in the new administration: unemployment is "part of the cure, not the problem."[7] Quite plainly, Stockman was saying that idle workers were an instrument of Reagan policy, particularly anti-inflation policy. The Reagan attack on inflation, in turn, was a critical step in the larger objective of enriching the rich.

It is the well-to-do who own bonds and large savings accounts. They are the *rentiers* and it is their assets that are damaged by inflation. For most Americans, savings are largely embedded in homes. Inflation tends to raise home values and reduce the real cost of mortgage debt. Middle Americans are not

percent,[11] Depression levels. It has been estimated that one worker in four suffered some unemployment in 1982, a sobering experience for all in the labor force.

Curbing demand, enforcing slack produced drastic consequences for prices. The consumer price index had risen 10.3 percent in 1981, Reagan's first year. It rose only 3.2 percent, less than a third as fast, in 1983.[12] If the Depression and World War II were the shaping experiences for a half century of policy makers, the slump inducted by the Fed in 1980–82 governed the thinking of the President and his men.

The President's Economic Report for 1983, the first compiled by Feldstein, warned against a recovery that threatened to relieve the slack. "If the slack in the economy declines too rapidly or capacity utilization is held at too high a level, inflation will tend to increase," Feldstein wrote.[13] More bluntly, high unemployment and idle plants were needed to curb price increases. Indeed, Feldstein warned that inflation would accelerate if unemployment was brought below 6 or 7 percent. He and others were now promoting a new target, a rate more than triple that reached in the war and more than 50 percent above the "interim" goal achieved by Kennedy and Johnson. Permanent unemployment was now a policy instrument.*

* The Reagan team never could decide on the target rate for unemployment, particularly when an election year brought it near 5 percent in 1988. The Committee for Economic Development, a collection of businessmen regarded as enlightened, said 6 percent was as low as you could go through expanded demand without increasing inflationary pressure. In mid-1988, Alan Greenspan, Reagan's choice to head the Federal Reserve, warned that "a leveling of the unemployment and capacity utilization rates is essential if more intense inflationary pressures are to be avoided."[14] The jobless level was then about 5.5 percent. A plausible conclusion came from William Niskanen, a member of Reagan's Council of Economic Advisers, who had resisted both Feldstein and Volcker for crudely linking inflation and unemployment. Niskanen said it appeared there was no longer "political concern" when unemployment reached 7 percent.[15] This appeared to be so.

For most of its eight years, the Reagan administration used this tool vigorously. Civilian unemployment was held comfortably above 6 percent until the last half of 1987.[16] Then, with an election looming, it slipped under 6 percent. Feldstein appeared to be a prophet after all. Inflation, which had been falling, now began to accelerate. But with a jobless rate still above 5 percent, there could have been excessive demand. In a competitive economy, any extra cash would have put idle men to work producing more goods. Instead, it appeared that corporations with pricing power had become bolder, exploiting the moderate increase in demand.

At least as early as 1968, Milton Friedman, the Nobel laureate who has insisted that all inflation is monetary, warned that there is a "natural" rate of unemployment.[17] Anything less would speed the pace of price increases. This view has been used by some conservatives to argue that tax and spending policies or monetary techniques to lower the actual rate below the "natural" rate doom the nation to disaster. Michael J. Boskin observed that unemployment in 1987 was 6.8 percent, that this would have been unacceptable twenty years ago. But now, he said, "most economists consider it fairly close to full employment."[18] Six point eight percent, he implied, was near the natural rate below which accelerating price increases threatened.

Mainstream economics has always been marked by a willingness to accept that whatever is is right, whether it is unemployment of 2 or 6 percent. Nevertheless, Boskin's claim that the idleness of 1 in 15 is full employment could only have been made in 1984.

Boskin, who became chairman of the Council of Economic Advisers for George Bush, is in a long tradition. In the 1930s, a prevailing view held that sticky wages, the stubborn refusal of workers to take deeper pay cuts, accounted for the massive joblessness of the Great Depression. More recently, Boskin and others have insisted that most jobless workers prefer to be idle on reduced pay. They can, after all, enjoy unemployment insurance (which covers fewer than one worker in three). Or they are women and blacks, unskilled or with loose attachment to the job market. Or they are young and cannot get jobs because of the minimum wage prices them out of the market. "Much unemployment was not involuntary; it was not due to insufficient demand for labor in our economy," Boskin said.[19] This no doubt comforted an administration so reliant on slack and helped convince some that joblessness was far less painful than described.

For workers stripped of dignity by enforced idleness, seeking work in markets that rejected them, the Boskin view could not have been so comforting. The remoteness of rich men in the Reagan administration from the misery of the jobless is explicable. The assurances offered by some academics is also a commonplace. But not all professors agreed. Another Nobelist, Franco Modigliani, said that Reagan's policy of slack abused history.

"We have been using the knowledge" learned in the Great Depression, "particularly in the United States, to create a lot of unemployment as a way to fight inflation," Modigliani said.[20] The Reagan team appeared to have stood Keynes on his head.

James Tobin gave a stern warning. We now fight inflation, he said, with "severe economic slack, unemployment of labor and excess industrial capacity, prolonged until business, workers and trade unions give way on wages and prices in desperate and often vain attempts to save jobs and avert bankruptcies. This will work as long as there is slack. But it destroys human capital, especially among youths and young adults, preventing them from attaining skills or dulling those they have. It discourages businesses and the state from investing. Business invests for expanding markets but is faced with shrinking markets. Local governments lose the revenue they need to pay for schools, hospitals, roads and libraries."[21] In the end, Tobin said, the economy becomes less productive.

Another obvious victim of the slack economy was the trade union, the workers' shield against income loss and sword to win gains. Unions in America had been enduring a colder climate for years, ever since the industrial or mass-production organizations of the more militant CIO merged with the historic craft unions, the labor elite of the AFL in 1955. A comfortable, well-paid union hierarchy, frequently installed for life, worked in comfortable offices and presided over a steady decline in members. There were enough dues payers to support the leadership in the style to which it became accustomed. Nobody worried very much. Leaders like George Meany, president of the merged group, were far more concerned with purging unions of Communists or expelling unions led by men that a Senate committee claimed were dishonest. This, no doubt, created a purer movement but also a feebler one, and technology weakened it further.

Late in the 1950s, the number of workers in clerical or white-collar jobs exceeded production workers with blue collars for the first time.[22] This threatened to slowly strangle many trade unions. White-collar workers are far harder to organize than blue, feel far less class solidarity, contain more women less firmly attached to jobs. Only a radically different, more imaginative leadership could enroll these people. The conventional Meany and his fellows were neither radical nor imaginative; if anything they feared that unorganized workers would cost money to bring into the union fold and might threaten the existing bureaucratic structure. At the height of their strength after World War II, unions embraced more than one in three workers outside agriculture. At the time of the merger, the union share was almost the same. But by 1975, union card holders were fewer than one in four. More recently, they had shrunk to one in six.[23] The drop was relentless.

The leadership was oblivious. As late as 1970, Meany said that "more and more people in the trade union movement—I mean at the highest levels—are thinking of other ways to advance without the use of the strike method."[24] Meany was implying that unions were so secure they could abandon the strike weapon, the withdrawal of their labor. More hardened unionists knew that only the threat of strike gives workers a voice in determining pay, hours, and conditions. Some economists might claim that all markets are competitive and all markets clear themselves, leaving no excess resources. Workers dealing with AT&T, GM, and others on capitalism's commanding heights knew otherwise. They understood that pay rates were not set in competitive markets but were bargained arrangements between an oligopolist, a large corporate employer in a market of few employers, and a would-be monopolist, a union.

As Meany spoke, corporate leaders were abandoning the tacit partnerships of the 1950s and '60s under which steel corporations increased steel wages and passed on the cost through higher prices. Or in which both corporations and unions lobbied together for protection against imports.

Even before Reagan, stagflation inspired business leaders to mount an assault on unions. Douglas Fraser, the president of the United Auto Workers, had been a member of a high-level discussion group of corporate and union leaders. Fraser resigned in 1978, charging that the corporate chiefs had broken an unwritten agreement and had now launched war against workers, the unemployed, blacks, the very young and the old.[25]

Reagan intensified the war. Slack was his principal weapon. A unionized force threatened with layoffs, fearful of mounting unemployment in its industry, tends to be docile. Its leaders make concessions, yield "give-ups" that worsen pay and conditions. In the Reagan era, unions signed contracts that cut pay, lengthened hours, scrapped work and safety rules, decreased welfare benefits. Nothing like this had been seen since the one-sided pay cuts imposed in the Great Depression.

The Reagan team celebrated its handiwork, declaring in the President's Economic Report for 1985: "Concessions have occurred in previous recessions, but the scale of recent concessions is unprecedented."[26]

The administration signaled that it was now open season on unions. In his first year, the President destroyed one union, firing 11,000 striking air controllers and replacing them with military men.[27] The action, popular and effective, crushed the Professional Air Traffic Controllers Organization, or PATCO. As it happened, these white-collar unionists had supported Reagan in 1980. The importance of their defeat did not escape the Reagan White House. Murray Weidenbaum, chairman of the Council of Economic Advisers, hailed the episode as "one of the most important labor events in the past decade." Reagan's "tough response to the illegal strike," Weidenbaum said, brought " a slowdown in labor demands . . . reducing inflationary pressure."[28]

This was precisely the point. The President had waged class war as policy. His was a successful stroke in the struggle to suppress wages and thereby induce corporations to restrain price increases.

This blunt demonstration was followed by daily lessons from the National Labor Relations Board, the NLRB. A New Deal creation set up to encourage unions and collective bargaining, the NLRB under Reagan became another weapon to harass unions. Claims of wrongful firing for union activity, an indicator of the intensity of the corporate assault, rose briskly. So did elections to force unions from plants.

Membership in major unions fell precipitously. The slump in Reagan's first two years cost the Teamsters, most truckdrivers, 400,000; the Auto Workers 100,000; and the Steelworkers 235,000.[29] Some came back in the modest recovery that followed,[30] but the Reagan era accelerated the unions' thirty-year decline.

The payoff is reflected in some dry statistics. Unit costs in manufacturing, the labor cost to produce one auto or computer or dress, advanced 3.4 percent a year after the war. In the stagflation period from 1973 to 1981, the rise was 8.2 percent. But in the Reagan years, after the recession trough in 1982, unit labor costs actually fell, by eight-tenths of one percent a year.[31] The battle had been won. Unemployment, slack, and the accompanying campaign against unions had brought down costs. This meant that most gains in the economy would go to the best-paid executives, professionals, and *rentiers*. Indeed, average weekly pay in factories and offices actually fell under Reagan, from $172.74 when he took office to $167.45 when he left, in dollars of constant 1977 buying power.[32]

Understandably, the Reagan team did not boast about its slack economy. Instead, as Murray Weidenbaum insisted: "The most obvious economic achievement of Ronald Reagan's administration has been to tame the inflationary beast."[33] The results were undeniably impressive. Inflation was more than 10 percent in the year before Reagan took office; it was reduced to 4.2 percent in the year he left. In the last seven years of Reagan, the consumer price index rose 3.6 percent a year, well below the 5.4 rate in the last seven years of the 1970s, although still far above the levels achieved in the Eisenhower and Kennedy period.[34]

The Reagan team, moreover, broke new ground in dealing with inflation. Earlier administrations had relied on a mix of weapons, fiscal as well as monetary, curbing aggregate demand with reduced spending, higher taxes, tighter credit, and—on occasion—direct or indirect price and wage controls. But the Reagan team resorted to a single instrument. "It was the tight money policy of the Federal Reserve System that directly squeezed the bulk of the inflation out of the American economic system in 1981 and 1982," Weidenbaum wrote.[35]

He was right. Indeed, the administration's expansionary fiscal impulses contradicted its anti-inflationary monetary measures. Reagan sought deep tax cuts for the best-off (with lesser cuts for others to make the thing politically palatable) and he wanted a huge increase in arms spending. Both enlarged aggregate demand, increased buying power. Nevertheless, said Weidenbaum, Reagan must be credited with suppressing inflation for he gave almost continuous support to the Federal Reserve.

If the battle with inflation was largely successful, it was won at a fearful cost.

The 26.6 million of officially recorded jobless from 1980 to 1982 could have produced an extra $490 billion in output with 1982 purchasing power, wealth for all.[36] For years thereafter, the country produced far below its potential. Empty plants and idle workers are goods and services that are never produced. To curb prices with monetary restraint, said Stephen Rousseas, a Vassar economist, "is very much like trying to stop a bleeding nose by applying a tourniquet around one's neck."[37] Robert Lekachman called the Fed's approach "calculated monetary sadism."[38]

Nevertheless, it appealed to Reagan. The Fed's stern restraint created the slack to discipline the labor force. Less painful methods to deal with prices would not have yielded such fruitful consequences in labor markets.

To be sure, the Reagan administration didn't always speak with one voice in these matters. Donald Regan, the stockbroker converted into Treasury Secretary, feared that the Fed's high interest rates were destroying the capital value of the bonds held by banks, insurance companies, and others. High interest rates do lift the price of what banks sell—loans—and that was no doubt a good thing. But at the levels fixed by Volcker, they destroy the value of all past loans with fixed interest charges. That is carrying a good thing too far.

Rising interest, moreover, draws speculators' funds from stocks to bonds, depressing stock prices and discouraging sales. No stock salesman can long enjoy this state of affairs.

Regan, former chairman of Merrill Lynch, Pierce, Fenner & Smith, the nation's biggest broker, told his aides early in 1981: "I don't know why we need an independent Federal Reserve Board."[39] He thought the Fed's policy was too tight. By mid-1982, he was threatening to unleash his Under Secretary, Beryl Sprinkel, a bank economist. Sprinkel, the Treasury warned, would launch studies of the central bank's independence, a hint that less might be welcome.

Despite Regan's sniping, the President evidently supported the Fed. Its drastic policy could not have been pursued for long without his assent. The central bank is independent only if it does not press a difference with the White House too far. Practically, the Fed cannot counter the President's expressed will. He is elected; Federal Reserve Board members are chosen, often by a previous President. They have no political legitimacy.

"What the administration wants or is perceived to want continues to dominate the Federal Reserve's conduct," wrote Robert Weintraub, a congressional expert on the central bank. This has been the case, he added, since the postwar accord that freed the central bank from supporting the price of Treasury bonds. Douglas A Hibbs, Jr., wrote: "The Reserve authorities act to preserve their nominal independence from explicit political direction by typically choosing 'independently' to pursue monetary policies accommodating strongly articulated preferences of presidential administrations."[40] In other words, the Fed doesn't need to be told; it anticipates what it would be told if it were told.

Milton Friedman has urged[41] that those who make monetary policy, the seven members of the Federal Reserve Board and the twelve presidents of the system's regional banks, have no particular competence and far too much power. Friedman is probably right, but the problem may be less severe than he suggests. If the central bank chiefs abuse the autonomy given them by law, if they push too long and too hard against the wishes of elected officials, Congress will transform the system. The central bank would be made a subordinate arm of the Treasury, whose Secretary holds office at the pleasure of the President, like the subordinated central banks almost everywhere else. (Germany's central bank is an exception and will remain independent of the government as far as anyone can see. But that is because German society was revolutionized by inflation in the 1920s and Germans want a central bank that errs on the side of tight money.)

Late in 1982, the U.S. central bank, again with Reagan's blessing, relented. It reversed policy and eased money, not because of the pain of unemployment or because of lost production. Those are the concerns of other bodies. The Federal Reserve turned around because Mexico stopped paying interest on billions of debt to the big New York banks, thereby threatening to wipe out those banks and several of their cousins in London. The Fed had driven interest rates so high that the bill for Mexico and other Third World debtors became insupportable. For years thereafter, the Fed, the Treasury, and others labored to shift this great burden onto the shoulders of unknowing taxpayers. *

The Fed also changed course because it had disastrously miscalculated the effects of its high rates on the velocity of money, the speed at which money changes hands. High rates made people hang on to pay, increase savings, and slow down velocity drastically. This reinforced the lack of credit, tightening money even tighter than Volcker wanted. So endangered banks and a grave miscalculation compelled the central bank to reverse course.

There was never any doubt that money, squeezed hard enough, could stop inflation. It was a technique particularly congenial to many in the administration who saw themselves as Friedmanite monetarists. They believed that prices could not rise unless the supply of money increased. Indeed, they went further, for this is a self-evident tautology. Monetarists thought that increased money was not only a necessary but a sufficient condition for price increases. Weidenbaum's first economic report said flatly: "Inflation is essentially a monetary phenomenon."[43] Since Weidenbaum had some experience of the real world, he also fretted over whether events like oil shocks and global food shortages could contribute to price increases. He decided they could, but not much, that they should not be blamed for our "basic inflation problem."[44]

---

* The preferred technique enables banks to swap their dubious Mexican paper for more solid, taxpayer-supported bonds of the U.S. or its global entities like the World Bank or the International Monetary Fund. Nicholas Brady, Treasury Secretary for George Bush, proposed doing just this, with the IMF and the World Bank guaranteeing a portion of the Third World debt.[42]

Curiously, Weidenbaum's successor, Sprinkel, another monetarist, turned the argument upside down. Sprinkel pointed to smaller oil-price advances and blamed them for the general rise in prices in 1987.[45] Economists have been explaining events to suit their master's political needs since Joseph modeled farm output for the Pharaoh.

The trouble with monetarism, as the Fed, which began practicing it in 1979 found out, is that it is useless for policy. It derives from a venerable formula invented by Irving Fisher of Yale. The general level of prices, he said, depends on the volume of money and the velocity or rate at which money passes from hand to hand. If velocity is fixed, a central bank can then control the level of prices simply by controlling the volume of money. A central bank can usually change the money supply, increasing or decreasing bank reserves, varying the fraction of bank loans against which reserves must be held. The trouble with all this is that velocity doesn't stay fixed. Fed officials and economists simply pretended that it did. But the appetite for cash varies with circumstances.

Velocity can't be anticipated or even computed until after the event, until all the transactions in a period are completed. All that economists know—not very much—is that the desire for cash changes from time to time. Besides the great miscalculation of 1982, velocity went wildly off course in 1986. It dropped nearly 30 percent below its supposed trend line.[46] The Fed has admitted as much. The board's monetary policy report to Congress in 1988 acknowledged that velocity "has fluctuated appreciably and rather unpredictably from year to year."[47]

The point is clear: a price level that depends on both the money supply and velocity can't be regulated by adjusting the money supply alone.

Volcker was perhaps the last great convert to monetarism as

a policy guide. He gave up in the last half of 1982 when he discovered he was endangering the big banks, that he had over-looked a large slowdown in velocity. Volcker's error was so monumental that financial writers almost everywhere hail his wisdom and scorn his critics in accord with the rule of success through catastrophe.

The monetarist view reflects a peculiar view of the world. Monetarists believe that markets are made up of flexible prices, responding to changes in monetary supply and demand. This implies competitive markets everywhere, that General Motors, General Mills and General Cleaners on Main Street are none of them big enough to affect prices and output. This is so for General Cleaners but not the others. As credit tightens and consumer demand for their products declines, General Motors and General Mills may reduce output, lay off men, and thereby sustain or even increase prices. This is commonplace, but can't happen, mustn't happen in the monetarist world, where firms are forced by competition to lower prices and maintain employ-ment when demand falls. Evidently, GM and General Mills are not as powerless as General Cleaners. They do affect prices and production in autos and packaged foods. They can thwart or reinforce a monetary policy.

In a more recognizable world, unions exercise some power over wages, large corporations exercise considerable power over prices.* Here, a monetary policy to cure inflation can only succeed if it is violent, exacts a painful cost in unemployed resources. There is no need for such pain, however. The course of wisdom is to treat with wages and prices directly as Roosevelt,

* Reagan's team implicitly recognized the existence of this world in its celebration over the destruction of PATCO. It was rightly seen as a blow to unions, a force that raises wages and thus encourages corporations to raise prices. If all markets were purely competitive, no independent union or corporate power would exist.

Truman, Kennedy, Johnson, Nixon, and Carter did at various times. (In the long run, prices of the strongest monopolies and oligopolies must bend to new entrants to an industry, new sources of supply, substitute products, and the like. But as OPEC demonstrated, waiting for the long run can be painful.)

Moreover, the monetarists assumed that the economy was overheated, that demand was too strong. In fact, all through the 1970s factories and workers were idle. The problem was excess supply, not excess demand: the Fed was fighting the wrong enemy.

The Reagan-Volcker approach created one more problem that persisted after Reagan left office. Tight money led directly to the payments imbalance that haunts so many commentators. High interest rates attracted tens of billions of dollars' worth of marks and yen from Germany, Japan, and other rich nations. Wealthy foreigners and their banking institutions bought up high-yielding Treasury i.o.u.'s—bills, notes, and bonds. This continuing demand for dollar investments bid up the price of the dollar on foreign exchanges. A Japanese bank, for example, would cash in 120 billion yen to buy $1 billion and purchase thirty-year Treasury bonds. Since foreign-exchange markets do resemble textbook markets, the Tokyo bank would increase the supply of yen in the world, decrease the supply of dollars, and thus lift the dollar against the yen. As this process was repeated elsewhere, the dollar climbed against all other currencies. The climbing dollar made American exports more expensive, Japanese imports cheaper. Lower exports and higher imports create a trade deficit. A balance was struck only because the foreigners exported capital to the U.S., bought those high-yielding notes, bills, and bonds. In effect, the Japanese swapped goods for American paper, an exchange that those untutored in economics might rightly applaud. The Federal Reserve had consciously sought a rising dollar to battle inflation in the early eighties; it had failed to perceive a side effect of its medicine, a sharply worsened trade deficit. At its peak in the 1970s, the deficit was $40 billion. After Volcker's ministrations, the level rose above $120 billion in 1984 and reached $170 billion by 1987.[48]

At home, the Fed's propensity to tighten money created a genuine near disaster late in Reagan's second terms. Once again, the Fed was tightening because of a wrong-headed preoccupation with rates of exchange, just like the disastrous tightening in 1931 to stem an outflow of gold. This time the Fed was troubled by the very fall in the dollar that was encouraging American exports and making American markets difficult for foreigners to penetrate. A cheaper dollar was precisely what was needed to cure the trade imbalance but that became a secondary issue. The sinking dollar was breaking a limit that the Fed had unwisely agreed upon with other central banks at a meeting in the Louvre palace in Paris. So the Fed squeezed hard, "dramatically," in October 1987 according to Reagan's economic report. The resulting burst in interest rates made yields on shares look meager; the stock market plunged in one day even further than it had in 1929.[49]

That, however, was a crisis a central banker could feel, not like a fall in output or jobs. So the Fed rapidly reversed course, eased money, halted the stock crash. Its leader, Alan Greenspan, was hailed as the savior of the market.

In Reagan's economics, it was right and proper to assign the visible central role in economic policy to the Federal Reserve. Inflation was blamed on money and the spending and taxing powers of the Federal government were said to have little to do with jobs, output, or price restraint. The fatal mistake of Roosevelt and his successors was to think otherwise. This, at least, was the official line.

In practice, nobody in the Reagan regime quite believed this, and so the induced slump of 1980–82 did not become a depression. If it had, Reagan could not have been reelected; he owed his political success to the fact that his administration ignored his proclaimed doctrine. In practice, Reagan was a closet Keynesian who invoked the countercyclical spending and taxing techniques of the past to recover from the slump and prolong modest growth for the rest of this time in office.

As with his discovery of slack, it is not clear whether Reagan consciously used fiscal techniques to expand output and jobs or whether other objectives led him to a happy result. He clearly wanted a huge increase in spending for arms because he thought it would frighten Russians. He embarked on this course just when the recession-hit economy badly needed a jolt of Federal spending. His first Economic Report noted as much. "The economy has ample slack to accommodate the beginnings of a major expansion in defense work," it said.[50] The slack could also have accommodated a major expansion in housing, highways, welfare, or pyramid building. The point is Reagan's men understood that enlarged government spending was required and Reagan's arms designs fit nicely.

Reagan did more. In a slump, standard Keynesian practice calls for cutting taxes as an alternative or addition to increased spending. Tax cuts like extra government spending put added income in the hands of citizens, who spend to enlarge the incomes of others. Take together, all this puts idle men and factories to work.

Reagan did not do things by halves. He put through a large, $177 billion tax cut starting in 1981, on top of his increase in arms spending.[51] It was this combine, bigger outlays, reduced taxes, and easier money from the Federal Reserve, that halted the economic recession in 1982 and launched the economy on a modest upward path of more jobs and more output.

Above all, Reagan wanted to reduce the burden for the wealthy men of his income class. But it is likely that more than chance determined the timing of his arms and tax maneuvers. Reagan evidently understood conventional countercyclical policy; he could not offend some of his zealots by saying so.

The cold budget figures, adjusted to fit the national income accounts, describe the dimensions of Reagan's heroic countercyclical impulses. The gap between spending and receipts, the deficit, was $61.2 billion in 1980 and little changed at $62.2 billion in 1981, Reagan's first year. Then it leaped to $147.1 billion in 1982 and $182.9 billion in 1983, a substantial Federal contribution to aggregate demand.[52] The military portion was important. Spending for guns climbed from $134 billion in 1980 to $185.3 billion in 1982 and $209.9 billion in 1983.[53] It is not clear whether this frightened Russians but it helped lift employment from 99 million in 1980 to 105 million by 1984.[54]

Rarely has a government's intention so closely matched its achievement. The Reagan administration announced, on taking office, that it wanted to increase military spending, after inflation, by 9 percent a year through 1987. This, it said, would lift weapons outlays as a share of the budget from 25 to 37 percent and increase the military's share of the nation's total output from 5.6 percent to 7.8 percent.[55]

Five years later, the Reagan team disclosed that the military now claimed 6.6 percent of total output,[56] a rise of 37 percent from the 4.8 percent share in 1978 when Carter launched his arms boom.[57] Reagan's yearly increase was 6.9 percent, not far from the 9 percent goal.[58] Moreover, all this was done at a time when international tensions were decreasing, arms-reduction agreements became the fashion, and the administration's Third World adventures—Nicaragua, El Salvador, Angola, Lebanon, Afghanistan, and Grenada—provided little outlet for big spending.

Some of the administration's own economists thought the outlays bore little relationship to any defense purpose. Chairman Weidenbaum described the program as "indiscriminately buying virtually every weapon in sight."[59] William Niskanen, the council member, thought that "the administration's defense budget was little more than a stapled package of the budget request from each service."[60]

Despite or perhaps because of the rapid buildup, the Defense Department found that its readiness to go to war had increased only "slightly" at most and in many areas was unchanged. Little was spent on operations and maintenance but purchases of weapons rose rapidly, 13.5 percent a year.[61] This then was essentially a public-works program to create orders and profits for weapons plants, related only incidentally to any military end. It was the purest kind of countercyclical spending. If the huge outlays had little to do with defense they did provide a floor under demand. Robert Lekachman described this as "military Keynesianism."[62]

The Reagan response to the slump he inherited yielded classic results. Output had fallen 2 percent between the first and third quarters of 1980 and 2.4 percent from the third quarter of 1981 until the end of 1982. Now it rose, quarter by quarter, gaining almost 29 percent by the end of 1988.[63] Some of Reagan's economists were compelled to break with the party line and acknowledge that the Federal government could after all affect output and jobs. The deficits "have a positive impact on the pace of recovery in 1983 and 1984," said the Economic Report for 1984.[64] Even more, the report continued, the tax cuts helped raise consumer spending which contributed so much to the recovery.

Although the deficit was a direct stimulus, Reagan's economists warned that future deficits would simply raise interest rates, crowd out new investment in plant and equipment, and hurt exports. The next year, with the slump safely over, the economists were far more cautious, edging back to Reaganite orthodoxy. They said, "Fiscal policy may have provided some support to aggregate demand . . . as the tax cuts gradually took effect and national defense purchase grew, but the stimulus was probably small.[65] Grudging as this was, it was nevertheless quite different from the orthodox Reaganaut view that government could not directly affect jobs and output.

Memories are short. What was learned in 1984 began to fade in 1985 and disappeared down an Orwellian memory hole by 1989. So Reagan's final report was curious. It offered a brief history of the economy in the twentieth century; it somehow omitted entirely World War II, with its powerful lesson of the government's ability to expand output rapidly, wipe out unemployment, and control inflation. For Reagan's entourage, that was an awkward story.

Successful politicians tend to be opportunists, wedded to no one theory, drawing on whatever is available to support the goals of the moment. Thus Hoover and Roosevelt wobbled between government intervention in the economy and budget balancing. Eisenhower sought to shrink government but employed modest anti-slump measures. Ford and Carter wavered between expansion and restraint. Despite the contradictions, a central thread can usually be discerned. In the end Hoover believed virtue lay on the side of budget balance, Roosevelt belatedly adopted the fiscal policies that led to the Depression's end, and all the postwar presidents through Carter believed and acted on the belief that government measures could avert disaster and bring prosperity.

The economics of Reagan, however, had puzzled many analysts. What picture of the economy did he hold? What theory or belief underlay his actions? Seldom has the gap between words and deed, rarely a close fit for any politician, been wider. How did he think things worked?

Michael Boskin, a sympathetic analyst, thought that Reagan was an eclectic philosopher king who drew on four strands of contemporary thought: monetarism, the Friedmanite doctrine that puts change in the money supply at the center of the economic solar system; rational expectations, a conservative doctrine that holds, among other things, that all unemployment is voluntary and no one is jobless because of circumstances beyond his control; traditional free market conservatism, with its distaste for budget deficits; and the most novel, supply-side economics, promising a fresh world by encouraging the factors that produce output rather than the Keynesian stress on aggregate demand.

An administration relying on four theories may be said to lack a certain coherence. But tidiness ought not to bother a politician. The real trouble is that there is little evidence that the Reagan White House gave more than lip service to any of these ideas. Rather it exploited the theoreticians to justify what it had already determined to do.

Monetarism, as we have seen, lost its usefulness as a policy guide in the Reagan portion of the 1980–82 slump. Then, it turned out, the central bank had tightened well beyond its intention or Reagan's desire because velocity plummeted. After that, the Fed abandoned attempts to guide prices by considering changes in the money supply alone. For practical purposes, monetarism died early in Reagan's tenure.

Rational expectations is a curious version of the simple classical model. It argues that all markets are purely competitive, that IBM has no more control over its prices and output than a Vermont hill farmer, that there are no unemployed men save by choice. Robert Lucas, a rational expectationist from Chicago, asked, "Why don't unemployed people get jobs as cab drivers? I guess they don't want to. They have better things to do with their time."[66] He apparently meant that the jobless prefer leisure to labor. This, scoffed James Tobin, [67] is the economics of Dr. Pangloss, Voltaire's philosopher who believed that all was for the best in the best of all possible worlds.

The supply-siders drew the most attention, partly because two of their prophets, Paul Craig Roberts and Norman Ture, won high positions in the Reagan Treasury and partly because a tireless publicist, Jude Wanniski, had been an editorial writer for the *Wall Street Journal*, where the doctrine frequently found a home in editorial columns.

If supply-side meant anything, it was an attempt to apply simple, first-year economic theory of the firm to national economic considerations—taxes, savings, and investment. Supply-siders argued that marginal tax rates, especially in the top brackets, discouraged work, savings, and investment, thereby curbing productivity advances, output, and income.

Taxes can be an incentive or disincentive to individual performance, although many other factors also govern human behavior. Taxes can help expand or compress national output, but other forces, notably changes in the supply of money and Federal expenditures, are easily as potent. What supply siders left out overwhelmed the little they put in to explain economic matters.

Supply-side theory ran into common-sense difficulties almost at once. A dedicated supply-sider like Roberts argued that lower taxes would induce machinists, doctors, architects, managers, bus drivers, and everyone else to work harder, increasing output and incomes.[68] Ture, equally dedicated, pointed out that unfortunately this wasn't clear. Higher after-tax income would surely encourage some machinists, doctors, and managers to work less, choosing leisure over labor.[69] You just don't know. Roberts called this "perverse," and the Treasury must have heard some hot arguments.

The supply-siders' claim for the effects of lower taxes on savings and investments were equally uncertain. Indeed, the Reagan tax cuts, with some special fillips to spur plants and machinery, failed to produce a burst of investment. Industry spent $315 billion on plants and tools in 1981, the year of the big tax cut. Despite the tax incentive, spending fell to $305 billion in 1983. Recovery from the deep slump lifted investment spending to $355 billion in 1984, and it continued to advance more or less in step with the economy.[70] This was not surprising. Corporations do not buy machines and plants because they receive tax breaks; they buy because they believe the demand for their products will increase.

If the supply-side theory was weak, some of its adepts were quite bold. Arthur Laffer, an economist from the University of Southern California, pulled out a napkin and drew a bell-shaped distribution curve. This, he announced, proved that lowering taxes would increase tax receipts. Laffer had rediscovered the principle of absolutely diminishing returns, another high point in first-year theory. This says simply that a farmer who adds fertilizer to his plot will get increasing yields up to the point of diminishing returns. Then added increments of fertilizer yield smaller increases in output until he burns out his land and the yield actually declines.

Why Laffer thought the nation was at the point of absolutely diminishing tax returns was never made clear. No one seems to have made an empirical test of his proposition. It had its polemical uses in supporting Reagan's tax cut. Unfortunately, as Herbert Stein observed, "it was almost certainly not true."[71]

Robert Heilbroner wondered out loud how so peculiar a set of beliefs as supply-side economics could gain attention. "The one convincing reason that occurs to me," he said, is that "supply-side economics has as its immediate objective the improvement of the conditions of the rich."[72]

The classical orthodox conservatives were represented by Martin Feldstein. He and they worried over alleged shortages of investment and savings, over budget deficits that were thought to eat up savings. Feldstein provided a useful excuse for upper-bracket and corporate tax cuts. But the large Reagan deficits suggested that his effect on policy was limited.

In fact, none of Boskin's four strands penetrated Reagan thinking very deeply. Monetarism died in action; rational expectations seemed less rational; supply-siders were too divided, too far from reality, to serve; the neoclassicals were undone by deficits that were both harmless and did not seem to affect investment.

In the end, Reagan's economists began to sound like conventional interventionists. "Clearly it is important to maintain policy momentum in the macro-economic area . . . when appropriate, judicious easing of monetary policy and increased spending on worthwhile public investments can contribute to demand and output growth without raising risks of inflation." This remarkable passage appears in the 1988 Economic Report.[73] It could have run unchanged in those produced by the economists for Kennedy and Johnson.

The confusing words, their mismatch with deeds, puzzled some of the Republican's highest priests. There is "current uncertainty about the meaning and the validity of the new macro-economic policy," Herbert Stein, Nixon's chief economist, wrote in 1986.[74] Later, he concluded that the Reagan administration simply had no fiscal policy, would not fix on a level of surplus or deficit to which expenditures and revenues were related. This theoretical vacuum surely came closer to the mark than Boskin's belief in four strands. The point is that Reagan and his top team were practical men, little troubled by theoretical coherence or consistency. If supply-siders supplied a rationale for cutting top-bracket taxes, splendid. If monetarists justified tight money to squeeze inflation, excellent. If orthodox conservatives and rational expectationists explained why the poor and unemployed can be ignored, good. Other Presidents, also practical men, sought some appearance of consistency between word and deed, at least as long as it caused no inconvenience. Reagan was not similarly troubled. He and his friends were lawyers, actors, salesmen for whom words are malleable. They are capable of playing any role, employing any script, to promote an end.

NOTES

1. *Economic Report of the President* (Washington, D.C.: U.S. Government Printing Office, 1989), pp. 3, 10.

2. *Ibid.*, p. 310.

3. William A. Niskanen, *Reaganomics: An Insider's Account of the Policies and the People* (New York: Oxford University Press, 1988), p. 137.

4. *Economic Report of the President*, 1989, p. 310.

5. *Ibid.*, p. 378.

6. *Ibid.*, p. 352.

7. Paul Craig Roberts, *The Supply-Side Revolution* (Cambridge: Harvard University Press, 1984), p. 225.

8. Martin Feldstein, "The Welfare Cost of Permanent Inflation and Optimal Short-run Economic Policy," *Journal of Political Economy*, vol. 87, no. 4, August 1979, p. 750.

9. Leonard Silk and David Vogel, *Ethics and Profits: The Crisis of Confidence in American Business* (New York: Simon & Schuster, 1976), p. 64.

10. *Economic Report of the President* (Washington, D.C.: U.S. Government Printing Office, 1984), p. 259.

11. Douglas A. Hibbs, Jr., *The American Political Economy: Macroeconomics and Electoral Politics* (Cambridge: Harvard University Press, 1987), pp. 46–7.

12. *Economic Report of the President*, 1984, p. 283.

13. *Economic Report of the President* (Washington, D.C.: U.S. Government Printing Office, 1983), p. 37.

14. David Wessel, "Fed Chief Warns Inflation Is Too High,' " *Wall Street Journal*, January 25, 1989, p. 2.

15. Niskanen, *Reaganomics*, p. 237.

16. *Economic Report of the President*, 1989, p. 352.

17. Milton Freidman, "The Role of Monetary Policy," *American Economic Review*, vol. LVIII, no. 1, 1968, p. 8.

18. Michael J. Boskin, *Reagan and the Economy: The Successes, Failures, and Unfinished Agenda* (San Francisco: ICS Press, 1987), p. 98.

19. Michael J. Boskin, "Economic Growth and Productivity," in *The Economy in the 1980's*, edited by Michael J. Boskin (New Brunswick: Transaction Books, 1980), p. 7.

20. Franco Modigliani, "Government Deficits, Inflation and Future Generations," in *Deficits: How Big and How Bad* (Toronto, Canada: Ontario Economic Council, 1983), p. 64.

21. James Tobin, "After Disinflation, Then What," in *After Stagflation*, edited by John Cornwall (London: Basil Blackwell, 1984), pp. 20, 21.

22. *Historical Statistics of the United States: Colonial Times to 1970: Bicentennial Edition* (U.S. Department of Commerce, 1975), p. 139.

23. Thomas Byrne Edsall, *The New Politics of Inequality* (New York: W.W. Norton & Company, 1984), pp. 142, 171.

24. George Meany quoted in Edsall, *The New Politics*, p. 155.

25. Samuel Bowles, David M. Gordon, and Thomas E. Weisskopf, *Beyond the Waste Land: A Democratic Alternative to Economic Decline* (Garden City, New York: Anchor Press, 1983), p. 109.

26. *Economic Report of the President* (Washington, D.C.: U.S. Government Printing Office, 1985), p. 33.

27. Frank Ackerman, *Reaganomics* (London: Pluto Press, 1982), p. 113.

28. Murray Weidenbaum, *Rendezvous with Reality: The American Economy After Reagan* (New York: Basic Books, 1988), p. 7.

29. Edsall, *The New Politics of Inequality*, p. 161.

171

30. *Ibid.*, p. 161.

31. *Economic Report of the President* (Washington, D.C.: U.S. Government Printing Office, 1987), p. 117.

32. James L. Sawyer, *Why Reagonomics and Keynesian Economics Failed* (London: Macmillan, 1987), p. 156.

33. Weidenbaum, *Rendezvous with Reality*, p. 9.

34. *Economic Report of the President*, 1989, p. 378.

35. Weidenbaum, *Rendezvous with Reality*, p. 10.

36. In 1982 dollars, assuming a 4% rate of structural unemployment.

37. Stephen Rousseas, *The Political Economy of Reaganomics* (Armonk, New York: M.E. Sharpe, 1982), p. 59.

38. Robert Lekachman, *Visions and Nightmares* (New York: Macmillan, 1987), p. 69.

39. William R. Neikirk, *Volcker* (New York: Congdon & Weed, 1987), p. 101.

40. Robert Weintraub quoted in Hibbs, *The American Political Economy*, pp. 8–9.

41. Milton Friedman in John H. Moore, editor, *To Promote Prosperity* (Stanford, California: Hoover Institute Press, 1984), p. 51.

42. *Facts on File Year Book* (New York: Facts on File, 1989), p. 178.

43. *Economic Report of the President* (Washington, D.C.: U.S. Government Printing Office, 1982), p. 54.

44. *Ibid.*, p. 4.

45. *Economic Report of the President* (Washington D.C.: U.S. Government Printing Office, 1988), p. 23.

46. Phillip Cagan, editor, *Deficits, Taxes, and Economic Adjustments* (Washington, D.C.: American Enterprise Institute, 1987), p. 139.

47. David Wessel, "Fed Chief Warns Inflation Is 'Too High,' " *Wall Street Journal*, January 25, 1989, p. 3.

48. *Economic Report of the President*, 1989, p. 428.

49. "Stocks Plunge 508 Amid Panicky Selling," *Wall Street Journal*, October 20, 1987, p. 22.

50. *Economic Report of the President*, 1982, p. 86.

51. Niskanen, *Reaganomics*, p. 76.

52. *Economic Report of the President*, 1984, p. 309.

53. *Ibid.*, p. 305.

54. *Economic Report of the President*, 1988, p. 286.

55. *Economic Report of the President*, 1982, p. 85.

56. *Economic Report of the President*, 1987, p. 69.

57. *Economic Report of the President*, 1988, pp. 48–9.

58. *Ibid.*, p. 28.

59. Weidenbaum, *Rendezvous with Reality*, p. 18.

60. Niskanen, *Reaganomics*, p. 33.

61. *Ibid.*, p. 30.

62. Lekachman, *Visions and Nightmares*, p. 82.

63. United States Department of Commerce, Bureau of Economic Analysis, *Business Conditions Digest*, February 1982, p. 63, and June 1983, p. 63.

64. *Economic Report of the President*, 1984, pp. 38–9.

65. *Economic Report of the President*, 1985, p. 29.

66. Robert Lucas quoted in Marc Levinson, *Beyond Free Markets: The Revival of Activist Economics* (Lexington, Mass.: Lexington Books, 1988), p. 52.

67. Tobin, *Policies for Prosperity*, p. 54.

68. Paul Craig Roberts, "The Breakdown of the Keynesian Model," in *Supply-Side Economics: A Critical Appraisal*, edited by Richard H. Fink (Frederick, Maryland: Aletheia Books, 1982), p. 7.

69. Rousseas, *The Political Economy of Reaganomics*, p. 73.

70. *Economic Report of the President*, 1989, p. 369.

71. Herbert Stein, *Presidential Economics* (Washington, D.C.: American Enterprise Institute, 1988), p. 240.

72. Robert Heilbroner, "The Demand for the Supply-Side," in Fink, *Supply-Side Economics*, p. 88.

73. *Economic Report of the President*, 1988, p. 125.

74. Herbert Stein, *Washington Bedtime Stories* (New York: The Free Press, 1986), p. 343.

VI

Country-Club Economics

"None of us really understands what's going on with all these numbers," David Stockman, Reagan's budget manager, told William Greider, the journalist, in a celebrated exchange. "You've got so many different budgets out and so many different baselines and such complexity. . . . People are getting from A to B and it's not clear how they are getting there. It's not clear how we got there."[1]

In his own account, Stockman renewed this theme. In budget making under Reagan, "one gimmick followed another," he said. "Numbers were written in sand."[2]

Manuel H. Johnson, a cooler figure, who succeeded supply-sider Roberts at the Treasury, told the same story. He explained how the Reagan administration invented wholly improbable and wildly varying increases in the velocity of money to make the deficit, money supply, and inflation forecasts add up.[3]

Reagan's indifference to budget arithmetic does not mean he lacked clear economic objectives. He had them but they simply would not fit any consistent accounting framework. Reagan and his colleague had impulses, gut feelings on which they acted. They knew that their class was taxed too heavily and this was a bad thing, particularly in the 1970s when shares in the stock market moved mostly sideways and a stiff inflation shrank their real value. Taxes at the top must come down. (The invaluable if self-serving Stockman tells us that the real object of the 1981 bill was to bring the top income-tax rate on interest and dividends down from 70 percent to 50 percent, that the tax cuts in the lower brackets were simply a "Trojan horse" to disguise this goal.)[4]

Reagan and his friends thought welfare rolls were loaded with loafers and cheaters. So Federal funds for the poorest must be cut drastically. Finally, there had to be a big increase in military spending. It would show the Russians and be good for business without threatening to create the socialism of welfare spending.

These feelings are a commonplace in the locker rooms of country clubs in affluent suburbs across the country. They reflect the wisdom of comfortable men drying themselves with terrycloth towels, standing on carpeted floors, enjoying a companionable drink at the nineteenth hole. They hardly add up to a theory. But the economics of the country club is a bond among most of its members. Reagan was unusually well placed, able to act on and enforce these sentiments.

In fact, a country club had been the setting for some of Reagan's most critical economics education. In the 1950s, a fading actor, Reagan hung out at his country club six months a year to attract the notice of producers and others.[5] There he likely discussed affairs of the day—Treasury Secretary Donald Regan wrote that the experience reminded both men how high taxes had penalized their success—heard sound men voice the belief that government was too much with them, that those who want work can get it, that the Russians should be taught a lesson.

Stockman reported that Reagan first learned of the joys of the single-bracket, flat tax from George Shultz, a certified economist, on the golf course.[6] Reagan's 1986 tax bill, drastically reducing the progressive quality of the income tax, evolved from this chat.

Stockman, who isn't always fair, insists that his colleagues were more ignorant than scornful of conventional economic thought. "The fiscal and economic illiteracy among the core White House group was simply too great." Secretary Regan and the White House senior staff "were almost entirely innocent and uninformed."*[7]

All in all, Reagan's cabinet and subcabinet were representative businessmen, frequently able at running their own firms, usually lacking a larger vision of public affairs, making false analogies between private and national business. Businessmen have held a disproportionate share of high government posts since Roosevelt. But presidents with a different sense of public purpose, aided by advisers of force and skill like Burns and Heller, have led administrations to adopt a more sophisticated view of class and national interest.

Perhaps nothing was simpler than Reagan's view of deficits. In 1981, he said that "excessive deficit spending has been the major contributor to inflation."[9] He was untroubled by the fact that he had created large deficits but inflation was declining. When Martin Feldstein, the chief economist, fretted over the deficits in his 1984 report, Treasury Secretary Regan dismissed Feldstein's document. "As far as I am concerned," Regan said, "you can throw it away."[10] That was a blunt response to an

---

* To be sure, Stockman did not know everything either. He and his deputy, Richard Darman, wanted to increase taxes in 1983, just as the nation was emerging from the deep slump induced by the Fed. Secretary Regan, Stockman relates, thought this was the wrong time for a tax increase, a view that common sense as well as economics would support. But to Stockman, Regan's opposition was "preposterous."[8]

awkward if wrong-headed belief held in locker rooms and some corners of academe. It underscored the wide gap between the economics Reagan preached and the economics he practiced.

Nevertheless, Ronald Reagan was the first president since Coolidge to enact into law at least some of the instinctive feelings about public affairs of the men in the country clubs. Given the small number of voters served, this was a stunning achievement.

Of all the rules in locker-room economics, none is stronger than the injunction to balance budgets. But Reagan flouted this on a monumental scale—at least as the deficit is counted conventionally—but the sky did not fall in on him. His deficits far exceeded those of the Great Depression. At the peak in 1983, Reagan's red ink was 6.3 percent of the gross national product. He then produced three more deficits of 5 percent or more. Apart from the war, past budget deficits almost never exceeded 3 percent, little more than half the Reagan level.[11]

An elaborate piece of congressional shadow play, the Gramm-Rudman-Hollings Act, pretended to force an inexorable end to the deficits. The law required President and Congress to agree on a *forecast* of future and diminishing deficits. That got in nobody's way. Reagan endorsed it enthusiastically. When the act threatens some worthy expenditure like bailing out fraudulent savings and loan banks, presidents try to remove that spending from the budget. That is just what George Bush did. Like the ceiling on the national debt, the balanced-budget law may be bad economics but it is stunning hypocrisy.

Just why deficits should mean doom has never been clear. Some economists like Lester Thurow have contended that deficits eventually "represent too large an infusion of aggregate demand and inflation results."[12] Thurow means that government deficits put money in people's pockets that can't bring forth new goods but must drive up prices on an existing supply. This is so only when there are no more goods to be produced, when all workers and plants are fully employed. In the rare and special case of full employment Thurow is right. If resources are idle, however, the extra money from deficits can put them to work, more goods flow, and prices need not change. Reagan presided over very high unemployment, gradually reducing it from a frightening 10 percent to a plateau at 7 percent, and then, in time for the 1988 election, 5 percent.[13] There were a lot of idle plants and the deficits could and did finance a lot of employment before inflation was renewed.

In Reagan's first term, a fashionable argument held that the deficits were crowding out private investment, threatening productivity, growth, and competitiveness abroad. Crowding out assumes that there is a limited fund of savings and government debt absorbs a disproportionate share. Not enough is left to finance new plant and equipment. This lay behind Feldstein's concern in 1984, the concern that Treasury Secretary Regan contemptuously dismissed. Regan knew that economic slack was real; he did not know, as Feldstein had professed, that unemployment was temporary or voluntary or due to the minimum wage which priced the poorest workers out of the job market and anyway didn't matter. Regan also knew that economic slack discouraged investment. Finally, he understood that large corporations don't depend on the savings of individuals to finance plant and equipment, that big firms get investment money from the prices they charge for products. Regan, like Feldstein, wanted lower taxes for corporations and the rich; but unlike Feldstein, he knew where plant and equipment come from.

Reagan lacked Regan's experience and panicked briefly over his deficits. So some of the 1981 tax cut was partly offset by tax increases, particularly for corporations, the next year. But thereafter Reagan ignored his deficits as blithely as Regan, apart from pretending that the Congress was somehow responsible.

Herbert Stein offered a more deft version of crowding out.[14] Great deficits, he wrote, mean high interest rates that attract foreign capital, which drives up the dollar against other currencies and makes exports dearer. Thus the budget deficit intensified the deficit in the balance of trade. This was ingenious. But since Stein himself has insisted that the trade deficit is not a matter of concern—a reasonable position as long as foreigners are eager to finance it—this consequence need not cause any loss of sleep.

Anyway, interest rates are determined by the supply as well as the demand for money, so Stein's concern is unwarranted. If the Fed wants to drive the dollar down, it can do so by expanding the money supply (assuming that velocity doesn't behave perversely and decrease), although it is probably a bad idea to let the exchange rate or gold or some external indicator determine the volume of domestic money. Far better to have the central bank obey the 1946 act and create enough money to sustain high employment as well as worry about inflation.

The less sophisticated insist that if a household must pay its debts or go bankrupt so must the government. But the government is not a household; it is sovereign and can print money, build dams or highways, create housing, schools, and other capital assets, as well as shift funds to the poor (or away from them), care for or neglect the aged and sick, spend on weapons. Future generations need not and must not pay off the Federal debt; it is the basis of changes in the nation's money supply. Future generations will indeed share in the debt's interest burden. They should. It has financed the building of much they will use and might even defend them against Russians or someone.

The fundamental point about crowding out was simply stated by Franco Modigliani. "If there is slack in the economy then the government deficit need not displace investment."[15] Under Reagan, there was plenty of slack.

Why then didn't the Reagan deficits bring about full employment as did those in the war and in the earlier slumps? The simple answer is that Reagan's deficits were too small, not too large. They were not big enough to generate jobs for more than a portion of the huge reserve army created by the Federal Reserve, too small to set at work all the idled plants.* After all, Reagan wanted slack.

Reagan's own economists grasped the point even if others did not. With some astonishment, the Reagan economists observed that their deficits had exceeded 5 percent of the gross national product for the first time in postwar history.[17] This means, they concluded, that deficits must be widened in a slump. If the opposite course is taken, contraction, it will further choke output and jobs. Beryl Sprinkel and the other Reagan economists made clear that their conclusion was distasteful, that they would like to greet the next slump with a lower deficit. But their argument against contraction brought them into the mainstream. So did their discovery that judicious government spending could promote growth without inflation. Between the two, it might now be truly said that at last we are all Keynesians.

Whether by design or luck, Reagan's touch was just right. He allowed deficits large enough to reduce the jobless misery created by the Fed; he avoided deficits big enough to create full

---

* James Tobin makes a distinction between active and passive deficits. A passive deficit is one created by the fall in tax revenues and rise in unemployment benefits in a slump. An active deficit changes the budget structure so that, for example, what had been a balance at full employment is now a deficit. Tobin argues that it is the change from passive to active deficit that puts men and plants to work.[16]

employment, which would have strengthened workers and unions. Herbert Stein no doubt is right to argue that Reagan had no fiscal policy. But his country-club instincts were sound enough to get what he wanted.

In terms of its declared objectives, the Reagan regime's most notable failure was its inability to increase the economy's efficiency. Reagan had claimed in his "world . . . born anew" that the engine of growth had been rebuilt, that the lagging productivity of the lean years had vanished, that new and more efficient factories and tools were spurring the economy to new heights. None of this happened. New plant and equipment, as a share of output, grew 9.5 percent a year in the stagnant Ford-Carter era; under Reagan, the pace was even slower, 9.3 percent. [18] Productivity, the yearly gain in worker output, averaged arithmetically 1.6 percent under Reagan and 0.5 percent in the eight earlier years. These minuscule gains lagged far behind the 4.4 percent achieved in the fat years. [19]

In the Reagan plan, this should not have happened. Special tax incentives had been given to large corporations to induce them to modernize factories and invest in the latest technology. They were given credits against their taxes for investment, a device invented in the Kennedy era. They were temporarily allowed larger and faster deductions against taxes for outlays on new machines. Some deductions exceeded the cost of the machines and so became outright subsidies, like those that had been stripped from the poorest families. Above all, high unemployment ensured a docile labor force, less likely to object to speeded-up assembly lines, agreeable to reduced manning levels.

The trouble is that corporate executives don't buy new plants and tolls because of taxes or compliant workers. From 1981 to 1984, forty large corporations that escaped all corporate tax over four years actually cut their investment by 4 percent; forty-three highly taxed corporations, however, increased their plant and equipment spending by 21 percent.[20] This summary by the Citizens for Tax Justice does not mean that Reagan had it upside down, that higher taxes yield more investment. It simply means that taxes have little to do with investment, far less than the state of demand. Respectable economic thought in the Reagan era declined to accept this view. Peter G. Peterson, a former chairman of the elite CED, was typical. He saw the critical problem in these terms: "We have chosen to consume, not invest."[21] This implies that consumption must be repressed to provide resources for investment. It also suggests the need for tax incentives to wealthy investors and corporations. It does not admit that expanded consumption is crucially required for enlarged corporate investment.

The Congressional Budget Office, a Capitol Hill think tank staffed largely by Reagan critics, spoke like Peterson. It said that deficits threatened to force aside private borrowers, drive up interest rates, damage productivity, curb growth, "limiting future standards of living and American competitiveness in the world economy."[22]

This suggests that savings are scarce. If savings are scarce, then their price must rise. But as Samuel Bowles observed,[23] real interest rates—the market rate less inflation—fell in the 1970s compared with the 1950s and 1960s. The investment-productivity crisis emerged in the 1970s, so a shortage of savings could not have been the cause. It was instead the sluggish level of demand.

Some economists do recognize that investment is not a function of tax benefits for the wealthy and the corporations but depends on the demand from customers. Barry Bosworth concluded[24] that the ratio of capital to labor—the amount of plant and tools employed per worker—is "highly sensitive" to the business cycle. This is an economist's way of saying that investment rises when demand rises. Lester Thurow estimated[25] that 30 percent of the notorious slowdown in productivity was due to idle capacity generally and another 30 percent to a decline in mining, building, and utilities, where demand has grown slowly. In other words, corporations don't enlarge their plant when they have unused plant on their hands. Herbert Stein said plainly that Reagan's tax cuts to promote investment were swamped by Reagan's slump.[26]

In the great debate over how investment is best stimulated, a critical point frequently goes unremarked. The capital spending of large corporations does not depend on the savings of individuals. Major firms extract the required funds from their customers. Balance sheets show these funds as retained earnings and reserves and they buy the new tools and plants.

So, in 1988, IBM had $7.8 billion left after paying all its expenses, dividends and taxes. It spent $5.3 billion on plant and equipment. In other words, IBM's customers paid for the firm's cost of production, selling, and administration; for its dividends and taxes; for all its capital investment. The customers still left IBM with another $2.5 billion. Individual savers did not finance IBM's capital spending; the customers did. In the same way, Exxon collected $6.9 billion after all expenses and dividends and invested $5.7 billion on capital.[27] Nine hundred large nonfinancial corporations took in $225.2 billion, invested $198.7 billion and had a tidy nest egg left over for new plant when demand would justify it.[28] None of this had to do with the loose change of citizen taxpayers. The large corporation does not rely on so uncertain a quantity except in a few textbooks and in the arguments of special pleaders. The established modern corporation finances plant and equipment outlays from the enforced savings it imposes on customers through prices. Large corporations use their power to impose prices at a level high enough to pay for capital costs. Consumers become involuntary financiers, involuntary savers, investing through no conscious delusion of their own in tools and factories.

A new firm, a small corporation, is differently placed. It usually can't control its product price, faces classical competition, and must raise capital through debt or shares, from savings. But this is not the corporation whose capital investment is usually discussed when alarm bells ring for declining U.S. industrial efficiency, Japanese competition and the rest. These things are blamed on the large, seasoned corporations because of their supposed inability or unwillingness to invest. Large corporations sometimes raise money through stock or bond issues. Typically they do so to take over other concerns, not to build plants or buy tools.

A peculiar rite of the big contemporary corporation underscores the small part played by individual savers in financing capital investment. Major firms like IBM use cash drawn from customers to buy up their own shares in the stock market. This bolsters share prices, pleases stockholders, and enhances the stock options of executives. It also reflects a judgment by IBM and others that no additional worthwhile investment exists in tools and plant to expand their capacity. Capital spending is not inhibited by a lack of savings; the corporations sit on so much that they use the money to buy pieces of paper. Corporate investment is held back by a lack of demand.

The Reagan approach, indeed the conventional business approach, to capital investment is wrong on two counts. The rich and their corporations do not need tax concessions to provide savings for new plant and equipment. Capital spending in corporate America is financed internally. No shortage of savings constricts plant and equipment outlays; it is a shortage of demand. Richard A. Musgrave summed up the productivity fiasco and said, "Bad economics, based on wishful thinking, has produced bad results."[29]

Reagan's tax incentives to spur capital spending played some role in feeding the great bull market of 1982 to 1987. There was no economic boom to explain the rise; the economy grew no faster than in past recoveries. But the incentives increased after-tax profits for corporations, an important source of higher share prices. By the time the stock-market boom ended, Reagan had withdrawn many of the corporate tax privileges. It didn't matter. In return, the businessmen had all gotten a stunning cut in personal top-bracket rates, from 50 percent to 28 percent. The bull market fed mostly on the Reagan income-tax bonanza for the best-off. They swapped old pieces of paper issued by established corporations, a traditional pastime for those receiving windfall incomes.

The central point is clear. The talk of productivity and investment by Reagan was an excuse, a Trojan horse in Stockman's terms. The real goal was to cut corporate taxes to provide a fillip for shareholders. The failure of investment and productivity to respond was, no doubt, regrettable. But this was not the purpose of the exercise.

In the end, the economics of Ronald Reagan enriched the rich at the expense of the poor. This was a bold break with the past. In an enterprise society resting on private ownership, with markets left largely to private owners or managers of capital, the wealthy are never likely to suffer. Those who own wealth and command high incomes did well under Roosevelt, Truman, Eisenhower, and all the other postwar administrations. Their control of capital assures them a sort of perpetual prosperity that varies only in amount. But the other presidents, from Roosevelt through Carter, also pursued other, broader economic goals. They sought high levels of employment, rapid growth in goods and services, a limit to misery, the elimination of poverty. None of these were inconsistent with the prosperity of the rich or they would have been stifled. But these other goals did require a large view of the economy, a conservative view that suggested that the continuing existence of the rich depends on providing jobs for all who seek them and a minimum standard of well-being for everybody. It was the genius of Reagan to scrap much of this, to pursue measures that shifted wealth and income from the poor to the rich.

This does not mean that Reagan deliberately sought the shift, that he wanted to impoverish the poverty-stricken. No doubt he genuinely believed his policies, or those that flowed from his impulses, would ultimately raise incomes at all levels. There is nothing to suggest that he is a cruel or heartless man. But he who wills the means wills the ends. He wanted lower taxes for the wealthiest, a cut in welfare rolls, high unemployment, less inflation, and a stock-market boom. He succeeded, and the perverse shift in wealth and income followed.

When Reagan came to office, most economists would have argued he could not alter the distribution of wealth and income. If there was a stable relationship in the economics of the West it was these relative shares. In peacetime, regardless of welfare and tax measures, the richest fifth and the poorest fifth received roughly constant percentages of national income year in and year out. War changes this. Higher taxes, fuller employment, and better wages typically shift income shares from the top group to the bottom. To be sure, war does not reduce the wealth and income of the richest; their share simply rises at a slower pace than that of the newly hired unemployed. But in peacetime nothing could change the shares, or so it seemed until

Reagan. From 1947 to 1980, the poorest 20 percent among American families earned 5 percent of all incomes with little variation in any of the thirty-three years; the best-off 20 percent collected between 40 and 43 percent.[30]

By the time Reagan had achieved his tax changes, cuts in welfare, and sustained unemployment, a profound change had taken place. Between 1980 and 1984, the after-tax income of the poorest 20 percent had dropped from $6,913 to $6,391, a fall of 8 percent.[31] Income for the best-off climbed, from $37,618 to $40,880, a gain of nearly 9 percent.[32] This was the Reagan revolution. He had succeeded in redistributing income in peacetime, from the worst-off to the best.

Reagan had remarkable success in controlling a docile Congress, in translating his impulses into policy. The redistribution of wealth and income may have been an unintended consequence, but Reagan's ability to achieve his ends was matched in the postwar period only by Nixon's election-eve conquest of unemployment and inflation.

The key to Reagan's coup came in his first year. He sought and won a large cut in income taxes that was advertised as a reduction of equal percent for all classes. But in a progressive tax system, with rates rising for larger amounts of income, the richest gained not only the largest number of tax dollars saved, but also the largest benefit in relation to income.

Those with incomes above $200,000 received a tax cut of $24,982 or 12.5 percent. Those with incomes under $10,000 received $58 or 0.6 percent.[33] In addition, the rich won a sharp cut in the tax on inherited wealth and benefited from a reduction in corporation levies.

The impoverished actually suffered tax increases. To qualify for aid to dependent children, surplus food, or education assistance, families must not earn more than a certain level. Reagan cut these levels. He thereby increased taxes on earnings for the poorest, discouraged them from working. Some 225,000 families lost aid for children and one million persons were stripped of food stamps. Other welfare programs were also cut back, a total of $112 billion between 1982 and 1985.[34] In the end, poor and rich lost some welfare benefits. Those with incomes under $10,000 lost $1,340 between 1982 and 1985. This was nearly three times the $490 loss suffered by those with incomes over $80,000.[35] It was the sort of equality described by Anatole France, who observed that rich and poor are equally prohibited from sleeping under bridges at night, begging in the streets, and stealing bread.

Reagan was politically astute. Welfare for the middle class—social security benefits, medical payments for the aged—was not touched, and was even increased. People receiving these benefits frequently voted for him.

The policies yielded an impressive increase in poverty. In 1980, 6.2 million families, or 10.3 percent, were below the poverty line. Despite the economy's modest growth, by 1987, the total grew another 900,000 to 10.8 percent of American families.[36] Few of those voted for Reagan, or voted at all.

No government openly acknowledges that it is transferring wealth from the bottom to the top. Reagan found more palatable terms for what he did. In his first economic report, he said, "People should be encouraged to go about their daily lives with the right and responsibility for determining their own activities, status and achievements."[37] In other words, less reliance on welfare and lower taxes for the rich would increase the responsibility of both for their actions.

Michael Boskin, who went from prophet for Reagan to chief economist for Bush, was frank about the shift. "Unquestionably, the Reagan economic program will lead to a more unequal distribution of income," he wrote. It is true that a "non-trivial" number of the poorest households will suffer a cut in income. But "this does not itself constitute an indictment," said Boskin. Cutting top-bracket taxes is "designed to restore incentives to produce income and wealth and help restore our long-term productivity growth."[38] In sum, the old arguments got another run. Give the rich more money and they will save and invest it in the plants and machines that will enable U.S. auto makers to compete with the Japanese, Brazilians, South Koreans, and the rest. The fact that none of this happens never weakens its attraction for the well-heeled.

Other Republican experts offered less involved explanations. Weidenbaum said that "arbitrarily redistributing income to the top of the income pyramid is . . . counterproductive" because it reduced incentives for all the other layers.[39] Stockman, a mischievous guide, called it simply "greed."[40] He told Greider, "The hogs were really feeding" when the bill to cut taxes was introduced. "The greed level, the level of opportunism just got out of control." The point of the 1981 bill, said Stockman, was to slash the 70 percent rate on interest and dividend income to 50 percent; other cuts were cosmetic, "to make this palatable as a political matter." But at bottom the bill's aim was "to bring down the top rate."[41]

Weidenbaum and Stockman are plausible. Reagan's aim was to make the rich richer and discipline the poor. Fancy explanations about savings, investment, and incentive were Trojan horses. Galbraith spotted the psychological acuity behind all this. The rich require more income to work harder; the poor need less income to work harder.[42]

There was still one more episode in the Reagan revolution. That was the 1986 tax measure, a marvelously complex affair that was advertised as reform and simplification. It had two principal purposes. The top-bracket rate was again brought down smartly, this time from 50 to 28 percent. Just as important, the number of tax brackets was reduced from fourteen to two.*

The Reagan team, heavily criticized for its deficits, tried to pay for this tax cut by closing a few tax loopholes and withdrawing several of the tax blessings bestowed on corporations, some of which had already been reduced. The owners of corporations, delighted with the prospect of 28 percent, did not find this too burdensome.

More important was the near-fatal blow to the progressive income tax, a reform introduced by Woodrow Wilson. The progressive tax, the graduated tax, assesses the rich more than the poor; it takes progressively more in taxes from higher slices of income. It can be argued that this is just, that the best-off should pay the most. Regardless of ethical considerations, the progressive tax has been the single biggest automatic economic stabilizer. More than unemployment benefits, more than anything else, the progressive tax kept the economy on an even keel without new legislation. In boom times, it deflated an overheated demand; in slump, it made up for a deficient demand. By moving toward a single-bracket, flat tax, Reagan committed a radical act. For doctrine's sake, he cast away a strong anchor.

It must not be thought that he undertook this step lightly, that it was merely a whim inspired by George Shultz on a golf course. As early as 1964, Reagan had asked whether the nation had the courage to "face up to the immorality of the progressive surtax and demand a return to traditionally proportional

---

* Because of the measure's peculiar structure, a third, higher bracket of 33 percent governs incomes between $71,900 and $149,250 and then disappears. This can affect decisions for those with incomes in the zone. However, the tax collector is left essentially with two bites for most incomes, 14 and 28 percent.

taxation."[43] A progressive tax is immoral, Reagan was saying. Twenty-two years later he took a giant step toward cleansing the code of sin.

Again the faithful Boskin found economic virtue in all this. "Progressivity may to a large extent conflict with efficiency," he wrote. And "the clamors for progressive taxation are historically dated."[44] Progressivity, he argued, interferes with the will to work, savings, and investment, the familiar cry. Boskin did not explain why higher taxes are good for the poor, although his support of consumption taxes suggests that he somehow believes this to be the case.

A simple explanation of Reagan's income revolution is politics. The rich pay for both the Republican and Democratic parties but their heart is usually with the GOP. Republican voters are wealthier and Democrats poorer. "We tend to get recessions during Republican administrations," said Paul Samuelson, an unofficial Democratic advisor. "The difference between the Democrats and the Republicans is the difference in their constituencies. It's a class difference. . . . The Democrats constitute the people by and large who are around the median incomes or below. These are the ones the Republicans want to pay the price and burden of fighting inflation."[45]

This would be a more compelling argument if there had been any serious Democratic opposition to the bills shifting incomes or compressing the progressive tax. There wasn't much. Walter Fauntroy, a black representing the District of Columbia, called the 1981 tax measure the "most extraordinary attempt by any President in modern times to redistribute income from poor to rich."[46] But few Democrats were this blunt and the opposition was mostly over details.

Professor Samuelson's median-income Democrats have changed. A substantial number of blue-collar workers own their own homes and are hostile toward blacks and others who are thought to rely on welfare. Some blue-collar conservatives vote Republican; others pull Democrats closer to Republicans. Stephen Rousseas of Vassar concluded that "Reaganomics is not about growth. It is a raid on the public treasury in favor of the rich . . . which may undermine the very interests of the highly privileged classes it seeks to promote."[47] He meant that the growing pauperization of an underclass through high unemployment, slow growth, and a shifting of income from poor to rich could create a swarm of derelicts, criminals, and diseased that threaten even the best-off and best-insulated.

Perhaps the best illustration of how little Reagan was troubled by theory, how much he responded to country-club wisdom, was his treatment of foreign trade, a relatively undramatic sphere.

"I reaffirm my administration's commitment to free trade," his first Economic Report proclaimed.[48] In fact, as Niskanen, his own economist, had noted, Reagan presided over the biggest increase in American protectionism since Herbert Hoover's time.[49] Indeed, Reagan's brand was more insidious than Smoot-Hawley. That measure simply raised the tariff or tax on a wide range of imports. Efficient foreign producers could get under a tariff, could still sell in the American market. But Reagan strengthened or erected quantitative curbs on imports, fixing the volume of cars or steel or textiles that could be sold in the U.S. There is no way to defeat a quantitative curb. Moreover, and unlike a tariff, it is disguised.

The General Agreement on Tariffs and Trade, another of the major postwar institutions in which the U.S. was a founding force, frowns on quantitative curbs. But Reagan's regime ignored international undertakings as blithely as it repealed the 1946 Employment Act.

The Kennedy administration launched the postwar wave of quotas and other cartel-like arrangements with its cotton-textile pact of 1962. The technique fixes a finite limit in tons, yards, or other physical units on the imports allowed a foreign competitor. From cotton textiles, quotas and market-sharing devices were extended to other industries. Reagan brought all this, euphemistically called "managed trade," to a new peak. His best-known measures curbed imports of steel, autos, textiles, and microchips. Some were officially described as "voluntary," between willing sellers like the Japanese and unwilling American competitors. This was Orwellian language since the Japanese and other foreigners were told to agree or else.

It is estimated that the steel and auto curbs cost American consumers more than $1 billion a year in higher prices.[50] Add in textiles, other "voluntary agreements," and the anti-dumping charges indiscriminately assessed against overly vigorous foreign competitors, and the contribution to inflation becomes significant. Weidenbaum concluded that at least one-third of all manufactured goods bought abroad enter under a quota or some quantitative limit.

Reagan claimed he was pressuring foreigners to drop their own protection, their own artificial barriers to imports. In fact, the rush to quantitative curbs in the U.S. simply encouraged the same practice abroad.

Reagan's quantitative curbs on imports reserved shares of the U.S. markets for foreign producers, the rest for the U.S. This is how cartels work to keep prices up. Despite the lip service paid to competitive virtues, business and unions like protection for their own industry much as they may deplore it in others. Competition is the life of trade and the death of business, an old saw holds. Adam Smith noted the business aptitude for price conspiracies more than two centuries ago. Reagan's market-share agreements and the like simply legalize them.

Reagan's trade curbs added to inflation and worsened relations between friendly nations. They were, of course, a classic instance of the heavy hand of government. They refuted his claim to have "reduce[d] . . . regulatory bureaucracy" and thereby "unleashed the creative genius of ordinary Americans."[51] It was cartel-minded Americans who successfully urged him to leash the feared foreigners.

Taken as a whole, the Reagan performance was a curious blend of country-club belief and the distilled wisdom of the war and postwar experience. Despite the claims, Reagan and those around him were too shrewd, too much men of the world to scrap all the lessons of the past fifty years. When Treasury Secretary Regan dismissed economist Feldstein's plea for a tax increase near the bottom of a slump, Regan was responding to a sound conservative instinct.

If the Reagan administration could compress graduated income taxes, weaken a great automatic stabilizer, it also embraced the basic Keynesian elements and ran large deficits with idle resources without fear of inflation. Big arms increases and tax cuts for the wealthy offset the curbs on spending for the poor and the central bank's squeeze on money. Despite locker-room convictions, Reagan found that deficits have uses.

In its own terms, Reagan's economics worked. After the deep slump that ended in 1982, a deliberate slump to shrink inflation, there were no more recessions. Growth was slow and there was much idle plant and many idle men. But things were supposed to run like that. In the year of the 1988 election, moreover, unemployment was brought down to nearly 5 percent, a level previous administrations would have regarded as deplorable but far better than the average 7.8 percent of the seven earlier Reagan years.[52] The improvement was due in part to some modest increases in defense spending that faithfully reflected past pre-election stimuli.

Reagan's greatest contribution to modern economics was political. Like Margaret Thatcher in Britain, and Helmut Kohl in West Germany, he found that voters in the 1980s tolerated far higher levels of unemployment than in earlier postwar decades. After the worrisome inflation of the 1970s, priorities had shifted. Citizens wanted prices curbed and were willing to sacrifice the jobs of others to achieve it. They no longer feared, as did the children of the Depression, that unemployment anywhere could become contagious, that their jobs and income were threatened. They sensed that Reagan, Thatcher, and Kohl could and would keep a floor under the economy, knew how to prevent a recession from turning into depression, understood how to support modest recovery. As long as joblessness didn't spread, most voters accepted it as a necessary evil to fight inflation.

Reaganite prosperity was limited and fragile. When unemployment came down even to 5 percent, corporate appetites for price increases grew. So prices rose over 4 percent in 1988; this was more than double the advance of 1986, when the jobless rate was 7 percent. Like his predecessors, Reagan had not learned how to combine high growth and employment with stable prices. But then he did not want to.

Reagan was lucky. He was not plagued with sharp and uncontrollable increases in oil or other commodity prices. If he achieved his principal end, rewarding the rich, the nation paid a high price. His policies meant a huge loss in potential output and income, more than $1 trillion.[53] This is the market value of the output that would have been produced if Reagan had run the economy with only 4 percent of the labor force out of work.

There were other losses too. Reagan's high unemployment encouraged recruiting for the guerrilla war now practiced by blacks against whites in large cities, a physical, social, and psychological cost of some dimensions. But then whites in country clubs believe they are largely immune from such trauma, so the Reagan constituency could dismiss this cost.

NOTES

1. Stockman quoted in William Greider, *The Education of David Stockman and Other Americans* (New York: E.P. Dutton, 1981), p. 33.

2. David Stockman, *The Triumph of Politics: How the Reagan Revolution Failed* (New York: Harper & Row, 1986), p. 173.

3. Manuel Johnson, "Are Monetarism and Supply-Side Economics Compatible," in *Supply-Side Economics: A Critical Appraisal*, edited by Richard H. Fink (Frederick, Maryland: Aletheia Books, 1982), p. 410.

4. Greider, *The Education of David Stockman*, p. 49.

5. Donald T. Regan, *For the Record* (San Diego: Harcourt Brace Jovanovich, 1988), p. 191.

6. Stockman, *The Triumph of Politics*, p. 361.

7. *Ibid.*, p. 92.

8. *Ibid.*, p. 363.

9. Ronald Reagan quoted in Stephen Rousseas, *The Political Economy of Reaganomics* (Armonk, New York: M.E. Sharpe, 1982), p. 90.

10. Michael J. Boskin, *Reagan and the Economy* (San Francisco: Institute for Contemporary Studies, 1987), p. 2.

11. *Historical Tables, Budget of the United States Government* (Executive Office of the President, Office of Budget and Management, 1989), pp. 17–18.

12. Daniel Bell and Lester Thurow, *The Deficits: How Big? How Long? How Dangerous?* (New York: New York University Press, 1985), p. 95.

13. *Economic Report of the President* (Washington, D.C.: U.S. Government Printing Office, 1989), p. 352.

14. Herbert Stein, *Presidential Economics* (Washington, D.C.: American Enterprise Institute, 1988), p. 289.

15. Franco Modigliani, "Government Deficits, Inflation and Future Generations," in *Deficits: How Big and How Bad* (Toronto, Canada: Ontario Economic Council, 1983), p. 63.

16. James Tobin, *Policies for Prosperity: Essays in a Keynesian Mode* (Brighton, England: Wheatsheaf Books, 1987), p. 173.

17. *Economic Report of the President* (Washington, D.C.: U.S. Government Printing Office, 1987), p. 66.

18. *Economic Report of the President*, 1989, pp. 308, 369.

19. *Ibid.*, p. 360.

20. Robert Lekachman, *Visions and Nightmares* (New York: Macmillan, 1987), p. 156.

21. Peter G. Peterson quoted in Samuel Bowles, David M. Gordon, and Thomas E. Weisskopf, *Beyond the Waste Land* (Garden City, New York: Anchor Press, 1983), p. 3.

22. *Reducing the Deficit: Spending and Revenue Options* (Washington, D.C.: Congressional Budget Office, February 1983), p. 4.

23. Samuel Bowles et al., *Beyond the Waste Land*, p. 58.

24. Barry P. Bosworth, *Tax Incentives and Economic Growth* (Washington, D.C.: Brookings Institution, 1984), pp. 23–4.

25. Lester Thurow, "Slow Economic Growth," in Fink, *Supply-Side Economics*, p. 359.

26. Stein, *Presidential Economics*, p. 277.

27. *Value Line Investment Survey* (New York: Value Line, Inc., 1989), pp. 410, 1009.

28. *Ibid.*, p. 296.

29. Richard A. Musgrave, "The Reagan Administration's Fiscal Policy: A Critique," in *Reaganomics*, edited by William Craig Stubblebine and Thomas D. Willett (San Francisco: ICS Press, 1983), p. 116.

30. Douglas A. Hibbs, Jr., *The American Political Economy* (Cambridge: Harvard University Press, 1987), p. 78.

31. *Ibid.*, p. 319.

32. *Ibid.*, p. 319.

33. Thomas B. Edsall, *The New Politics of Inequality* (New York: W.W. Norton, 1984), p. 205.

34. *Ibid.*, pp. 227–8.

35. *Ibid.*, p. 206.

36. *Economic Report of the President*, 1989, p. 342.

37. *Economic Report of the President* (Washington, D.C.: U.S. Government Printing Office, 1982), p. 3.

38. Michael J. Boskin, "Distributional Effects of the Reagan Program," in Stubblebine and Willett, *Reaganomics*, pp. 193–8.

39. Murray Weidenbaum, *Rendezvous with Reality* (New York: Basic Books, 1988), p. 18.

40. Greider, *The Education of David Stockman*, p. 58.

41. *Ibid.*, p. 49.

42. Rousseas, *The Political Economy of Reaganomics*, p. 43.

43. Ronald Reagan quoted in William A. Niskanen, *Reaganomics* (Oxford: Oxford University Press, 1988), p. 86.

44. Boskin, *Reagan and the Economy*, p. 145.

45. Paul Samuelson quoted in Hibbs, *The American Political Economy*, p. 213.

46. Walter Fauntry quoted in *ibid.*, p. 296.

47. Rousseas, *The Political Economy of Reaganomics*, p. 121.

48. *Economic Report of the President*, 1982, p. 8.

49. "Talking Loudly and Carrying a Crowbar," *Economist*, April 29, 1989, p. 23.

50. Phillip Cagan, editor, *Deficits, Taxes, and Economic Adjustments* (Washington, D.C.: American Enterprise Institute, 1987), p. 115.

51. *Economic Report of the President*, 1989, p. 3.

52. *Ibid.*, p. 352.

53. Assuming a 4% rate of structural unemployment.

VII

Keynes Armed

Seven months after the Soviet Union exploded its first nuclear device in 1949, the Truman administration ordered a new plan to assure national security, to counter the breach in the U.S. monopoly of nuclear weapons. Paul Nitze, head of the State Department's Policy Planning Staff, a key Cold War figure for nearly forty years, was chosen to head a team of State and Defense Department officials. Like many government committees, the officials were agreed before they began. Quite simply, a vast increase in military outlays was required to regain U.S. supremacy. The committee's task was to provide a rationale, a justification for what had already been decided. Their report, perhaps the single most important strategic document in the postwar period, was designated NSC 68.

NSC 68 did not call for a specific increase in arms spending, but Nitze and the others had a clear goal in mind. They wanted to increase the Pentagon's budget from $13 billion to $35 billion,[1] nearly tripling expenditures. Inevitably, the Nitze group had to answer this question: could the U.S. afford it? The answer was quite clear. NSC 68 said: "From the point of view of the economy as a whole, the program might not result in a real decrease in the standard of living, for the economic effects of the program might be to increase the gross national product by more than the amount being absorbed for additional military and foreign assistance purposes."[2]

The central lesson of World War II had been fully absorbed, at least in the higher reaches of government. A big increase in military spending need not reduce civilian living standards. Instead, the military stimulus could expand total output and actually leave consumers better off than before. Expanded output, the document said, "would permit and might itself be aided by, a buildup of the United States and the free world; furthermore, if a dynamic expansion of the economy were achieved, the necessary buildup could be accomplished without a decrease in the national standard of living because the required resources could be obtained by siphoning off a part of the annual increment in the gross national product."[3]

Here was the best of all possible worlds. Stern necessity compelled confronting the Russians with more force; virtuous behavior would yield material rewards for all. Although the document was stamped top secret, there was nothing original in its economics. The war had focused the minds of serious men on the link between arms, spending, and prosperity in an economy prone to high levels of unemployment.

Three years earlier, another top-secret committee, the Special "Ad Hoc" Committee, faced a similar problem. The Secretary of State, George C. Marshall, was deeply troubled by the precarious state of politics and economics in France, Italy, Greece, Turkey, and other nations, mostly in Western Europe. Encouraged by Under Secretary Dean Acheson, Marshall was thinking early in 1947 of giving the Europeans large amounts of dollars to better withstand Soviet designs. The "Ad Hoc" Committee, W. A. Eddy of State, Brigadier General George A Lincoln and Rear Admiral E. T. Wooldridge, had to decide among other issues whether the U.S. could afford a Marshall Plan. It reported that American customers abroad were running out of dollars and could not sustain the 1946–47 rate of imports beyond twelve to eighteen months. The Committee said: "The President's Council of Economic Advisers has indicated that a slight business recession may be anticipated sometime within the next twelve months. A substantial decline in the United States export surplus would have a depressing effect on business activity and employment . . . if the export decline happened to coincide with weakness in the domestic economy, the effect on production, prices and employment might be most serious."[4]

Thus, an aid scheme to provide dollars for friendly foreign customers would not only serve the anti-Communist crusade but also benefit the domestic economy. U.S. exporters of farm and industrial produce would be assured of a demand for their goods—effective demand, desire backed by cash—at the very moment that the domestic economy was threatened with slump. Virtue and interest had again united. A few months later in early June, Marshall went to Harvard and announced his program of aid.

It is important not to misunderstand what happened here. The Marshall Plan and NSC 68 were decisive stages in the Cold War. But they were not designed primarily to shore up the American economy. The Cold War was not, as Marxists have sometimes claimed, primarily a device to rationalize military outlays for an economy otherwise threatened with slump and unemployment. The Cold War was politically motivated, partly by a wish to perpetuate the postwar dominance of the U.S., partly by a genuine fear of Russian expansion across Western Europe. Even a casual reading of the "Ad Hoc" Committee report and NSC 68 makes clear that geopolitical considerations came first. Happily, the authors of the large aid program and the big expansion in military outlays discovered that their schemes had useful side effects for the domestic economy.

The fact is that arms spending and its related programs for foreign aid and space have been a great bulwark to the postwar economy. In fat years and lean, high levels of military outlays (ranging from 5 percent to 3 percent of the economy since 1950)[5] have put a floor under effective demand, a brake on every slide. It is spending that can be turned on rapidly, although it is hard to turn off. The mere announcement of a speedup in defense orders will expand hiring, improve the bank balances of large contractors, stimulate the economies of communities where arms plants are located, and multiply its blessings by increasing incomes for the providers of goods and services to the newly hired.

Before the end of the war, Sherwood Fine, the Treasury analyst, predicted that military outlays would and must remain high in peacetime to counter the cutbacks of demobilization.[6] As it turned out, demobilization did not harm the economy because of suppressed demand backed with cash. But over the long postwar period, Fine was right. High arms outlays have limited the damage from a drop in demand. In the postwar period, the Federal government has sustained about 20 percent of all spending. Military and space outlays now account for about three-quarters of the goods and services bought by the government.[7]

After 1948, the economy's output rarely matched its potential except under the stimulus of war outlays. Even in the fat years, Robert Aaron Gordon observed, unemployment was well above the 3.3 percent average of the booming twenties. Indeed, joblessness fell below 4 percent only during and immediately after World War II and in the Korean and Vietnamese wars.[8] Eisen-

204

hower's brief boom from 1955 to 1957 was the sole period since 1929 when the jobless rate even approached the 4 percent target without enlarged military spending or the suppressed demand created by war.[9]

Some economists, particularly liberal Democrats, are distressed at suggestions that postwar prosperity is linked to arms and wars. James Tobin of the Kennedy council has vehemently insisted that a wall separates guns and civilian wealth. "Postwar prosperity obviously did not require defense spending on anything like the scale observed," he said. However, he added, "It is true that the postwar size of the Federal budget has made economic stabilization an easier task than it was before 1940." But "these stabilization dividends of large defense spending were certainly unintended."[10]

Wilfred Lewis, the Brookings expert on postwar cycles, also argued that the defense outlays that spurred recovery from the 1958 and 1961 recessions were "fortuitous."[11] This raises a question: how often in economics must two events occur together before more than coincidence is involved?

Tobin contended that each large increment in arms outlays could be traced to some international crisis. He offered a chronology in support. The trouble is that his chronology includes crises when no arms buildup took place as well as those when it did. Moreover, what is a crisis lies in the eye of the beholder. In the past, the Navy ritually announced that a Soviet sub had been sighted off the Atlantic Coast at appropriations time in early spring. This "crisis" assured swift passage of the Navy's request.

Charles Schultze, Carter's chief economist, is another defender of the orthodox faith. "The American economy does not need the stimulus of a war to reach and maintain economic growth and prosperity," he said in 1967.[12] This was the peak of

Vietnam spending, which finally brought unemployment below the Kennedy target of 4 percent. Schultze was literally correct, but politically naïve. The economy does not require an arms stimulus but it is easier to obtain than a national program of health care.

Arthur Okun, Johnson's economic adviser, noted that there had been a modest fall in defense spending in mid-1962 and yet the economy expanded. This was so. But there had already been an increase in arms spending in 1961 for the Berlin crisis and other reasons. It had helped pull the economy out of the last Eisenhower slump and laid the basis for Okun's 1962 expansion.

The postwar history is clear. Recovery from every slump has been stimulated by increased Pentagon spending.[13] Tobin's argument that all this was unintended seems to stretch chance beyond prudent limits.

Keynes, the author of modern fiscal policy, was much less squeamish than his disciples. In 1940, he wrote in *The New Republic*, "It is, it seems, politically impossible for a capitalist democracy to organize expenditure on the scale necessary to make the grand experiment which would prove my case—except in war conditions."

Addressing the U.S., he said, "Your war preparation, so far from requiring a sacrifice, will be the stimulus which neither victory nor the defeat of the New Deal could give you, to greater individual consumption and a higher standard of life. You can still invest more and spend more."[14]

Adam Smith, who seems to have anticipated almost everything, said: "In the midst of the most destructive foreign war, therefore, the greater part of manufactures may flourish greatly; and, on the contrary, they may decline on the return of peace. They may flourish amidst the ruin of their country and begin to decay upon the return of its prosperity."[15] Smith might have admired the contemporary fashion: spending on arms to prevent the decay of manufactures, rarely spilling blood in war.

One of the earliest and most pungent descriptions of the new economy came from a sociologist, Daniel Bell. He saw that economic stabilization "will be maintained by government" spending, about 20 percent of total output. "This high federal budget is fixed—for the foreseeable future—by the nature of the international tensions and by the indebtedness of the past." There is a Republican and Democratic agreement on "semi-war," and "it inevitably casts government in the role of controller and dominator of the economy."[16] Bell is clear; the wide agreement on the Soviet threat forces arms outlays to a level that stabilizes the economy.

Conservatives, on the whole, have been far readier than liberals to acknowledge the economic importance, even the gains, from arms spending. Some have been almost lyrical. Frank Pace, the Army Secretary, said in 1957 that "defense spending per se might be countenanced on economic grounds alone as a stimulator of the national metabolism."[17] He spoke just as the metabolism was running low, with another recession looming. Frank Carlucci, a Reagan Defense Secretary, observed in 1983 that less than 70 percent of the country's manufacturing plant was at work and more than one worker in ten was unemployed. In such circumstances, he said, "defense investments are an important factor in a stronger GNP. . . . We estimate that each $10 billion cut in defense spending leads to the loss of 350,000 private sector jobs."[18] There was the customary disclaimer. "Impressive as some of these economic benefits may be . . . they should not be seen as a justification for defense spending. Only the military threats we face should justify the amount of money we spend."[19]

Similarly, Charles J. Hitch, comptroller for McNamara at the Pentagon, and Roland H. McKean said that arms spending "makes a deficiency of total demand less probable." And "We do not have to have defense programs in order to avoid unemployment. . . . Nevertheless . . . a large security budget is an anti-deflationary force."[20]

John Connally, at various times a leading Democrat and a Republican Treasury Secretary, was blunt. Asked what Lockheed, a large arms seller, was required to perform in return for a $250 million government loan, Connally replied scornfully, "What do we care whether they perform. We are guaranteeing them a $250 million loan . . . so they can provide employment for 31,000 people . . . at a time when we desperately need that type of employment."[21] Hoover would have understood. This was an RFC-style loan, keeping a bankrupt manufacturer afloat.

To be sure, some of these conservatives were special pleaders. The Pentagon officials, Pace, Hitch, Carlucci, praised the economic consequences of arms spending to defend their budgets, seeking more funds to enhance their agency's prestige and power. Nevertheless, businessmen adopted their view, even executives with little direct stake in military spending. Colby H. Chandler, the chief executive officer of Eastman Kodak, spoke for legions. Manufacturing, he said, benefits from increases in Pentagon spending, is hurt by cuts. "Defense cutbacks," he warned, "will . . . lead to rather concentrated employment reductions."[22] The business community was evidently pleased with Reagan's arms stimulus and feared that successors might be more grudging.

From a corporate standpoint, there is one drawback to arms outlays. They are too volatile and disturb long-range planning. They rise and fall, igniting slumps and booms. Bert Hickman of the Brookings Institution found that military spending is twice as unstable as business investment, commonly thought to be the great variable in total demand.[23] If weapons outlays could only increase by a fixed yearly amount, the problem would disappear. But that would reveal the unpleasant fact that this spending has more to do with economic than military security.

There is anyway an ambivalent strain in business thinking. Military outlays are welcomed for the lift they give to the economy but there is a feeling that this is somehow illegitimate. This vague concern affects Republicans and Democrats. Gabriel Hauge, an Eisenhower economist, said he didn't want a "military WPA to keep the economy fully employed." Hauge said, "If we can't keep the economy humming without that, we had better turn in our suits right now."[24]

As it happened, Eisenhower fought two of the three slumps in his tenure with enlarged arms or space outlays. His chief economist, Arthur Burns, embodied the contradictions.

"At at time of general economic slack," Burns wrote, "the government may begin to look upon military spending as if it were a favored public program. . . . Fortunately, our government officials have generally been reluctant to tamper with something so fundamental to the nation as its defense establishment."[25]

Burns must have forgotten that a few years earlier he was a high government adviser when Eisenhower accelerated defense orders to help end the 1954 slump. A few years later, moreover, Burns urged Nixon to seek enlarged arms spending to save the 1960 election.

It is hard to avoid using the Pentagon for domestic economics and politics. As Hitch said, "Certainly the defense budget is a large and powerful tool for the government, and one is tempted to seek its uses to solve an array of problems."[26]

Temptation is the crucial word. How can the most high-minded political or business leader resist so splendid a device to cure slump, a lack of demand? In fact, not many can.

In the prosperous postwar years, American presidents and their advisers were keenly conscious that the new U.S. role, defender of nations everywhere against potential Communist aggression, entailed little economic sacrifice. As early as the Marshall Plan, high officials in all spheres understood that geo-political outlays in an economy running below full employment could only strengthen output and income. Whatever the public reasons advanced for this spending, leaders knew it brought an economic dividend.

The first President to use the Pentagon as a countercyclical device was Eisenhower in 1954. It wasn't much. Eisenhower ordered a step-up in Federal spending of only $545 million, of which $400 million was military.[27] But it broke with the past and it was done on the advice of both Hauge and Burns.[28]

This may seem to contradict Eisenhower's farewell speech and his warning of the political danger from the military and its industrial suppliers. Eisenhower, a man far more complicated than his public pose, was of several minds about the complex he named. He had even assisted at its birth. As Army Chief of Staff in 1946, he wrote a memorandum urging that the wartime collaboration of scientists, businessmen, and military should be continued. "This pattern of interrogation [apparently meaning an exchange of ideas] must be translated into a peacetime coun-terpart," he said.[29] Contracts should be given to scientists and industrialists to conduct fundamental research into military re-quirements. They should be freed from simply responding to the Army's demands for weapons with given characteristics, Eisenhower said. This is one key to the strength of the complex today. Private contractors rather than the Pentagon frequently determine the threat and design a system to combat it. The military and its suppliers enjoy a common interest in maximizing defense outlays.

So Eisenhower did not hesitate in the 1958 slump any more than he did in 1954. His economic report for 1959 said tersely, "the acceleration of defense procurement, which was being undertaken in line with national security policy, exerted an expensive effect."[30] The defense speedup in 1958 was dwarfed by outlays for the newly launched space race. It is commonly held that the Russian Sputnik, the first vehicle in orbit, solved the 1958 recession. It certainly launched a vast new spending program in the U.S., but Eisenhower was probably too sophisticated to believe that space outlays contributed much to national defense. Sherman Adams said that the President was particularly skeptical about a lunar probe. Adams reported that the President said he would rather have one good nuclear-armed Redstone missile than a rocket that could hit the moon. We have no enemies on the moon, Eisenhower observed tartly.[31]

No matter. Eisenhower understood that spending for space was easier to get through Congress then than spending for guns, planes, or ships. For the second time, Eisenhower used military money or its space equivalent to end a slump.

Why then did he deny Nixon, urged on by the prescient Burns, in 1960? There was no philosophical reason for Eisenhower to reject his Vice President's plea for an injection of military spending that could ward off a slump and save Nixon's electoral prospects. Actually, in that third and last recession of his tenure, Eisenhower did resort to arms for a countercyclical spurt in demand. But he moved too late to help Nixon. In August of 1960, just three months before the election, Ike released $476 million that had been appropriated for the Polaris missile, the Strategic Air Command, faster development of the B-70 bomber, and other items.[32]

The reason Eisenhower moved so late is buried in the troubled relationship between any President and his Vice President. Rexford Guy Tugwell's remarkable *The Art of Politics*, based on firsthand observation of Roosevelt, La Guardia and Muñoz Marin, suggests that great leaders can't stand the thought of succession, of yielding their places.[33] Eisenhower anyway preferred Treasury Secretary Anderson to Nixon; Anderson had urged restraints on spending even in the slump. So Eisenhower's belated use of the military stimulus in 1960, too little and too late, offered a major issue to the young Democrat who did succeed.

Eisenhower then was not only the first Keynesian president in fact, he was the first military Keynesian as well.

Walter Heller, Kennedy's chief economist, said that "the big income tax cut in 1946 . . . is rightfully regarded as the most overt and dramatic expression of the new approach to economic policy."[34] That is certainly the popular view. But the Kennedy team used arms and space spending even earlier to counter slump, although it was reluctant to say so. To be sure, Heller himself was candid enough to recognize the Pentagon's role in ending the recession that Kennedy inherited from Eisenhower. Heller's economic report in 1962 said that "increased Federal activity . . . was a major force—probably the principal driving force—of our recovery of 1961.[35] . . . The largest increase in expenditures," the report said, "came in the areas of defense and space exploration."

Of course, "The programs were expanded, for reasons of national security, not for economic stabilization."[36] Whatever the motive, the Kennedy team enlarged defense and space outlays by $11 billion from 1960 to 1965.[37] As it happens, this was just equal to the more heavily advertised slash in personal income taxes. For Kennedy, the arms stimulus was as important as the innovative tax cut.

Hugh G. Mosley regards the Kennedy era as "the paradigm of military Keynesism in recent U.S. economic policy."[38] He wrote, however, before the great burst of arms outlays in the Reagan presidency.

Under Johnson, military spending was too much of a good thing. His failure to attack the Vietnam inflation drove the economy to its lean years. As President, Nixon used every available tool but principally military outlays to reduce unemployment and provoke a boomlet in time for his reelection. Herbert Stein, Nixon's economist, was frank. Many government agencies simply weren't spending enough but "finally the Department of Defense came to our rescue when they expended much money, which was probably some phony outlay," Stein recalled.[39]

James Schlesinger, Defense Secretary for President Ford, was also open. Schlesinger said he had inserted from $1 to $5 billion in his new budget for 1974, "as a measure of economic stimulation."[40] Later, with the economy again in recession, Schlesinger told his top assistants they must speed the pace at which funds were obligated or committed.[41] The Pentagon's comptroller would oversee all this to ensure that the money poured out.

Under Reagan, of course, Pentagon money flooded a deeply depressed economy. The administration's own officials have acknowledged what was anyway apparent. There was no attempt to fix priorities, no military rationale for much that was spent. There was, however, a sound economic reason. With the tax cut, military spending was the source for recovery.

Nixon, both the most blunt and most secretive of presidents, once let the cat out of the bag at a press conference. Stung by charges that he had not done enough to reduce unemployment, Nixon retorted, "We want to remember. We did not have low unemployment except at the cost of war between 1961 and 1969."[42] This was partisan, focusing on years when Democrats were in the White House. But it probably reflected the view of all presidents since Truman, that high employment can be achieved only with a big increase in arms outlays, the kind associated with war.

In 1972, the Congressional Joint Economic Committee objected to Nixon's implicit strategy. "The defense program should not be used for purposes of stimulating the economy. The only legitimate function of the defense program is to provide the military requirements for national security."[43] The committee, a powerless vehicle, could take the moral high ground here. In practice, Congress rarely opposes and frequently demands even more spending for arms.

The Arms Control and Disarmament Agency is the governmental unit charged with negotiating accords to reduce military budgets. It has testified that its task is virtually hopeless.

"It is generally agreed," ACDA said in 1962, "that the greatly expanded public sector since World War II, resulting from heavy defense expenditures, has provided additional protection against depression, since this sector is not responsive to contraction in the private sector and has provided a buffer or balance wheel in the economy."[44]

The peace agency records fact. All presidents since Truman have used defense outlays to fight slump.[45] They play a decisive role in stabilizing the economy.

There is no simple way of determining whether the $4 trillion outlay[46] for arms since the end of the war has been spent chiefly for defense or for economic stabilization. Both motives have clearly played a part. So have the bureaucratic concerns of flag-rank officers. If arms are bought primarily for nonmilitary reasons, economists and citizens can ask why the money isn't better spent on civilian purposes or by civilians through tax cuts. One clue to the real purpose of arms outlays lies in the history of the wartime maneuvers by the Army Air Corps to transform itself into an independent Air Force. A thoughtful account by Colonel Percy McCoy Smith, a West Point instructor, makes clear that the highest-ranking officers were far more concerned with bureaucratic power, gaining an independent status, than with national defense.[47]

The Air Force began its drive to become a separate and equal service in 1943. The planners, directed by General Henry H. Arnold, aimed not only for a separate service but also a major share of the postwar military budget. To achieve these goals, Arnold's team fixed on the bomber as the centerpiece for their strategy. Unless they could make a case for a large bomber force, they feared they would lose the battle for independence. If, for example, they urged tactical aircraft and support of ground troops, the Army might argue it should retain the air branch. So all postwar planning was based on the critical importance of the bomber.

The trouble with this was that World War II had shown that the bomber has limited use. The U.S. Strategic Bombing Survey demonstrated that German weapons production actually increased under the pounding of Allied bombers. Frills were cut; output was rationalized. German armament production tripled between February 1942 and the peak of July 1944, when the ground invasion of Europe finally brought it down.[48] Strategic bombing, the destruction of war industry, had failed. The Air Force planners, however, had to pretend this critical fact was not so or risk their bid for independence.

"Instead of making the common mistake of planning to fight the next war with weapons and techniques that had been effective in the last, the Air Corps planners were laying plans to conduct the next war using weapons and techniques that had been proven largely ineffective in the present war," Smith wrote.[49]

To support the case for bombers, Arnold's team claimed that prostrate Germany and Japan were the likeliest postwar enemies because they could one day manufacture opposing bombers. Any potential Soviet threat was dismissed with flat-earth, Mercator-projection maps that grossly exaggerated the distance across the North Polar route. To increase the number of planes in the new Air Force, the planners pushed for bases in the Pacific and the Caribbean where there were no threats against the U.S. Arnold's team even urged a large Air Force to keep war plants busy in peacetime.

The assorted fictions worked so well that the Air Force was created with 70 groups and 400,000 men. The older services, filled with jealousy and admiration, learned to copy the Air Force techniques to win their share of the defense budget.

Air Force planning, Smith concluded, was "not based on trying to analyze postwar international relations in order to design an Air Force that would meet the dangers to the United States national security. . . . Instead the planning was done to gain autonomy for the postwar Air Force."[50]

The Naval equivalent of the big bomber is the aircraft carrier with a large protective flotilla that provides jobs for admirals and work for contractors, at multi-billion-dollar prices. By 1984, there were fifteen carrier groups that cost $9.5 billion each.[51] Apart from expense, General James Doolittle observed that the carrier has "two attributes. One attribute is that it can move about; the other attribute is that it can be sunk."[52] Doolittle was contending that the carriers have the same military value as the bombers he flew.

Indeed, writers on strategy like Edward Luttwak have argued that it is not clear why the U.S. needs a large Navy at all. A blockade against Russia, the putative enemy, must be ineffective because the Soviet invasion routes are overland. There is no vulnerable Soviet coast nor are there strategic Soviet islands to defend. Total defeat of the Soviet Navy, Luttwak said, could not halt a Soviet invasion of Western Europe.

The Army relies on equally dubious weapons. In Vietnam, infantrymen threw away the complicated M-16 rifle and seized the more reliable Soviet AK-47. Army tanks, notably the Sheridan, perform badly in combat and endanger their own crews.

Indeed, it is hard to find many postwar weapons that serve a combat purpose. The Poseidon missile for submarines was built to penetrate what was advertised as a Soviet defense against missiles, an anti-ballistic missile system or ABM. The Soviet ABM was in fact an AA, an anti-aircraft defense against planes. At a cost of $18 billion,[53] the SAGE Air Defense system was constructed to guard against Soviet bombers. The Soviets, it turned out, had only a few and some, flying at low altitude, could get inside SAGE. The Navy ordered an F-14 fighter complete with Phoenix missile to fly at a distance from their carriers to destroy Soviet bombers. But as it happens, the Soviets do not have enough bombers to pose any threat against the fleet at sea. The F-14 was unneeded.

Military need is one thing, however; economic and political requirements are another. Candidate John Kennedy campaigned strongly against a "missile gap," an alleged Soviet superiority in missiles. In office he found there was no gap but anyway ordered an increase in U.S. missiles. The White House historian Arthur Schlesinger said Kennedy did so to soothe Air Force generals upset at the loss of a new bomber project.

The Central Intelligence Agency frequently supports the Pentagon's mission to gain more funds by producing inflated estimates of Soviet arms expenditures. The agency has calculated Soviet outlays by assuming that a Russian tank or plane costs the Soviet Union what a similar weapon costs in the inflated environment of military contracting in the U.S. This, of course, has nothing to do with intelligence and a great deal to do with marketing. The cost to the Soviets of a weapon is the opportunity cost of using the resources for some civilian good.

The CIA method is useful, however, for producing an artificial gap. Thus the agency assumes that the Soviet military-pay bill is twice that of the U.S. because Soviet services are twice as large. This is a remarkable fiction since Soviet soldiers and sailors are badly paid even by Russian standards. But when the Congress increases pay of American servicemen, the CIA can show an instant gap, contending that the Soviet outlays have expanded by twice the U.S. increase.

The gaps are closed by more spending but not by stronger defense. Richard Stubbing, a veteran analyst in the Budget Bureau, looked at the electronic brains of planes and missiles beginning in the 1950s. Only 4 of 13 were reliable. In the next decade, Stubbing found not a single one of thirteen weapons was up to standard.[54] In the 1980s, the analyst discovered still more weapons were breaking down more frequently than promised.[55] The costliest may well be the Stealth bomber, which could emerge as the first billion-dollar plane. It had been assigned three different missions and nobody is quite sure what it is for except to spend money on.

It should not be assumed that the generals and admirals in

charge of procurement and their nominal civilian masters are knaves or fools. They do not deliberately equip pilots, sailors, or soldiers with weapons that don't work against threats that don't exist. They are rational men and some rational purpose must lie behind trillions of dollars of production with a limited and sometimes negative military value.

What then is going on?

Some of the answers can be found in the Air Force's postwar plans. The planners dismissed genuine potential threats and chose the bomber as their weapon to promote careers. Personal interest drove Air Force generals to select a weapon of dubious utility.

In other services, weapons are similarly chosen to protect a traditional mission or stake out a claim for a new one. The Soviet Union may have little to fear from a carrier or a Navy of six hundred ships but admirals must fear for their jobs if these vessels are sunk in the appropriations skirmishes. Eisenhower again understood the forces at work. In his State of the Union address in 1958, he said that service rivalries "find expression in Congressional and press activities which become particularly conspicuous in struggles over new weapons, funds and publicity."[56]

If power and promotion drive the flag officers, their civilian colleagues in the Pentagon and the White House approve the outlays because they serve broader political interests. At this level, few can believe that a vulnerable plane, a slow-moving tank, or a defective rifle protects the nation against an aggressor. The outlays, however, do serve to nourish a large aerospace industry and its suppliers. They prevent an increase in unemployment, desirable even in a Reagan administration that uses the idle to suppress wages and prices. Increased military spending, quickly turned on, is especially helpful at election time, when every politician in office wants a rising economy. Arms outlays, as Arthur Burns recognized, are an easy way to counter a slump.

It must not be thought that bureaucratic, economic, and political considerations are the sole determinants of Pentagon purchasing. The admirals, generals, assistant secretaries in the Pentagon, the President and his aides, are surely as patriotic as any and must believe at least some of what they say about defending against a Soviet or Libyan or Iranian or Grenadian or Lebanese or Afghan or Cuban or Nicaraguan or Panamanian threat. No doubt they wished the weapons worked better and were better suited for their task. But in the end what matters most is protecting or expanding a service mission, countering slump, winning an election. These are the priorities.

There is an interesting implication in all this. The Pentagon really does not believe in war. If the admirals and generals thought a conflict with the Soviet Union or anyone else of size was likely, they could not countenance inappropriate and ineffective weapons and go to such lengths to cover up the defects of the arms. If they thought war was imminent or even possible, they would surely seek to obtain the maximum military effectiveness for each outlay of dollars, more bang for a buck. But flag-rank officers know better than most that war is unthinkable, that a conflict with a major power threatens to obliterate both.

A. Ernest Fitzgerald, an industrial engineer who works for the Air Force, has written that the Pentagon doesn't really like war. In wartime, outlays for boots, blankets, beans, buttons, and bullets push aside the more expensive, costlier, gaudier electronic weapons. "The Pentagon prays that war will never really happen," Fitzgerald writes, "but it loves its main mission in life, eternally preparing for war." Fitzgerald once heard an Air Force general complain that he saw little point to the war in

Vietnam "except that it's helping to buy us a new tactical air force."[57] There speaks the authentic voice of a modern military bureaucrat.

The view at the top of the Pentagon is relaxed. Joseph Sherick, the Defense Department's civilian inspector general, has explained the loose attitude toward performance. The generals and admirals in charge of procurement, said Sherick, "salve their conscience [by saying], 'Well, we'll never have a war and we won't use that and if we do, we'll always fire 10 of them anyway.' "[58]

What is envisaged and indeed practiced is a "relentless, implacable but ultimately benign struggle with the Soviet Union," John Kenneth Galbraith has written.[59]

Above all, however, are the politico-economic concerns of the civilians at the Pentagon and in the White House. The inutility of the arsenal, the invention of threat, the use of military budgets for private purposes can only be understood if the higher levels of civilian and military government tacitly agree that major war has become technologically obsolete.

If the weapons work badly they do cost a lot. To understand postwar economic policy, it is necessary to see why. The usual reason given is that modern weapons are very intricate, at the frontiers of science. They are systems, not weapons. There are simpler explanations. Contractors, suppliers, have no incentives to hold costs down; quite the reverse. Most work on cost-plus contracts that pay for all costs of production and overhead plus a percentage for profits. The higher the cost, the greater the profit.

The buyers, the military, have no reason to hold down costs either. A Navy captain or admiral is promoted for expanding his program. Limiting costs will get him nothing except perhaps an uncomfortable assignment. The same is true for Army and Air

Force colonels and generals. Their rank depends on the size of their program, the number of people they supervise. This is a well-recognized principle in private industry.

There is an even stronger incentive for the captains and colonels to approve the mounting costs, test failures, and substandard performance of the weapons they supervise. Many look forward to a future with the contractors they are supposedly supervising. Hundreds of officers and ranking civilians retire from the Pentagon each year to be hired promptly by the arms makers. It abuses human nature to expect that the colonel in charge of developing a weapon at Lockheed, Grumman, McDonnell Douglas, General Dynamics, or anywhere else is likely to complain of waste or deception or inefficiency when he counts on Lockheed, Grumman, McDonnell Douglas, or General Dynamics to provide him with an agreeable career after he leaves the service. Military contracting is a collusive world, with the agents of the Pentagon buyer collaborating closely with the seller to the mutual profit of both. This is no trivial affair. The General Accounting Office counted 30,000 majors or higher officers who retired from the Defense Department in 1983–84. No fewer than 5700—almost one in five—found berths in the aerospace industry.[60]

The Pentagon signals its indifference to economy and efficiency by choosing contractors on the basis of their economic need rather than selecting the best design. The Air Force thought McDonnell Douglas had produced the best blueprint for a successor to the C-5A transport. But Defense Secretary Caspar Weinberger overruled the generals because Lockheed needed the business.[61] One of his predecessors, Donald Rumsfeld, did much the same with a tank. Chrysler proposed a costlier model than its rivals but Chrysler was in deep trouble in 1976 and got the order.[62]

The purpose of much Pentagon spending is not to procure an increment of defense but to spend. Spurred by its research and development teams, urged on by contractors, Pentagon purchasing aims at producing the costliest machine, not the most reliable or efficient one.

There is no conspiracy in this arrangement, uniting a handful of producers, an oligopoly, with a single buyer, the Pentagon, a monopsony, an arrangement blessed by the executive and legislative branches of government, most unions and all business. This is, said Walter Adams, "a natural coalition of interest groups with an economic, political or professional stake in defense and space."[63] The arrangement operates without checks because there is no countervailing force, no group with an interest in controlling it. The contractors, the instruments for distributing funds, Adams continued, are "protected, privileged and subsidized by the state . . . a form of private socialism—a type of social planning . . . blending private economic power and public political power."[64]

The intimacy between the Pentagon and its large suppliers is wasteful but not catastrophic. As long as no serious war is contemplated, the military machine can be employed chiefly to spur domestic spending and bureaucratic ambition.

Military spending, however, is not uniquely endowed; other forms of spending could also bolster the economy. If stimulus is required, why not employ some other fiscal policy? A tax cut, as Kennedy and Johnson demonstrated in 1964, can stimulate demand. Those who receive it save a modest portion of their enlarged income and spend the rest, increasing the demand and hence the output of goods and services. The trouble is that a tax cut, unlike a spending program, is a discrete or unique event. It does not lend itself easily to renewal, year after year, like a program to produce Stealth bombers. Moreover, there is a finite limit to tax cutting. A 10 percent cut for seven successive years would wipe out more than half the tax base. Each succeeding cut would produce a decreasing stimulus and therefore provide a successively weaker increment to demand. A large, almost self-renewing spending program suffers from none of these defects.

Why not substitute civilian expenditures for military? Surely there are great unfilled needs to house the homeless or the badly housed, treat the sick, teach those in inferior schools, provide comfortable and rapid mass transit for the tens of millions suffering daily in New York, Chicago, and elsewhere.

Galbraith offers the answer: "It was long a commonplace of Keynesian economics that civilian spending, similarly supported by a progressive tax system, would serve just as well the goals of fiscal stability as military spending. This argument which, alas, I have used myself on occasion was, I am now persuaded, wrong—an exercise in apologetics. Civilian spending does not evoke the same support as does military spending on a large scale."[65]

Hitch, the McNamara comptroller, and McKean said much the same thing.[66] The big defense budgets of World War II and after Korea strengthened the economy. Perhaps other means could have been used; they weren't found or applied.

The central point is that civilian spending not only lacks support, it provokes strenuous opposition. Large government outlays for civilian purposes challenge the business belief that economic decisions and economic welfare flow from private markets. Even the businessmen most heavily subsidized by government, aerospace contractors, fervently hold to this faith.

Moreover, Federal spending in most civilian sectors must compete with private concerns or at least threaten them with regulation. The construction industry and private home builders would have mixed emotions about a large public-housing program; it could cost them at least a part of their market. Public support for mass transit would displease General Motors, Ford, and the other makers of autos, who, as it happens, are also substantial defense contractors. Makers of steel and cement who provide raw materials for cars and their highways cannot welcome mass transit either. Builders of schools would prefer to deal with school districts and county authorities; Federal authority might prove irksome. Hospitals would say the same. Tanks, missiles, carriers, and bombers compete with nothing in the private sector. These outlays are applauded by the business community.

The urbane Committee for Economic Development pointed out in 1958 that of course the economy could flourish without defense spending. There were unfilled civilian needs for urban renewal, for education. "There is in fact no end of desirable uses to which the resources freed by a reduced armament burden could apply," the elite business group said. But its central message was that more should be spent on defense. "The risk that defense spending of from 10 to 15 percent of the gross national product, or, if necessary, even more, will ruin the American way of life is slight indeed."[67] Like the drafters of NSC 68 and the Marshall planners, the CED saw more virtue in arms outlays than in spending for the deprived civilian sectors.

Galbraith has suggested that the exotic products made for the military and space, employing a substantial share of the nation's scientists and engineers, are another reason that Pentagon outlays are preferred over housing, schools, or hospitals. Peaceful spheres offer less scope to the professionals of technology. Finding employment for scientists and engineers in mass transit, even if Congress put up the money, would not be easy.

In the same way, the large aerospace contractors—Northrop, General Dynamics, Grumman, McDonnell Douglas, Rockwell International, United Technologies, and Lockheed—could become technologically unemployed if Federal spending switched to civilian goods. These firms can't convert to civilian markets. The only major contractor that sells successfully to civilian customers is Boeing, the plane maker. The others have lived and worked too long in a cost-plus world, where all expenses are covered, all mistakes earn profits, and workmanship and skill have been eroded under the relaxed demands of the military.

There is little prospect that these large firms could survive without space and defense orders. They are an obvious and important force behind large Pentagon budgets. Collectively, they speak with a powerful voice. They have plants in the districts of many congressmen, who then have a constituency interest in keeping production lines running. The firms contribute money directly to House and Senate members, particularly those on the Armed Services Committees and the Defense Appropriations Subcommittees. There is feedback here. Taxpayers provide the companies with profits from cost-plus contracts. The companies use the money for, among other things, buying political support to assure more contracts. Thus, taxpayers finance the demand for and the supply of arms.

In theory tax cuts or civilian spending could replace the Pentagon budget. In practice, as Samuel Huntington of Harvard noted, defense spending is the vehicle of choice.

"Such increases avoid the controversies which are inevitably stimulated by most other anti-recession actions," Huntington wrote. "They do not get caught in the cross-fire between liberals and conservatives, domestic spenders and tax reducers, the defenders of consumer buying power and those of business expenditure. A severe recession is likely to be caused in part by reductions in defense spending. It is even more likely to be remedied in part by an increase in defense spending."[68] Huntington has wide support. Arms spending in the U.S. has become a great social emollient. Public housing, public schools, and public health cause far more trouble.

There is a view among some supporters of arms reduction that society pays a price for military outlays. The Pentagon, it is said, absorbs an overwhelming quantity of scientific and engineering talent, depriving civilians of skills that could enhance the good life. Arthur Burns, a frequent advocate of defense outlays to counter slump, complained eloquently that the Pentagon distorts the nature of education and inquiry, fostering physics at the expense of humanities, imposing secrecy on inquiry, stifling curiosity.[69] The military certainly does pay for a large share of industrial research. In 1986, the Pentagon spent $37 billion on research and development, two-fifths of all research outlays. More than two-fifths of the nation's scientists and engineers were probably at work on military contracts where efficiency is low.[70]

But the serious question is whether these human and physical resources, these talented people and their laboratories, could have been employed elsewhere if the Pentagon had not claimed them. The answer is far from clear. If military research and development shrank or disappeared, it is not certain that private firms and private markets would employ the scientists and engineers freed from military tasks. The released research technicians would find jobs only if demand in the private sector expanded, if private firms found some reason to hire them. Since business and Congress are suspicious of public spending—arms apart—it is quite likely that a reduced military share would merely free resources indefinitely. The Pentagon deprives the economy of engineers and scientists only if there is an effective demand for them in some other civilian work.

No doubt the Pentagon has other, corrosive effects on the economy. Its engineers learn to maximize costs, minimize efficiency, and cultivate indifference to the quality of their products. This is precisely the opposite of what they are taught in engineering schools. As they circulate between the defense and the civilian world, moving from North American to General Motors, the curious lessons learned in the defense sphere must weaken their skills for civilian markets.

Of course, the amount of interchange is probably limited. Just as defense contractors can't sell in civilian markets, engineers formed in aerospace probably become badly suited for civilian producers.

Defenders of Pentagon science point to a long list of civilian products that have derived from defense contracting. These spinoffs are said to include transistors and computers. But, "if you want the by-product, you should develop the by-product," said W. K. H. Panofsky.[71] His logic seems impeccable.

In the end, it is impossible to assess the damage done to civilian output by the large arms expenditure. It is possible that any qualitative decline is more than offset by sheer quantitative gain. Remove or reduce arms spending and a substantial portion of demand is also reduced. This increment, moreover, must be multiplied by some factor to account for the respending of the money the military spends. If there is no civilian component to replace the reduced military outlay, demand falls, men and plants are idled, living standards fall. The business-Pentagon argument that the military expands output and employment in civilian markets is true as long as the economy works below high employment, as long as slack is the national policy to control prices.

Forty years after the Air Force successfully promoted an obsolete bomber that won the service its independence, the more or less stable economic structure built on expanding arms outlays was threatened by a crisis of astonishing proportions. The enemy vanished. The Soviet Union, under new management, concluded it could not improve its stagnant economy unless military resources were converted to civilian use. President Mikhail Gorbachev successfully pressed the United States to limit output of some weapons. The Soviet Union's new turn unleashed long-suppressed democratic forces in Eastern Europe, the buffer Stalin had built after World War II against renewed German aggression. Communist regimes fell rapidly along the East–West divide. The great threat, the chief justification for the West's heavy arms spending, disappeared with a speed matched only by the change from friend to foe in Orwell's *1984*. A menacing, aggressive Soviet Union and its obedient bloc of satellites was transformed. The Russians were now seen as the deprived and troubled people of a backward state, so feeble that it was threatened with internal breakup on several borders. Clearly, Moscow could not prevent what had been yesterday's obedient satellites from embracing the values of what had been the enemy West.

This breathless conversion must not obscure the postwar facts. There had been a Soviet menace, and the great arms buildup had some basis in reality. The Red Army had created a vassal zone in Eastern Europe, whether for defense or offense, and stationed armies there. The aspirations of Poles, Czechs, Hungarians, Rumanians, and East Germans for an independent existence were ruthlessly suppressed. The West was compelled to regard Soviet military might and its deployment along the German border as a threat. It was in this spirit that the Marshall Plan and NSC 68 were conceived. To be sure, a conviction rooted in fact soon took on overtones of fantasy. It was thought that Moscow, in league with Beijing, directed North Korea's attack on South Korea and North Vietnam's invasion of the South. These were convenient beliefs. Later, it was inconvenient to appreciate that the Soviet system could not provide tanks and soap, so little attention was paid to the unraveling of Soviet society, and the ever-mounting arms outlays in the U.S. enjoyed a measure of plausibility.

Now the Russian empire's lack of clothes is plain for all to see. The U.S. defense industry faces its greatest crisis since the end of World War II.

More importantly, stability of the U.S. economic system is threatened. A large arms budget has put a sturdy floor under demand; increased arms outlays have provided rapid relief from slumps. Even before Reagan left office, the drastic change in Soviet policy halted fresh increases in the swollen military budget. Under Bush, talk of cuts, large cuts, appeared in the public prints.

The apocalypse has not arrived, however. Military spending is largely divorced from military need, and expenditures could continue at a high level with little military reason. Strategies or scenarios have been floated to ensure that the U.S. keeps up its guard. A complex that survived the Vietnam peace can survive a vanished Soviet enemy. One scenario holds that Gorbachev will fail, that he will not make the Soviet economy more productive. A Baltic or a Moslem Soviet state will break away. The twin crises will lead to Gorbachev's overthrow by traditional Stalinists, and the Soviet Union will reemerge as an unchanged, aggressive enemy. A more extreme version of this scenario holds that nothing has changed, that Gorbachev is a master illusionist who craves world domination. Either or both versions provide a rationale, no matter how implausible, for expanding arms.

A more sophisticated version echoes the Marshall Plan and warns that a letdown in U.S. armaments will discourage West Germans and other Europeans from maintaining their defenses. So the U.S. must spend, regardless of Russian behavior, to encourage other allies.

None of this is very convincing, and other possible enemies have been canvassed. Unfortunately, none seem formidable enough to justify vast outlays on technologically elaborate weapons. Libya, after all, is a backward desert country with a pool of oil and its military failed in Chad. Castro is the aging chief of a small Caribbean island. Guerrillas in Latin America rate little more than some conventionally armed troops. There is nothing in this to explain spending more than $250 billion a year on the Pentagon's suppliers alone. They are, moreover, unlikely to regard the most theatrical war against the narcotics industry as a useful source of demand.

But military spending is too important for its direct beneficiaries and the economy generally to disappear easily. The first Pentagon announcements of potential budget cuts showed how the uniformed spenders were digging in. Defense chiefs spoke of cuts after taking account of price increases. By expanding the arms budget at a rate less than a self-proclaimed inflation increase, the Pentagon could spend more and claim it was spending less. If the military calculates inflation at 5 percent, it can add $9 billion to a total budget of $300 billion and still claim a "cut" of 2 percent.

Arms spending had become a unique force in American life. No serious political group opposed it. All—unions, corporations, engineers, scientists, local politicians, Congressmen—supported it enthusiastically and complained bitterly over the loss of a contract or a base. To be sure, military spending has twice damaged the economy. Truman had to cope with a Korean War inflation he quelled through controls. Johnson failed to act and his Vietnam inflation contributed heavily to the stagflation plaguing the economy ever since. But these unfortunate side effects were more than outweighed by the utility of arms as provider of jobs and income.

The ingenuity of the Pentagon and its contractors must not be underestimated. Perhaps the complex will yet find the formula to continue increased outlays even with a retreating Russia. If they fail, the U.S. will surrender a second great economic stabilizer. Reagan's erosion of the progressive income tax was the first. Without military outlays to sustain them, it is conceivable, if unlikely, that hard-pressed corporations might then become less hostile to government outlays for civilian purposes.

NOTES

1. Paul A. C. Koistinen, *The Military–Industrial Complex: A Historical Perspective* (New York: Praeger, 1980), p. 13.

2. Robert W. Degrasse, Jr., *Military Expansion, Economic Decline* (Armonk, N.Y.: M.E. Sharpe, 1983), p. 3.

3. Thomas H. Etzold and John Lewis Gaddis, editors, *Containment: Documents on American Policy and Strategy, 1945–50* (New York: Columbia University Press, 1978), pp. 407–8.

4. *Foreign Relations of the United States, 1947*, Volume III (Washington, D.C.: Department of State, 1972), p. 210.

5. *Economic Report of the President*, 1989, pp. 308–9.

6. Sherwood Fine, *Public Spending and Postwar Economic Policy* (New York: Columbia University Press, 1944), p. 142.

7. *Economic Report of the President*, 1989, pp. 308–9.

8. Robert Aaron Gordon, *Economic Instability and Growth: The American Record* (New York: Harper & Row, 1974), p. 25.

9. *Ibid.*, p. 120.

10. James Tobin, *The New Economics One Decade Older* (Princeton: Princeton University Press, 1974), pp. 44–5.

11. Wilfred Lewis, *Federal Fiscal Policy in the Postwar Recessions* (Washington, D.C.: Brookings Institution, 1962), p. 23.

12. Charles Schultze testifying before the United States Congress Joint Economic Committee, "Economic Effects of Vietnam Spending, April 1967" (Washington D.C.: U.S. Government Printing Office), p. 32.

13. *Economic Report of the President*, 1989, p. 309.

14. John Maynard Keynes, "The United States and the Keynes Plan," *The New Republic*, July 24, 1940, p. 158.

15. Adam Smith, *The Wealth of Nations* (London: Dent, 1970), p. 390.

16. Daniel Bell, *The End of Ideology* (Glencoe, Ill.: Free Press, 1960), pp. 83–5.

17. Frank Pace quoted in Degrasse, *Military Expansion*, p. 3.

18. Frank C. Carlucci, "An Economic Defense of the Budget," *Directors and Boards*, Winter 1983, p. 25.

19. *Ibid.*, p. 27.

20. Charles J. Hitch and Roland N. McKean, *The Economics of Defense in the Nuclear Age* (Cambridge: Harvard University Press, 1960), p. 69.

21. John Connally quoted in Seymour Melman, *The Permanent War Economy* (New York: Simon & Schuster, 1985), p. 55.

22. Colby Chandler quoted in A. Ernest Fitzgerald, *The Pentagonists: An Insider's View of Waste, Mismanagement, and Fraud in Defence Spending* (Boston: Houghton Mifflin, 1989), p. 302.

23. Bert G. Hickman, *Investment Demand and U.S. Economic Growth* (Washington, D.C.: Brookings Institution), p. 7.

24. Gabriel Hauge quoted in Sherman Adams, *Firsthand Report: The Story of the Eisenhower Administration* (New York: Harper and Brothers, 1961), p. 153.

25. Arthur Burns, "The Defense Sector: An Evaluation of its Economic and Social Impact," in Arthur Burns, Charles J. Hitch, and Jacob J. Javits, *The Defense Sector and the American Economy* (New York: New York University Press, 1968), p. 78.

26. Charles J. Hitch in Burns et al., *The Defence Sector*, p. 54.

27. Lewis, *Federal Fiscal Policy*, p. 178.

28. Adams, *Firsthand Report*, p. 153.

29. Seymour Melman, *Pentagon Capitalism* (New York: McGraw-Hill, 1970), p. 232.

30. *Economic Report of the President* (Washington, D.C.: U.S. Government Printing Office, 1959), p. iv.

31. Adams, *Firsthand Report*, p. 416.

32. Samuel P. Huntington, *The Common Defense* (New York: Columbia University Press, 1961), p. 264.

33. Guy Tugwell, *The Art of Politics as Practised by Three Great Americans* (Garden City, New York: Doubleday, 1958).

34. Walter W. Heller, *New Dimensions of Political Economy* (New York: W.W. Norton, 1967), p. 71.

35. *Economic Report of the President* (Washington D.C.: U.S. Government Printing Office, 1962), p. 59.

36. *Ibid.*, p. 83.

37. Military spending increased by $6 billion—*ibid.*, p. 309; spending on space programs increased by $5 billion—U.S. Department of Commerce, *Historical Statistics of the United States, Colonial Times to 1970: Bicentennial Edition* (1973), p. 1116.

38. Hugh G. Mosley, *The Arms Race: Economic and Social Consequences* (Lexington, Mass.: Lexington Books, 1985), p. 14.

39. Herbert Stein in Erwin C. Hargrove and Samuel A. Morely, editors, *The President and the Council of Economic Advisors: Interviews with CEA Chairmen* (Boulder, Colorado: Westview Press, 1984), p. 395.

40. Schlesinger quoted in Melman, *The Permanent War Economy*, p. 315*n*.

41. Fitzgerald, *The Pentagonists*, p. 80.

42. Richard Nixon quoted in James M. Naughton, "President Vows Action to Spur Economic Upturn," *New York Times*, May 2, 1971, p. 2.

43. U.S. Senate, *1972 Joint Economic Report*, Report No. 92–708 (Washington D.C.: U.S. Government Printing Office, 1972), p. 5.

44. *Report from Iron Mountain on the Possibility and Desirability of Peace* (New York: Dial Press, 1967), p. 35.

45. *Economic Report of the President*, 1989, p. 309.

46. *Economic Report of the President*, 1989, p. 309.

47. Perry McCoy Smith, *The Air Force Plans for Peace, 1943–45* (Baltimore, Maryland: Johns Hopkins University Press, 1970), p. 114.

48. *The Effects of Strategic Bombing on the German War Economy* (Overall Economic Effects Division, U.S. Strategic Bombing Survey, October 31, 1945), p. 7.

49. Smith, *The Air Force Plans for Peace*, p. 27.

50. *Ibid.*, p. 114.

51. Edward N. Luttwak, *The Pentagon and the Art of War: The Question of Military Reform* (New York: Simon & Schuster, 1984), p. 28.

52. Doolittle quoted in Smith, *The Air Force Plans for Peace*, p. 69.

53. William Proxmire, *Report from Wasteland: America's Military Industrial Complex* (New York: Praeger, 1970), p. 85.

54. Richard A. Stubbing, "Improving the Acquisition Process for High Risk Electronics Systems," *Congressional Record—Senate*, January 7, 1969, p. 3171.

55. Richard A. Stubbing and Richard A. Mendel, "How to Save $50 Billion a Year," *The Atlantic*, June 1989, p. 55.

56. Adams, *Firsthand Report*, p. 406.

57. Fitzgerald, *The Pentagonists*, p. 42.

58. Sherick quoted in Rick Atkinson and Fred Hiaff, "To Prepare for War, We Need a Revolution," *Washington Post*, December 15, 1985, p. C1.

59. John Kenneth Galbraith, *The New Industrial State* (Boston: Houghton Mifflin, 1978), p. 339.

60. J. Ronald Fox, *The Defense Management Challenge* (Boston: Harvard Business School Press, 1988), p. 234.

61. Richard A. Stubbing with Richard A. Mendel, *The Defense Game: An Insider Explores the Astonishing Realities of America's Defense Establishment* (New York: Harper & Row, 1986), p. 35.

62. *Ibid.*, pp. 166–8.

63. Walter Adams, "The Military–Industrial Complex and the New Industrial State," *American Economic Review*, May 1968, pp. 654–5.

64. *Ibid.*, p. 656.

65. John Kenneth Galbraith, "Military Power and the Military Budget," in *The Political Economy of Federal Policy*, edited by Robert H. Haveman and Robert D. Hamrin (New York: Harper & Row, 1973), p. 114.

66. Hitch and McKean, *The Economics of Defense*, p. 81.

67. *The Problem of National Security* (New York: Committee for Economic Development, July 1958), p. 27.

68. Huntington, *The Common Defense*, p. 277.

69. Burns et al., *The Defense Sector*, pp. 75–6.

70. *Statistical Abstract* (Washington, D.C.: U.S. Bureau of the Census, 1988), p. 557.

71. Panofsky quoted in Harold L. Nieburg, *In the Name of Science* (Chicago: Quadrangle Books, 1966), p. 78.

VIII

The Hobbled
Economy

Fifty years after Roosevelt's belated attack on the Great Depression, the American economy had reached a peculiar equilibrium, an uneasy balance. The massive drop in production of the 1930s, unemployment that struck more than one in four, above all a feeling of helplessness against overwhelming economic forces—all this had vanished. Only blunder on an unthinkable scale could make it return. Now, more than nine of ten who wanted jobs had them.

But incomes—material well-being—for half the country had been falling steadily for nearly a generation. This lower half drew little consolation from the fact that the rest of the nation, particularly those at the peak of the income pyramid, enjoyed handsome gains; the rise in pleasure boats, art prices, second homes, and jet-propelled vacations abroad amply testified to the good life for some.

Prices generally continued to climb at a rate disturbing those whose income flows largely from the interest on bonds. But taxes had been rearranged so that inflation had become a lessened burden for the recipients of passive interest income. There was no longer a higher bracket into which they were driven by prices, thanks to Reagan's low ceiling of 28 percent. It was now well understood that if prices rise too rapidly, a recession will be induced, passing the burden of inflation to unemployed workers. This reflected the most important change in policy since Roosevelt's first term.

Until recently, any administration, Democratic or Republican, felt obliged to resist slump. All postwar administrations had some knowledge of how to tame economic forces, how to deploy monetary and fiscal policy to overcome a notable fall in demand or curb a runaway rise in prices. Eisenhower and Nixon used slump briefly to check inflation but both were compelled by political necessity as well as some notion of proper public behavior to reverse their ground. Even the radical Reagan administration, which had claimed it could not guide the economy, exploited monetary and fiscal measures—pressing the Fed for easier money, cutting taxes, and expanding arms spending— to undo the overly rigorous Volcker recession.

But Reagan, partly anticipated by Carter, introduced a new term in the policy maker's vocabulary. He invented the notion of prolonged slack to restrain prices, a permanent pool of jobless to hold off inflation.

The new stability was very different from that promised by the 1946 Employment Act. The new equilibrium had been achieved largely at the expense of the country's poorer half. Thus, leading Western regimes began to embody two of Karl Marx's most dubious propositions, that capitalism increases the misery of the working class and depends on an industrial reserve army of unemployed. To be sure, U.S. workers were relatively worse off, not absolutely. But the need for a reserve army was reflected directly in the use of unemployment to restrain inflation. These are radical doctrines, for they run the risk of creating an alienated, mutinous class of those with eroding incomes and those without jobs. The postwar governments that sought high employment were far more conservative defenders of the private-property system.

The characteristics of the new economy are evident. Growth in output continues at about 2.5 percent a year, but it is 30 percent below the rate in the fat era of the fifties and sixties.[1] Employment is far from full. Some 6 million or more are now kept jobless;[2] a high-employment economy would idle perhaps 3 to 4 million, only those between jobs or out of work because of weather, like farm workers and loggers.

It has become fashionable to define high employment as the rate of joblessness consistent with an unchanged inflation level. This is a counsel of despair. It means accepting an intolerably high rate for both unemployment and inflation. It implies that most of those unemployed aren't fit for modern jobs, are structurally unemployed. But in years of high output, these unemployables are much in demand, are trained and put to work. The phrase "structural unemployment" is largely a semantic device to dismiss intolerably high levels of joblessness.

Price inflation now running near 5 percent a year is surely better than the 12 percent in the last half of Carter's term;[3] but it will still halve the value of money every 8⅓ years. The most stunning change from fat years to lean is the sharp reversal in workers' fortunes. Average weekly pay, in dollars of 1977 buying power, rose from $123.43 to $198.35, or 61 percent between 1948 and 1973. Wages then fell steadily to $167.45 by the end of 1988.[4] The combination of slower growth, higher unemployment, and stifled demand shrinks workers' well-being almost every year.

Their plight was eased somewhat by wives who left homes and child rearing to seek work. Two incomes made bearable what one had provided before. But only just. The middle or median family income in 1973 was $30,820 a year in terms of 1987 buying power. By 1987, it was the same, $30,853.[5] Sending wives to work, with extra expenses for traveling, baby care, and the like, still left half the nation's families with an income unchanged for at least fourteen years.

None of this—slower growth, persistent inflation, many jobless, and the erosion of workers' incomes—seemed to disturb American society. As long as the change was gradual, Americans did not protest. Reagan's radicalism could be made to appear a natural evolution so there was little complaint. Indeed, the economics of most presidents are exercises in modest change. Hoover and the first-term Roosevelt fit together far better than the hagiographers of either allow. Both were interventionists, casting about for ways to break the Depression's grip, willing to use government against slump but inhibited by balanced-budget fantasies. Then came the war. Its lesson that spending, taxes, and credit creation can erase slump was absorbed by all postwar presidents. From Eisenhower through Kennedy ran a clear line, although Kennedy's stimuli were bolder than any Eisenhower attempted. Nixon studied Johnson's inflationary boom and cut through Johnson's frustration by scrapping global currency arrangements and substituting price controls for markets. Stagflation restrained Ford and Carter and led Carter to try an innovation that Reagan made his own: deliberate slack. But even Reagan was careful not to repudiate the tradition entirely. So arms outlays and tax cuts for the wealthy sustained demand and limited unemployment.

The Great Depression made clear that there is little room in America for the radical temper. Despite massive misery, no revolutionary movement developed that threatened the political and economic order. Huey Long in Louisiana and Father

Coughlin in Detroit had large followings but neither built a lasting movement. The Communist party, gaining tens of thousands of members, provided organizers for the industrial unions of the CIO, in steel, autos, rubber, and maritime. But the party organizers either worked under traditional leaders like John L. Lewis or survived only as long as they promoted conventional demands—wages, hours, and conditions. Communists could negotiate contracts, not revolution.

Whether the system could have survived continuing catastrophe, what would have happened if Roosevelt's cautious experiment with increased spending in 1938 had not been intensified by the war, is of course unknown.

There is little to suggest in either the immediate prewar or postwar U.S. history that government and those who do well from it have much to fear from the current arrangement. Large gains for those in the upper half, steady losses for those at the bottom have built no barricades in the streets.

The bottom half appears narcotized. As it happens, roughly the same proportion have dropped out of the electoral system. About half do not vote even in widely advertised presidential contests. The bottom half of the income ladder is not identical with the nonvoters, but there is considerable overlap. Nonvoters tend to be disproportionately black or Hispanic, poorly educated, more heavily unemployed than others. This group gets much of its information about public affairs from television. That medium, with its exciting pictures, hypercharged language, and snippets of coverage, creates confusion and cynicism among those who rely upon it most heavily for information. Studies reported by Austin Ranney have confirmed this.[6] Television news thus plays a key role in the political process, although not the one conventionally assigned to it. It unintentionally alienates working-class voters from the electoral process, strengthening the pattern of not voting. By promoting cynicism and confusion, television implicitly persuades these people, the core of a potential protest, that voting does not advance interest. *

The disappearance of the poor, ill-educated and minorities from national political life has driven Democrats and Republicans closer together. In national elections, it is increasingly difficult to distinguish between the economic programs of the major candidates. Both typically deplore deficits in the budget, the lack of U.S. industrial competitiveness, and similar diversions. Neither candidate addresses slower growth, higher jobless rates, or the growing maldistribution of incomes. In the Congress, Democrats vie with Republicans to undo the progressive income tax and distribute the benefits of arms spending. Both parties more or less faithfully represent the half of the population that does well out of the present state of affairs and that votes.

The trade unions, a source of strength for Democrats (officials of the Teamsters and building trades prefer Republicans), are largely quiescent. They are weakened by slack and make little effort even to hold their declining share of the labor force. They often join employers to resist foreign competition. The unions engage in only token ventures to attract nonvoters to the

---

* The transformation of the press in the last generation provides indirect confirmation of the fact that workers increasingly rely on television for public information. In many cities, notably New York, Los Angeles, Boston, Washington, St. Louis, and Philadelphia, upmarket newspapers have thrived and the popular blue-collar press has gone under. Evidently television gratifies popular tastes for entertainment even though its political content confuses. This suggests that politicians' infatuation with television, the outlet for most of their large campaign funds, may be misguided. Political ads may confuse and repel potential voters. However, politicians, like advertisers generally, carefully control their messages, and this material may get through and influence while the buzzing, blooming confusion of the nightly news show does not.

polls. This activity, like organizing the unorganized, is expensive. Outlays for such purposes might threaten the pay and perquisites many union leaders now expect. A generation ago, major newspapers closely followed union affairs, with one or more specialists working a full-time beat. Today, few such reporters are left. Unions play a diminishing part in American political and economic life. They are instruments neither of radical change nor of reform.

No society with widening inequalities can be wholly anesthetized. In several unions, notably the United Auto Workers and the Teamsters, well-organized rank-and-file movements have been formed. They challenge the leadership on everything from corruption to collaboration with management at the workers' expense. But the spread of such movements is limited by the fear of layoffs. In the thirties, workers were bolder because none had a secure job; in the nineties, more than 5 in 100 may be out of work but more than 9 of 10 have jobs. Few will put these jobs in peril by challenging a union-management alliance.

Minorities, particularly blacks, Puerto Ricans, and other Latin Americans, make up a large share of the 50 percent in the nonvoting underclass. They might be a force for political change but they are reduced by their unstated belief that it is not worth the effort to vote. So they tend either to be ignored by the politicians in national contests or used as a focus for hostile racial feelings by whites. Local politicians frequently but not always cater to the demands of blacks and Hispanics. They, however, can't touch unemployment, which is determined at the national level.

As recently as the 1960s, blacks were a political force of some consequence and were courted by some white urban politicians. Their alliance created a social revolution that broke down discrimination in many public activities, particularly voting rights. But black failures in the economic area—they are usually first to be laid off in hard times—appear to have soured many on the utility of the vote. In towns where blacks are a majority, or a large minority, they do turn out to elect black mayors and share in some of the spoils previously monopolized by whites. There, a clear link can be seen between voting and benefits.

Not all of the underclass are passive. Some conduct guerrilla raids—murder, rape, and robbery—usually against each other but occasionally in white enclaves. Growing crime, violence, and conventional prejudice create a growing number of No-Go areas in the great cities, districts where whites prohibit entry to blacks except for servants, where blacks bar whites, especially at night. A major source of crime is the participation by some entrepreneurial blacks in an elaborate network distributing drugs or illicit addictive mood-changing substances to satisfy appetites that appear to require a white level of income.

Dropouts from the underclass, white and black, beg on city streets. An increasing number sleep on the streets, as in Bombay or Calcutta. Epidemic disease spreads.

In this climate, it might be thought that the creation of more and better jobs, public housing for the underclass rather than the use of public-housing money as a slush fund for politicians, abandoning the policy of slack to curb prices—all this might have some appeal.

Not many people seem to agree. The notion that a healthy economy could reduce crime or homelessness is regarded as sentimental. Just as arms have provided a stabilizer against slump, so military solutions are popular to suppress social anarchists. Concentration camps, not housing, are urged for criminals. The Supreme Court, still following the election returns, has narrowed the rights of the accused[7] and strengthens the police arm of the state. Similar tactics are employed in other societies with troublesome ethnic groups, Israel and, until recently, South Africa.

On all sides, the forces supporting things as they are remain strong. The bottom half loses ground to an upper half, but is still mostly housed, clothed, fed. There are bread and circuses, fast food and an abundance of televised professional sport from college and other subsidized arenas. Black and Hispanic minorities extract least from the system but, even when jobless, are provided with welfare covering a minimum of material needs. Illegal commodity markets, crime remains an outlet for the boldest. Traditional instruments of change—unions, politicians —are controlled or purchased. It is hard to detect any prospect or much demand for significant change.*

Perhaps the demand of Soviet and other Eastern European citizens for food, housing, and other amenities could stimulate change in the U.S. A serious Russian effort to switch resources from the military to civilians might undermine the large U.S. arms budget. Despite formidable political obstacles, it is conceivable that a reduction in U.S. arms could encourage other public programs to sustain demand. That in turn could launch popular support for a return to policies of the fat years, for a reversion to high employment.

This does not seem likely, however. Soviet rulers may after all decide that a garrison state is preferable to restructuring and

---

* One hint of this lack of demand for change comes from a wealthy financier, a friend, who lost one son from a college campus, perhaps to drug dealers. In an unrelated episode, his daughter was dragged into an alley and raped. He does not favor a high-employment economy with better schools and housing. He wants a freer hand for police and the execution of murderers. A beneficiary of the system's economic arrangements and a stark victim of some of its consequences, he largely favors the status quo and opposes drastic change.

try to reinvent the past. The great constellation of U.S. forces—military, industrial, union, and political—that promote weaponry could discover new threats justifying continued arms outlays. A sustained reduction in the U.S. military budget would contradict nearly fifty years of postwar history.

In any case, a smaller arms budget would make more difficult the task of high employment and high growth required to restore city streets to the citizens and dignity to the lower reaches of the underclass. The economy's record since Roosevelt is clear. Full employment and rapid increases in output depend on aggregate effective demand, the sum of all demands backed by cash, private and public, for goods and services. The $300 billion arms budget is a major source of that demand.[8]

But because unemployment is high and plants are idle, even with a large military outlay, the economy has room for expansion, space for extra demand that is not now forthcoming because of a lack of cash. Citizens, particularly those with low or little income, would evidently buy more if they had the means. Business would invest more if it foresaw an increase in demand. The way to achieve both ends, to expand consumption and investment, has been demonstrated again and again since 1938: launch a government program to build homes, schools, hospitals, promote medical research, bury dangerous wastes, serve the arts, and engage in one thousand and one other useful activities. The funds the government spends for doctors, teachers, bricklayers, computer programmers, lathe operators, supervisory bureaucrats, and the rest will enlarge employment. As the newly hired spend their incomes, more people will find jobs. The spending side of fiscal policy can lift a slack economy as it did during the war and postwar years.

There is another equally direct route to high employment

and faster growth, through tax cuts. These would enlarge the spending of those with incomes high enough to pay taxes. The same benign circle would begin again. A politically prudent program would probably embrace both elements, substantial multi-billion-dollar outlays in new civilian spending and multi-billion-dollar tax cuts.

The government would, of course, require the support of the Federal Reserve. Instead of tightening money to compress demand, the central bank would have to expand the money supply to accommodate the increased spending, output, and employment. A government attempt to embark on a course of expansion might well provoke a classic confrontation with the deflationist Federal Reserve. In the end, the rules may have to be redrawn so that the nonresponsible central bank is subordinated to the policy of elected officials.

An increasing number of commentators dismiss the tested remedies of fiscal and monetary policy for the nation's sluggish growth. In their view, a profound malaise has overtaken the actors in the American economy. Comfortable managers shun risk and innovation. Complacent workers won't extend themselves, even for larger rewards. The U.S., the cliché holds, has lost its cutting edge. Drive and discipline are found abroad, in West Germany a generation ago, in Japan, in Asian nations on the Pacific.

This is a literary argument not susceptible of proof. If it has any merit, it must show up in a key measure of efficiency, in productivity or output per worker or unit of investment. It is quite true that the fat years ended and the lean began with a marked slowdown in productivity. This is the prime source for the contention that the American economy is decadent.

In logic, faster growth rate can come only from a bigger work force or a more efficient one. Increased productivity is the key to an expanding economy. But how to turn that key is a source of prolonged debate. The slowdown in productivity is frequently blamed on a decline in the capital available for each worker, the tools at each worker's hand. The conventional wisdom holds that a lack of savings inhibits the production of capital needed to elevate productivity. This is a convenient argument for the well-off. Lower the taxes on their incomes and their capital, it is said, and productivity will flourish again. This line of argument of course illustrates a well-known law of economics: he who pays the piper calls the tune. It ignores the simple fact that new plants are built to satisfy new customers, not to absorb savings. Create more customers, and corporations will build the new plants to serve them with dollars taken from retained earnings.

If the productivity-savings-capital link can be treated with an appropriate skepticism, some stubborn facts remain. Productivity suffered a sharp drop in 1973, the dividing point between fat and lean years. This book has traced the sharp, discontinuous break in the economy to three factors. There was first the timid Johnson policy in the Vietnam War, his refusal to pay for growing military expenditures with increased taxes. If there had been slack in the economy, unemployed men and empty plants, the failure to raise taxes, to withdraw income, would have been a blessing and not a curse. But employment was high and plants were working; Johnson's war spending could only raise prices, not expand jobs. His inflation was reinforced by the sharp rise in oil and food prices at the start of Nixon's second term. They served both to inflate prices generally and depress demand.

The third great force creating stagflation was the loss after 1971 of a permanently overvalued dollar. Americans had to work longer, produce more to buy the goods and services of Germans, Japanese, and others; conversely, importers in advanced nations could spend fewer marks and yen for American goods. The process was inevitable; prosperous defeated nations would not accept undervalued currencies forever. But when they shifted ground, Americans suffered a loss. Together, inflation and currency changes and the demand-depressing effects of oil forced the Ford and Carter governments to tread warily. Their restraint meant less-buoyant American demand. Incomes grew slowly or fell. All this struck at investment. Corporations do not buy new cost-cutting machines or build more efficient plants if there are no new customers. The failure to invest in more-productive plants and machinery meant workers were less equipped to turn out more goods in less time. The productivity of workers does depend to a critical extent on the quality of the tools with which they work. The three forces held back the introduction of new tools that would have expanded productivity.

Edward F. Denison, a leading growth analyst, looks at a different set of forces.[9] He measures the internal, domestic economic factors that produce change in the potential national income. The most important, he finds, is change in the volume of work performed. Evidently, more workers or more time worked increases output. Second is gains in knowledge and management. These two together account for 60 percent. They far outweigh private capital, a third factor. The last consequential force flows from increases in the education of workers. Together the four produce 90 percent of the change in potential output, the output that can be reached at a high level of employment. The central point is that all four of these critical forces depend crucially on demand. The slack economy launched by Carter and perfected by Reagan may curb prices and gratify the psychological needs of managers. But it is the enemy of growth.

Of Denison's four forces, the amount of work done obviously depends on the volume of jobs. A high-employment economy not only puts more of an existing labor force to work, it expands the labor force. It draws in those who want to work but are discouraged by the difficulty in finding it, those who believe they lack skills for a modern economy, those working part time only because they can't find full-time jobs. World War II was a striking example. Civilian labor increased despite the huge military buildup. This also illustrates how the grim statistics of the Great Depression badly understated the depth of unemployment, misery, and waste.

In the same way, an economy under pressure is likely to spur advances in knowledge and better management, Denison's second growth force. When labor is tight, managers tend to economize on it, find more efficient ways to produce. They will seek better materials and even new products. Slack demand confirms workers and managers in routine, less productive ways.

The source of private capital has been examined. Most American industry does not rely on the voluntary savings of the rich to pay for tools and plants. It extracts savings from consumers through prices. But no rational firm invests in new tools and plants without expecting more customers. A high-employment, high-growth economy promises new customers and therefore induces more capital spending, more machinery and factories.

Denison's last big factor, the education of workers, also depends on a high employment demand. General Motors, General Electric, and other major corporations will train workers when they are hard to find. A high-growth economy, high levels of demand, make it worth a corporation's while to convert the unskilled to the skilled. Rosie the Riveter of World War II is the paradigm. With men in service, women were trained and performed traditional masculine jobs. Rosie was a forerunner of the structurally unemployed in the Eisenhower era who found jobs in the intensified demand of the Kennedy-Johnson period.

In sum, all four of Denison's forces to spur higher potential national income are closely linked to demand. An economy with high-level employment will increase the amount of work done, advance knowledge, stimulate private capital, and enlarge workers' education. Economics teaches what most already know: the more people at work and at better jobs the larger the national pie, the larger the slices for all.

Still another Denison calculation measures the cost of unemployment. He estimates that each 1 percent change in the level targeted for high employment changes the potential rate of total output by 1.6 percent. [10] In other words, a government that aims at 3 percent unemployment instead of 5.5 percent can expand the gross national product in 1990 by about $200 billion. That would provide almost as much goods and services as the defense budget.

The notion of a high-employment target has almost disappeared from public discussion. Instead, serious talk centers on other issues of uncertain relevance: whether American manufacturers can compete with the Japanese at home and abroad; the deficit in the balance of trade; the deficit recorded for the national budget. The issue of manufacturing competitiveness is probably the least consequential. It is unclear why anyone should want workers in advanced society to produce steel, autos, or ships when Korea, Brazil, India, and other emerging industrial states make these things more cheaply with less costly labor. Many industrial plants, moreover, are noisy, dirty, monotonous, and dangerous. To be sure, in an economy below full employment, one that fails to cushion the move of workers from inefficient to efficient tasks, any job is better than none. So steel and auto managers demand—and frequently get—quotas, cartels, and other devices to block foreign competition, preserve backward industries, and their uncomfortable jobs. But in a high-employment economy, in an advanced society, where citizens are educated and trained to levels that come close to exploiting their talents, the managers and workers in traditional industry are replaced by men and women likely to engage in more satisfying and better-paid work. Factory labor will be found more and more in newly industrializing states. They will make most of the steel, autos, and ships. In advanced societies, more and more will engage in banking, insurance, publishing, education, entertainment, science-based industry, health care, and the like. Indeed, this has already happened. In the U.S., white-collar workers exceeded blue-collar workers 30 years ago, and the gap widens every year.[11] Just as agriculture, once a major employer of U.S. workers, gave way to industry, factories yield to offices, laboratories, and studios.

The balance of payments seems to touch an especially raw nationalist nerve, as if a failure to export more goods than are imported raises some question about a nation's economic virility. In fact, the U.S. exports relatively fewer goods and more services all the time. It sells its skill in education, finance, entertainment, and science; it buys cars, toasters, and toys abroad because they can be made more cheaply in Japan or South Korea. The export of U.S. services doesn't match the import of foreign goods, or at least it hasn't in recent years. This is hardly cause for alarm. The sellers—Japan, Taiwan and others—are content to invest surplus dollars in American real estate, plants and Treasury bills. There is not a shred of evidence to suggest that this process will soon come to an end. Nor is there any evidence that foreign investment in a developed nation diminishes its sovereignty. Japanese purchase of Rockefeller Center or an American auto plant in Tennessee increases Washington's influence over Tokyo, not the reverse.

Over time, and if exchange rates are left to fluctuate with markets, changes in the dollar's value should correct any deficit in the balance of payments. This means, of course, that the cartelist instincts of finance ministers and central bankers, who usually favor fixed exchange rates, must be restrained. Then a surplus of dollars will cheapen dollars to the level where exports of U.S. services and goods will rise, imports will fall, and payments will move to balance. In the contemporary world, this simple relationship is overwhelmed by capital flows, the billions deposited by global corporations seeking the safest currency or the best yield. This money floods into the U.S., dwarfs the trade deficit, and automatically balances U.S. foreign payments. If, however, global corporations think the dollar is healthier than the yen or the mark, that is hardly reason for concern.

Perhaps the most persuasive device to inhibit increased spending for full employment is the repeated emphasis on the perils of the national deficit in the domestic budget, the gap between revenues and Federal outlays. A species of neo-Hooverism has returned to the U.S., making a balanced budget the nation's most precious goal. To begin with, the deficit of conventional discussion is grossly exaggerated, an accounting monstrosity, as Robert Heilbroner and Peter Bernstein have explained.[12]

For example, in the 1988 budget year, the deficit was reported to be an impressive $255 billion. But this made no allowance for inflation, which balloons the number. Nor did it take into account the substantial surpluses run by state and local governments. Much of their black ink flows from the programs of the Federal government. It must be subtracted from the U.S. deficit to measure the real impact of the Federal budget. Finally and most important, the budget fails to distinguish between capital outlays and operating outlays, between spending for highways and dams, which yield income streams over many years, and spending for unemployment or health care, which are consumed at once. Every business differentiates between capital and current outlays; a peculiar convention inhibits the Federal government from doing so. After allowing for these and other items, Heilbroner and Bernstein concluded that the 1988 deficit was really about $3 billion.[13] In other words, the budget was far too tight for high employment; it was inhibiting growth.

The budget, as conventionally counted, represses government investment in transportation, power and communications—infrastructure—that raises productivity and output. Realistically counted, the deficit is negligible and curbs productivity and growth by holding demand below high-employment levels. Picturing the conventional budget deficit as an outsized monster is one more technique to serve the best-off by sustaining an economy of slack.

All during the 1980s, the crusaders for higher savings and lower taxes on the rich had things largely their way. But it is possible that change is ahead. The crusaders warned repeatedly that the two deficits, trade and budget, spelled disaster, that collapse lay around the corner. Even so sober an economist as Paul Samuelson spoke of "the new devil in American life—the basic structural federal deficit."[14] The corner was not turned; disaster did not happen. Reagan kept the economy running far below capacity, but, once recovery began, without slump. The two deficits began to be taken less seriously, although President Bush argued for a lower capital-gains tax on the ground that less tax would mean more tax and reduce the deficit.

At least in the beginning of his term, Bush like Reagan presided over a stable equilibrium—ignoring the slack—that did not arouse demands for change. There were, however, a few signs that an economy resting on joblessness and a maldistributed income was no longer so popular. The Congress temporarily delayed Bush's plea for a lower capital-gains tax largely on the grounds that the rich would benefit. But there did not appear to be any strong cry for a turn back to the policies of the fat years.

There is a different and, perhaps, a more attractive path to follow, one that assures jobs for all who seek them and expands the national wealth for everybody. No arcane knowledge is needed to recreate prosperity, although there is little popular demand for it. An expansive monetary and fiscal policy, some combination of enlarged spending and lower taxes, could, however, restore a high-employment economy. This is a well-worn path, marked out in the twenty-five years after the war. Despite occasional lapses, these techniques worked well and could work again.

It is true that no policy comes without cost. For high employment growth, these are symbolic and real. Initially, there would be an increase in the budget deficit, a budget that now constrains the economy. But a realistic measure of the deficit, one that reflected the capital generated, the surpluses of state governments and inflation, would reduce the conventional number, put it in perspective. Once the economy regains and holds the high ground of full employment, less will be spent to compensate the jobless, and the extra incomes generated will yield more tax to erase the deficit. What matters is not an artificial accounting that exaggerates the deficit at low levels of employment. What matters is the wealth of the nation, which depends on balance at high levels of employment.

There is a serious problem, however, created by lower levels of unemployment. Prices will come under added pressure. The

255

economy of slack designed by Carter and Reagan is intended to hold prices down. Although slack has been far from a complete success—inflation during Reagan's recovery averaged 3.4 percent[15]—there is little doubt that a monetary and fiscal stimulus will further spur price increases. As the jobless go to work, as others work at higher pay, as business borrows and invests more, anticipating new customers, the demand for goods and services will increase. Union workers in a high-employment economy would regain some strength and successfully demand higher wages. Corporations in concentrated industries would exploit enlarged demand to cover these wage costs and expand profits. Price power could incite a spiraling inflation.

This is a dilemma: how to combine high employment with a tolerable level of price increase, the modest levels of the prosperous postwar years. There is no easy answer to this problem, although the fat years offer some clues. Kennedy in the U.S., Harold Wilson and Edward Heath in Britain, both major parties in West Germany and other Europeans in the 1960s and 1970s, experimented with a new technique, incomes policy. They sought to restrain prices set by the major economic actors through persuasion. In the U.S., Kennedy set a wage and price standard and used presidential persuasion to enforce it. Nixon turned to outright controls. The Europeans preferred techniques that avoided compulsion. All these devices worked for a time, then broke down. Inevitably, and no matter how indirectly, incomes policy constitutes some interference with free markets, some interference with the price and wage determination of private actors. The policy will bring less than an optimum allocation of resources. Prices are no longer ideal signals, directing resources to their best use. Incomes policy will not create, will in fact interfere with, the textbook ideal in which every factor of production is guided by an impersonal price system and pure competitive markets to its best use, when every worker is paid an amount precisely equal to the value of his marginal product and every product is produced and priced at the point where supply and demand intersect.

It is evident that this ideal state never existed outside of textbooks, that incomes policy will not distort in the real world anything that resembles so abstract an ideal. The optimum allocation of resources and optimum pricing depend on pure competition—no one seller or buyer has enough weight to influence price or output. Pure competition rarely exists in any market in the real world. In most markets, competition is imperfect and prices can't fulfill their textbook role. In electrical machinery, for example, General Electric and Westinghouse dominate the market and each has a lot to say about the prices the industry charges and the volume of production. Labor markets are frequently controlled by a single seller, the union of electrical workers in New York or the Teamsters for over-the-road haulage. They too play a part in determining wage and other costs. In none of these cases does pure competition rule.

If the structure of markets prevents less than optimum results, interferes with the competitive allocation of resources, there need be no great alarm over an incomes policy to restrain pricing power. Against this, some economists propose restoring textbook competition, pursuing a rigorous antitrust policy that dissolves large corporations and unions. That is unthinkable; these large institutions are the essence of modern economic life. It is quixotic to urge the use of antitrust laws to recreate Adam Smith's world.

The public restraint of economic power by incomes policy is a more realistic alternative. It is untidy; there is no reason to think it can be sustained over a long period. It involves more interference with free choice than anyone who applauds competitive markets can welcome. It is clear, however, that the fiscal and monetary policies to bring about and maintain high employment and growth require some new institutional frame to contain prices. Or high employment and high growth must be abandoned for the Carter-Reagan solution, high slack.

A promising form of incomes policy is TIP, the tax-based incomes policy. Under this, the President would fix a yearly goal for price or wage increases. Corporations and unions that met the goal might be rewarded with a tax bonus; those that breached the standard could suffer a tax penalty. Carter proposed a version of TIP but Congress refused to approve it.

There is no popular demand for incomes policy now. It is unlikely that more than a few of the 4,157 political action committees that Philip M. Stern found had paid for Republicans and Democrats in the 1986 election[16] want a return to past prosperity. The country's voting half, the half that enjoys rising real incomes, certainly does not want unsettling change and prefers a world in which workers and inflation are curbed by substantial unemployment.

In a peculiar way, the slack economy is a form of incomes policy. It tacitly recognizes that large corporations have considerable power to fix prices and levels of output. It implicitly assumes that if wage costs can be held down, this power will not be exerted with maximum force. So corporations are induced, not pressed, to restrain price increases, using jobless labor to curb labor costs. The unemployed serve to remind those at work how precarious their pay is; the employed temper their demands accordingly. This turns the incomes policies of the sixties upside down. The techniques of the Germans, Kennedy, Wilson, and Heath aimed at repressing pricing power to permit full employment without inflation. The inverted incomes policies of Reagan rely on unemployment to curb inflation; incomes policies properly used restrain inflation directly and promote high employment.

Up to now, the electing fraction of the electorate has been willing to tolerate an underemployed world and its deformations: illegal drugs; disease; derelicts in doorways and parks; burglary, rape, and murder. There is, of course, no assurance that a richer, faster-growing society with jobs for all would reduce these afflictions. An economy that fully employs its workers and plants is not Utopia. It can't rescue the environment, revive unions, or even ensure that elected officials fix monetary policy. It need not house the homeless, make medicine available for all, provide for a fairer distribution of wealth or reduce crime.

But an economy based on expansion, on employment and growth, can make easier the resolution of these problems. When all incomes rise, political resistance to a larger share for public purposes diminishes. It is conceivable that better schools and decent jobs may draw recruits from the anarchical guerrillas now terrorizing the great cities. A legal economy might attract some portion of the substantial number whose incomes flow from the illicit economy. Provided of course that the legal economy offers jobs with dignity for those who want them. Restoring a high-employment economy, abolishing the slack economy that has overturned the prosperous postwar years, is only a necessary, not a sufficient, condition for a decent society.

NOTES

1. *Economic Report of the President* (Washington, D.C.: U.S. Government Printing Office, 1989), p. 310.
2. *Ibid.*, p. 346.
3. *Ibid.*, pp. 373, 378.
4. *Ibid.*, p. 359.

5. *Ibid.*, p. 342.

6. Austin Ranney, *Channels of Power: The Impact of Television on American Politics* (New York: Basic Books, 1983), p. 76.

7. See for example Elizabeth Kolbert, "On Rights, New York Looks to State, Not U.S. Law," the *New York Times*, January 8, 1990, p. 1.

8. *Economic Report of the President*, 1989, p. 309.

9. Edward F. Denison, *Trends in American Economic Growth 1929–82* (Washington, D.C.: Brookings Institution, 1985).

10. *Ibid.*, p. xxv.

11. U.S. Department of Commerce, *Historical Statistics of the United States, Colonial Times to 1970: Bicentennial Edition* (1975), p. 139.

12. Robert Heilbroner and Peter Bernstein, *The Debt and the Deficit* (New York: W.W. Norton, 1989).

13. *Ibid.*, p. 78.

14. *Ibid.*, p. 116.

15. *Economic Report of the President*, 1989, p. 373.

16. Philip M. Stern, *The Best Congress Money Can Buy* (New York: Pantheon Books, 1988), p. 24.

Index

output of, 27
in World War II, 36
Gorbachev, Mikhail, 229, 230
Gordon, Robert Aaron, 66, 204
Government
  business alliance with, 35–36
  expenditures of. *See* Government
    spending
  goods and services purchased by, 35,
    38
Government spending, 17, 19–23, 33,
    40. *See also* Budget, balanced;
    Budget deficits; Budget surpluses;
    Defense spending
  prosperity and, 41
  tax cuts vs., 47–48
  for Vietnam War, 96–99
  in World War II, 34–35, 53
Gramm-Rudman-Hollings Act, 178
Great Britain, 9, 14, 36, 45, 119
Great Depression, 1–28, 38, 60, 65,
    66, 75, 83, 240–41. *See also* New
    Deal
  Friedman's views on, 12
  Hoover's assault on, 4–8
  Mellon's welcoming of, 5
  Roosevelt's ignorance about, 1–2
  unemployment in, 2, 7, 10, 14–15,
    16, 24, 26, 28, 33, 34, 45
  World War II and, 34
Great Society, 98, 99
Greece, 50
Green, William, 39
Greenspan, Alan, 111–14, 147n, 161
  stagflation and, 113–14
Gross national product (GNP), 15, 33,
    73
Growth. *See* Economic growth

Hanna, Mark, 72
Hansen, Alvin, 40, 42, 43, 65–66
Harris, Seymour, 40, 70, 85
Harrison, George, 9
Hauge, Gabriel, 79, 209

Hawkins, Augustus, 115
Heilbroner, Robert, 34, 169, 253–54
Heller, Walter, 84, 90, 94, 212
Hibbs, Douglas A., Jr., 156
Hickman, Bert, 208–9
High employment (high-employment
    economy), 250–52. *See also* Full
    employment
Hitch, Charles J., 208, 209, 224
Homelessness, 244
Hoover, Herbert (Hoover administra-
    tion), 1–12, 14, 47, 49, 81
  budgets under, 3–5
  New Deal anticipated by, 4–8
  Roosevelt compared with, 1–5, 11,
    14, 16, 18
  as Secretary of Commerce, 5–6
Hoovervilles, 8
Hopkins, Harry, 25
Housing, 23, 25
Hull, Cordell, 12
Humphrey, George M., 70–74, 77, 78
Humphrey, Hubert, 115
Huntington, Samuel, 226–27

IBM, 184, 185
Imports, 93. *See also* Foreign trade
Income, 12, 17, 26. *See also* Wages
  growth of, 1, 4, 65
  multiplier and, 6
  national, 25–28
  redistribution of, under Reagan, 143,
    187–93
Incomes policy, 131–33, 256–58
  Carter's, 133
  Kennedy's, 91–97
  tax-based (TIP), 133, 258
Income tax, 49–50, 67–68, 99. *See also*
    Tax cut(s)
  corporate, 88–89
  inflation and, 114
  progressive, 86, 191–92
Inflation, 3, 8, 17, 19, 38, 52–59, 65,
    72. *See also* Stagflation